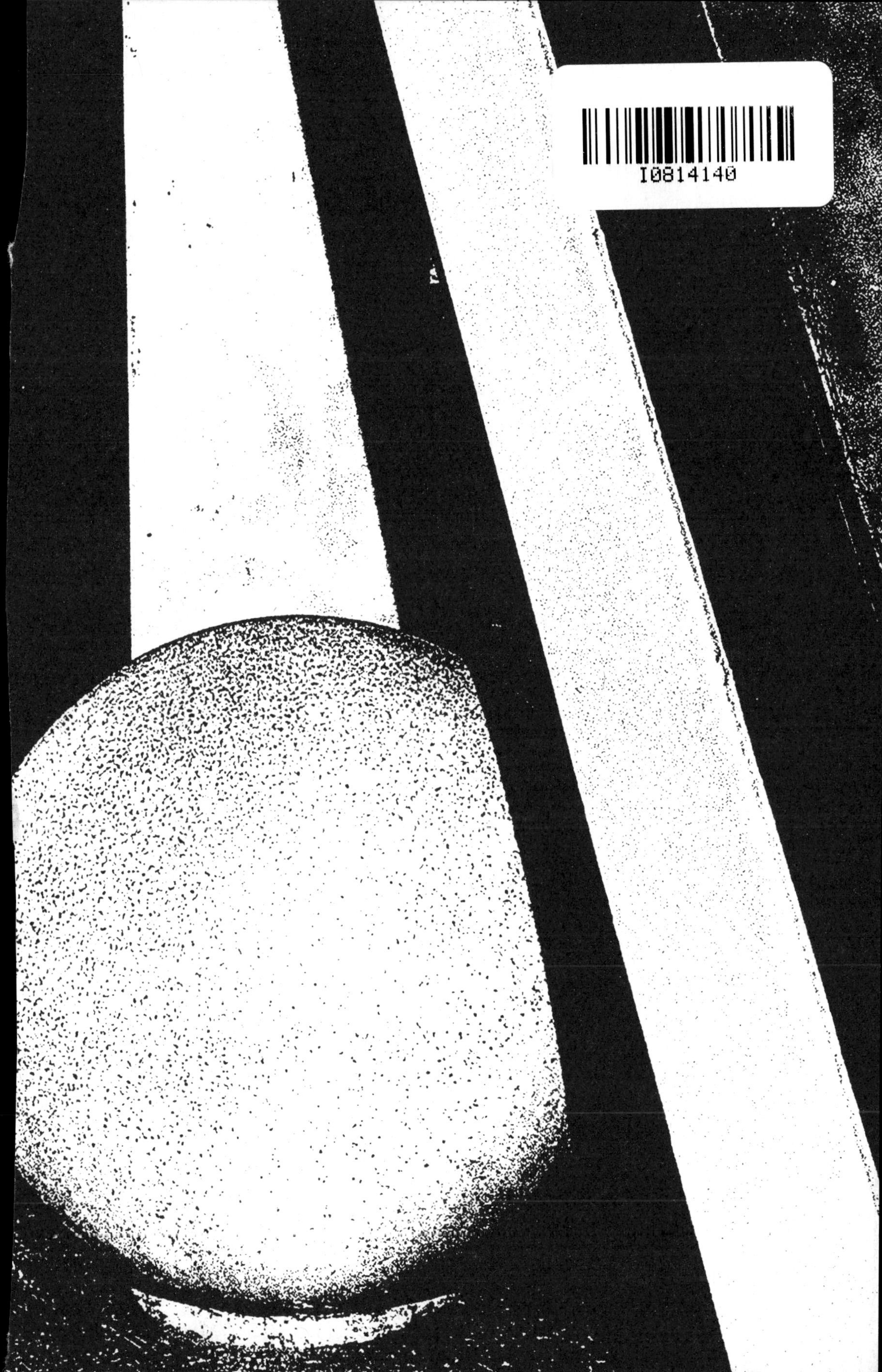

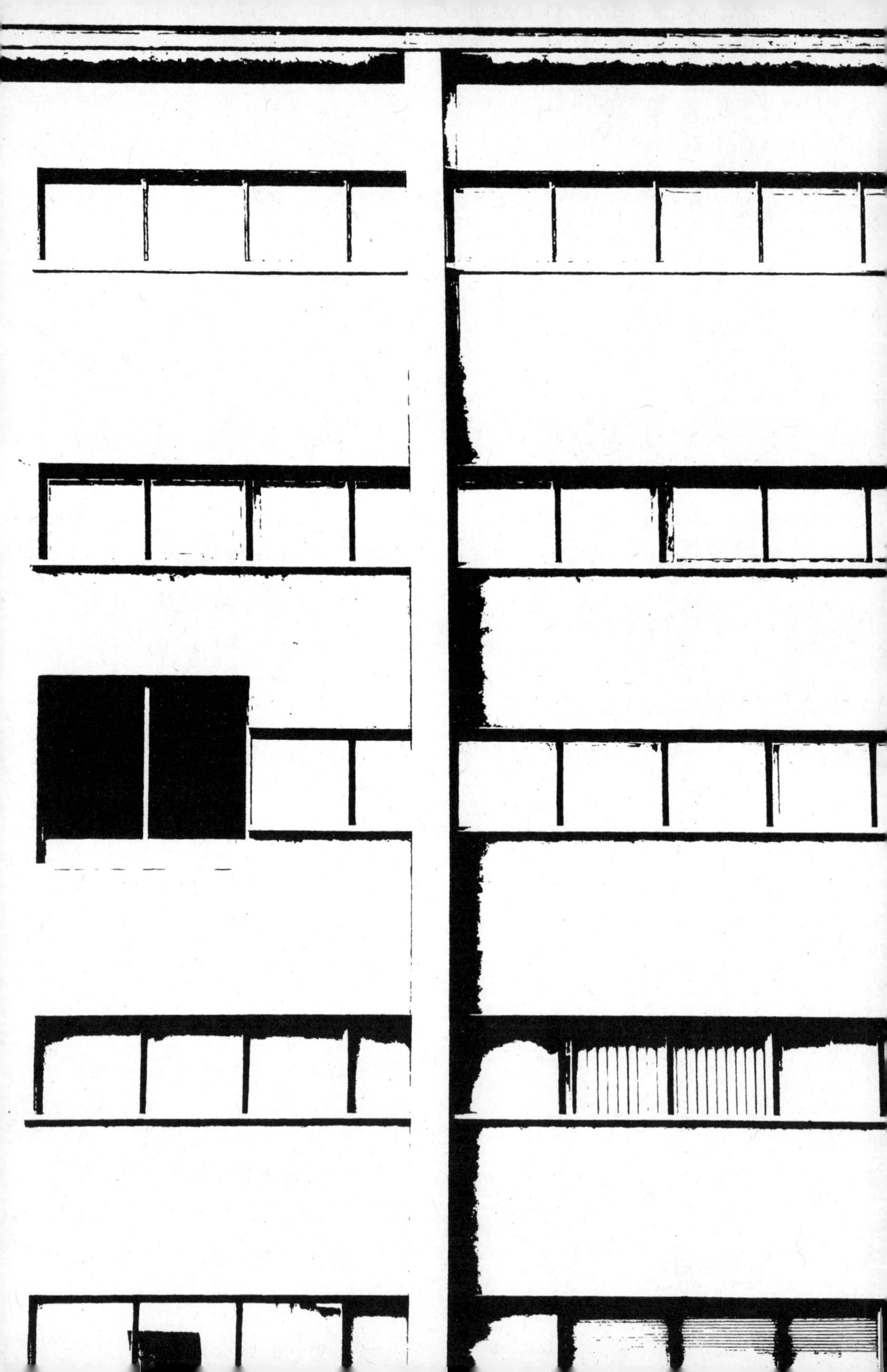

AILEN

NUEVO

PLUG-INS

DESIGN FOR CITY MAKING IN BARCELONA

PLUG-INS
DESIGN FOR CITY MAKING IN BARCELONA

Ezio Manzini, Albert Fuster, Roger Paez
Ramon Faura, Ed.

Published by ACTAR
A project by ELISAVA

OPENING

This book showcases some of the projects developed by Elisava's Design for City Making Research Lab, a research institute that investigates the role of design in the material and social construction of our habitats, focusing on spatiality, temporality, interactions, meaning, citizen engagement and social impact. Elisava Research has been exploring the design for city making concept since 2017, and some of its milestones include the exhibition *D×CM, in Barcelona* (Elisava 2018), the book *Operative Mapping: Maps as Design Tools* (Actar 2019), the public events *The City of Inter-actions* (in collaboration with Barcelona City Council 2019), the research projects *Civic Placemaking* (financed by La Caixa Foundation 2018-2022), *FURNISH* (financed by EIT 2020-2022) and *Open Schools* (financed by Erasmus+ 2022), and the book you now have in your hands. The Design for City Making Research Lab researches and tests the expanded capabilities and the growing relevance of design disciplines to contribute to a better city for all.

The concept of design as plug-ins is the core idea of this book. This notion of plug-ins results from a renewed approach to how design can be a key agent in city making. Given that the city is a system of relationships, design for city making means understanding, reinforcing and articulating this network. We posit plug-ins as situated design outcomes that aim to enrich the complex system of the city and expand its potentialities. Based on the effects these plug-ins produce in an urban system, their role can be that of a *generator* (introducing new elements in a pre-existing urban context, transforming initial conditions and opening up new expectations and possibilities); a *mediator* (distilling existing practices into new landscapes and producing new relationships that activate the urban system); and an *identifier* (recognizing, visualizing and describing existing spaces and practices, contributing to maintaining or enhancing a level of conscious urban awareness). This book's central argument is that plug-ins are a solid yet supple conceptual framework for rethinking design's agency in the city –the main aim of Elisava's Design for City Making Research Lab.

A POSSIBLE INSTRUCTION MANUAL

This book can be understood as the addition of four layers.

LAYER ONE: CORE TEXT

The first layer is the core text, written by Ezio Manzini, Albert Fuster and Roger Paez; it offers a theoretical, speculative and cultural framework for the material generated by the Elisava D×CM initiative over the course of three years.

LAYER TWO: GUEST ARTICLES

In the first part, the central text is enriched with contributions from other authors (Bravo, Bohigas, Baur, Faura, Torrens, Díez, Carbonell and Rueda) who, in their "interferences", offer a reply or an elaboration, or provide a complementary viewpoint.

In the second part, the catalog, five texts written by Elisava faculty members with ties to D×CM (Monjo, Tomico, Benini, Esparza and Valtchanova) expand on the reflections from the first part, focusing on the specific projects in which they were involved.

LAYER THREE: IMAGES

The final layer focuses on the projects. Given the impossibility of explaining each of the almost 100 projects in detail, we offer a collection of images from a selection of projects to portray, in broad strokes, the social, urban and experimental imaginary of the D×CM. The images are organized into three parts (one for each type of plug-in: *identifier*, *mediator*, *generator*), which, like the guest contributions, spark a dialogue with the all the texts in the book, interfering with them.

LAYER FOUR: CATALOGUE

The second part is an indexed catalogue of most of the projects that were developed.

SEARCH ENGINE

The catalog that opens the second part of the book indexes each project (project leaders, stakeholders, educational context), but it also works as a search engine for locating information about the indexed projects, whether in the central text, in the interferences, in the images, or, of course, in the texts written from the front lines.

Design for City Making

PART I

DESIGN FOR CITY MAKING (INTRODUCTION)

This book presents design research on urban regeneration and on the contribution that design can offer. The activities on which it is based took place in the framework of Design for City Making (D×CM): a platform started in 2018 by Elisava Barcelona School of Design and Engineering.

The city in which and with which we operated is Barcelona: a city with its own unique and unmistakable character. But which, at the same time, is also representative of an urban typology definable as low rise-high density: a dense city in which density is more horizontal than vertical. There are good reasons to assert that this urban form offers a better balance between livability and environmental sustainability. And it is precisely for this reason that Barcelona is an excellent testbed to experiment with urban regeneration initiatives that are also concrete steps towards resilience and sustainability.[1]

This book therefore delves into density and diversity; the built city and the lived city; social innovation and public policies —all through the prism of what design can do to contribute to the desired city. And it does so by describing a city in which new artefacts and processes are inserted into the existing urban fabric to reconnect parts that have been torn apart, to reinforce parts that are weak, to consolidate parts that are already strong, and to enrich the city with new possibilities.

In this discussion, the book talks about design and its role as a city making plug-in. In other words, design is conceived as a component (hard or soft) that adds a specific feature to an existing system: the city.

1 This book is an explicit contribution to a radically important issue: how to make cities and human settlements inclusive, safe, resilient and sustainable. The relevance and timeliness of this approach align with the United Nations' 17 Sustainable Development Goals, "adopted by all United Nations Member States in 2015, providing a shared blueprint for peace and prosperity for people and the planet, now and into the future." (UN SDG11 Sustainable Cities and Communities).

Specifically, this book discusses how design contributes to the quality of the urban fabric (both material and relational) in which it acts by opening up opportunities and creating favorable conditions for the interaction between people; between people and places; and, hopefully, between people and the Earth —that is, between people and that wider intertwining of human and non-human relationships of which we are a part. Our experiences operating in Barcelona have led to the recognition of a meta-typology of design processes and outcomes, which we have called *plug-ins*, whose characteristics seem generalizable to all morphologically compact and socially dense cities. This proposal takes as its foundation the following reflection: if the city is a system of relationships, design for city making means reinforcing and articulating this network, making it more dynamic and resilient. To do this, design can conceive and create new physical and relational entities which, by interacting with existing urban networks, engender a new, denser and more diversified urban ecosystem. The image of plug-ins came from this observation.

Formally, the book is made up of four distinct yet related layers: core text, guests' articles, project images, and project catalogue. In a very basic sense, the book proposes two levels of reading to express the dual nature of the activity carried out during the research developed at Elisava: vertical projects on specific themes, and horizontal reflection activities. In practice, it is proposed as a double book. On the one hand, the book offers a collection of design material, notes and information sheets relating to Barcelona, relevant issues in the city's agenda, and a sample of the academic and research projects developed within the framework of Elisava D×CM. On the other hand, the book offers a transversal reflection on the projects, with the aim of distilling the core issues addressed by the practical design research and offering this general reflection to a wide audience. The double book expresses and dialectically articulates two approaches to the same experience.

There is no preeminence of one over the other, and the differences between both approaches to the content are mostly formal: while most of the book is vertical and demonstrative, presenting specific material and standalone projects, the core text is horizontal and reflective, build-

2 United Nations 2018; United Nations 2019.

3 We owe this conceptual shortcut to informal exchanges with David Bravo. For the core idea that social fairness should be necessarily related to environmental sustainability and vice versa. See: Dobson, 1999; Pelletier 2010, 1887-1894; and Bravo, Schrader, Yera 2012, 119-136.

ing a general discourse based on the experiences of Elisava's Design for City Making initiative.

WHY THE CITY?

Due to the massive demographic growth and the concentration of population in cities, rethinking urban habitats is and will remain one of the main issues humanity and the planet need to address. Most current projections forecast that, if there are no major discontinuities (i.e., no major catastrophes), we will see sustained global population growth and an even more dramatic concentration of people in cities worldwide. In 1950, only 30% of the Earth's 2.5 billion human inhabitants lived in cities, some 0.7 billion people. By 2050, 68% of the Earth's 9.7 billion human inhabitants are expected to live in urban areas, amounting to 6.6 billion people, that is, the entire global population from 2007.[2]

Today, the world is facing a number of wicked problems that are endangering the planet's delicate dynamic balances and the very continuity of humankind. Most of these problems can be traced back to two, often inter-related, main factors: the abuse of nature and social inequality. The first of these factors is associated with problems of survival and the damaged legacy we are leaving to the coming generations: the climate emergency, energy waste, and contamination. The second refers to problems of coexistence: abuses of power, the concentration of wealth and opportunities, spatial segregation, and alienated governance. These structural problems also identify society's main challenges —we call them, respectively, the 'eco' and 'equi' challenges.[3] 'Eco' challenges affect the diachronic transfer of wealth from present to future, while 'equi' challenges affect the synchronic transfer of wealth among the world's population —where wealth is understood as material and energetic resources, but also social, cultural and memory-related heritage.

Given this complex framework, we can safely say that the fate of society is playing out in urban milieux —more now than ever before. Cities are the single most important theatre where the present and immediate future of humankind and the planet are being played out. On the one hand, cities are depredatory entities, accumulating human

4 "Wo aber Gefahr ist, wächst / Das Rettende auch", Friederich Hölderlin's second verse from the poem "Patmos" (1803) is directly quoted by Martin Heidegger in "The Question Concerning Technology", and indirectly by Walter Benjamin in "Theses on the Philosophy of History". See Heidegger 1994; Benjamin 2019, 129; and Benjamin 2013, 179-80.

population and material resources, consuming massive amounts of energy and producing huge amounts of waste, including greenhouse gases, one of the decisive agents behind the current climate emergency. On the other hand, cities are liberating entities, fostering sociality and rich webs of interactions unsubsumed (although not unaffected) by traditional forms of domination (family, clan, class, religion), potentially resulting in better societies.

Following Hölderlin's famous dictum,[4] salvation comes from the heart of danger. Seen along these lines, cities are, simultaneously, the world's burden and its potential relief. This is the case when it comes to environmental sustainability, but also social equitability and political freedom. Due to the world's growing population and to the emancipating potential of urban life, cities may well be at the core of the world's problems, but they are also at the basis of potential solutions, which is why designers involved in city-planning and city-making have a special responsibility.

The relevance of this approach is rooted in the undisputable importance of the urban horizon, given the sustained trend towards global urbanisation. Its timeliness is linked to the fact that cities in general, and dense and mixed cities in particular, are possibly the only viable long-term organisational system to tackle the current climate emergency and global sustainability challenges.

The City as a Complex Phenomenon

The city is a complex phenomenon, simultaneously *urbs*, *civitas* and *polis*. Urbs refers to the built space, the morphological framework of the city, made up of buildings and infrastructure. Civitas, on the other hand, refers to the social reality construed by citizens inhabiting the city. Finally, polis refers to the political sphere articulated around the city and city-life.[5]

To a great extent, we still plan, manage, and imagine our cities following the functionalist tenets of the Athens Charter. Its original value notwithstanding, Le Corbusier's vision (1933)[6] has been widely criticised since the Team X's Doorn Manifesto (1954),[7] and yet —albeit in an updated and revised version— it still holds sway. The clarity of the

5 Capel 2003, 9-22.

6 CIAM, 1933.

7 From Smithson, 1982, 33: "Urbanism considered and developed in the terms of the Charte d'Athene (sic) tends to produce 'towns' in which vital human associations are inadequately expressed. To comprehend these human associations we must consider every community as a particular total complex. In order to make this comprehension possible, we propose to study urbanism as communities of varying degrees of complexity" (emphasis added). See also pages 13, 34.

categorical segregation of the city into four basic functions (dwelling, recreation, work, transportation) and the pre-eminence of a material approach to the city, disregarding both the socio-cultural and the political axis, align it precisely with modern and contemporary technocratic tendencies and, specifically, with the bureaucratic apparatus of city and regional planning.

CLEAN CARS DON'T EXIST: THREE ARGUMENTS TO UNMASK THE FRAUD OF ELECTRIC CARS

David Bravo

The private vehicle is an *urbicidal* invention. Its mass use during the 20th century has made it increasingly difficult for us to go on thinking of cities as the greatest example of cooperation and coexistence that humanity has ever come up with. When Henry Ford applied the principles of Taylorism to the manufacture of the Model T, making it affordable enough for the working classes, it unleashed the biggest urban transformation the world had seen since the Neolithic Revolution. The "democratization" of the automobile made us forget how to build good cities. Before then, since time immemorial and all over the world, cities had been mixed and compact. It is the best geometric solution for the occupation of finite territories that are also subject to demographic explosion, a scarcity of resources and the generation of waste. Today, urban compactness and mixicity are some of the most powerful tools for combatting global crises like climate change and rising inequality. However, with the invaluable help of urban planners who roll out the red carpet, Fordism traded compactness for dispersion and mixture for segregation. In its wake, there has been a proliferation of large-scale monocultures that are completely dependent on cars. Some take the form of low-density housing developments that plunder large tracts of land, drive consumption and emissions through the roof, and hike up the costs of infrastructure and services. Others are social ghettos (for the rich or the poor) or large, specialized single-use sectors like commercial areas, bedroom communities, fairgrounds, university campuses, or cultural complexes. Both urban dispersion and the segregation of uses and populations exacerbate private mobility and obstruct active or shared mobility options. Ultimately, we don't need cars because we work far from home; we only began working far from home when cars came into our lives. What's more, in addition to wresting the art of making good cities out of our hands, cars have also turned us into abusers of the neighborhoods we've inherited from the past. Being invaded by cars has made them dirtier, louder, less comfortable, and more dangerous. They have become places to flee at the earliest opportunity. And, in a cynical turn, the car itself has become the vehicle for that escape, the guarantor of a Sunday mass getaway to faraway, more placid, less asphalt-covered places. To landscapes we've also spoiled by building highways, roundabouts, shopping centers, and vacation homes.

And now, suddenly, the "clean car" has come onto the scene. After playing dirty for so long, the motor industry lobbies are now coopting the concept of "sustainable mobility". Inexplicably, the electric car —sometimes also "shared", "connected" or "self-driving"— is supplanting public transportation, walking or cycling in the debate about the most environmentally friendly, healthy and efficient ways of transporting people. The same corporations that played a starring role in the Dieselgate scandal, the same ones that, for decades, have warmed the planet, ransacked the territory, torn up neighborhoods, drained the public coffers, and decimated public health now claim to be the bearers of a magic recipe that will put an end to the messes they themselves have made. Beyond the usual techno-euphoric circles, their proposal has taken root in the collective imagination and managed to win over a large part of public opinion, the media, and the administrations dedicated to urban planning and mobility. At the 26th UN Climate Change Conference in Glasgow (COP26), for example, the electrification of vehicles was the focus of all the roundtables on transportation. Something similar is happening in Pedro Sánchez's administration, allegedly the most progressive and eco-friendly in the history of Spanish democracy. As a star measure to offer a light at the end of the pandemic tunnel, the Council of Ministers has just approved what they call PERTE, a plan that will allocate 14% of Next Generation EU funding —some 10 billion euros— to the promotion of electric cars. With similar enthusiasm, and despite the tensions brought on by the Catalan independence movement, both the Spanish king and the pro-independence parties in power in the Catalan government have coincided in offering a *Marshallian* welcome to the battery factory Volkswagen hopes to set up in Martorell. Even the City Council, led by Ada Colau —the anti-car mayor who has set off many a media firestorm with proposals like the superblocks, connecting the trams along Avinguda Diagonal, or expanding the network of bike paths— is bragging about the installation of 600 electric charging stations in Barcelona for new supposedly "clean cars". In reality, however, the electric car revolution is just another iteration of the Lampedusian motto: "If we want everything to remain as it is, it will be necessary for everything to change." A top-down social engineering operation, for the benefit of the few, and running counter to the interests of the majority —including future generations. A scientific fraud that needs to be unmasked, using common sense and objective data, by way of three solid arguments.

ELECTRIC CARS ARE JUST AS DEADLY AS GAS-POWERED CARS

First, electric cars are just as deadly as gas-powered cars. It's true that the lack of an exhaust pipe means that these new vehicles don't release any fumes locally, but it's no less true that they contaminate at the other end of the electric cables that power them. That's why Vaclav Smil, one of the world's leading experts on energy, asserts that electric cars should be called "nuclear" cars in France or "carbon" cars in China. Indeed, several studies have shown that in more than 30 major Chinese cities, higher levels of contaminating emissions can be attributed to electric vehicles than gasoline or diesel cars, because the energy that powers the electric vehicles is generated largely by burning coal. Moreover, not all the air pollution associated with cars comes out the exhaust pipe. Some of the emissions that are most harmful to public health are the fine particles released by the friction between car tires and the asphalt. Aside from the fact that electric cars also have tires, they are heavier than gas-powered cars and thus generate greater friction. Those fine particles remain suspended in the air for long periods of time and, when we inhale them, they cross into our bloodstream through our alveoli. According to data published by the WHO, these particles are more dangerous to human health than even the dreaded cholesterol. Globally, they are responsible for 36% of deaths from lung cancer, 34% of deaths from strokes, and 27% of deaths from heart disease. The European Environment Agency (EEA) attributes to them the astronomical figure of 399,000 premature deaths every year in the EU. Some studies even warn that they have negative effects on children's lung and brain development and that they can harm the fetuses of pregnant women. Perhaps we should have begun wearing masks a long time ago, and not precisely indoors.

On the other hand, air pollution is not the only deadly effect cars can have, whether they are electric or gas-powered. Noise pollution, for example, has a negative impact on people's quality of sleep and causes high levels of stress, which is a risk factor for serious diseases like cancer, psychopathologies, immune deficiencies and multiple sclerosis. At first glance, it might seem like electric cars are quieter than traditional cars, but the truth is that, at certain speeds, most traffic noise doesn't come from engines, but from friction with the air and the asphalt. Bad news for the people who live near the ring roads or carrer Aragó. Cars can even be held responsible for a large portion of marine pollution. Research by California scientists has shown that a majority of the microplastics in the San Francisco Bay come from fragments shed by car tires. Those fragments enter the food chain through the fish we eat. It is estimated that each of us ends up ingesting the equivalent of a credit card in plastic every week, which affects our metabolism and can have adverse consequences such as the early onset of menstruation in girls.

But the deadly effects of private cars are even more far-reaching. For example, there is nothing to indicate that electric cars have the potential to reduce the accident rate of conventional cars, which have left a dramatic swath of death and lifelong disability in their wake, both among the vehicles' occupants and among innocent cyclists and pedestrians. Electric or otherwise, cars play an undeniable role in sedentary lifestyles and obesity, plagues of biblical proportions that have given rise to countless chronic illnesses and premature deaths. Even among the people who do exercise, any number of contradictory habits have taken root —like riding a motorcycle to the gym instead of sweating on the way there. The loss of biodiversity, a potential trigger for viral pandemics like the one caused by COVID-19, is also largely due to the ubiquity of the automobile, either because of the environmental impact of pollution or as a result of the territorial dispersion of low-density suburbs, which would have been utterly unthinkable before the automobile era. Finally, the contribution of private vehicles to the proliferation of pathologies associated with global warming is no small thing, including tropical diseases and the suffering of the most vulnerable populations during heat waves or cold spells.

In terms of the climate crisis, we should recall that the responsibility of the automotive industry stretches far beyond the useful life of vehicles. To begin with, calculations show that nearly 30% of the emissions attributable to an individual car —even more in the case of an electric car— are released before it even leaves the factory. The processes of extracting and transporting heavy materials, as well as melting plastic, glass and metal, are very intensive in terms of energy consumption and contaminating emissions. Consequently, we should question the public policies that discriminate against older cars and encourage the renovation of the existing fleet, such as Barcelona's Low Emission Zone (ZBE). On the one hand, they are unfair because they penalize drivers with less purchasing power while making it easier for car companies to boost their sales. On the other hand, they ultimately increase the emissions of greenhouse gases by favoring the premature obsolescence of vehicles that have already been manufactured, leaving their remaining useful life and embedded energy to go to waste. Moreover, a common mistake when assessing the climate impact of cars is to focus only on the characteristics of the cars themselves, without taking into account the externalities attributable to the infrastructure they require. Highways, roads, roundabouts, bridges, tunnels, and underground parking lots require pharaonic quantities of reinforced concrete, a highly polluting material, which is responsible for

6% of global CO_2 emissions. And, obviously, the infrastructure for electric cars won't be made of wood. Plus, since we're looking at infrastructure, we can't forget streets. Whether parked or in motion, private vehicles occupy a disproportionate amount of public space, which greatly reduces cities' possibilities of incrementing their plant mass to capture atmospheric carbon. Parked cars on the streets of New York City, for example, occupy twelve times the surface area of Central Park. And it's clear that electric cars won't be parking on or driving through leafy flower beds. In that sense, no; there are no clean cars. Cars are killing machines; and that won't change just because they're running on batteries.

ELECTRIC CARS ARE AS UNJUST AS GAS-POWERED CARS

A second weighty argument against electric cars is that it they are as unjust gas-powered cars. To begin with, their widespread use would only perpetuate the dispersion and segregation that has characterized town planning in the automobile era. On the other hand, and despite the efforts of automotive industry propaganda to present them as vehicles that are respectful of urban life, there is nothing to suggest that electric cars will be any more compassionate than gas-powered cars when it comes to the mixed and compact neighborhoods we have inherited from the past. The urban highways that segregate neighborhoods by creating insurmountable barriers are just example of this abuse that would have no reason to cease. One of the most notorious cases of this *urbicidal* trend was the dispute between Robert Moses and Jane Jacobs in New York City the 1960s. The planner intended to raze Greenwich Village to make room for the Lower Manhattan Expressway, but the activist managed to stop him with the slogan "Downtown is for people!" Another form of abuse perpetrated by cars is the overcrowding of public space. When Henry Ford succeeded in putting the 80 passengers from a city bus into as many private vehicles, he also amputated much of the urban area devoted to active or shared mobility. In Barcelona, for example, private vehicles, which transport an average of 1.2 people each, occupy more than 60% of public space, even though they account for less than 20% of all trips. And, unlike buses, cars don't only occupy space when they're in motion. They also take up space when they are parked, which accounts for 95% of their useful life. In a totally unjustified way, the motorization of society has gone hand-in-hand with the assumption that, when someone buys a car, they are also acquiring a piece of public space to park it on. This lopsidedness in the uses of space translates into injustices like the fact that buses run much slower, pedestrians are forced to cross the Eixample in zigzags, and bicycles and scooters have to share the sidewalks instead of being given their own lanes on the road. And, aside from questions of mobility, the privatization of the streets by cars also hampers other civic uses that are essential to urban life, like social interaction among the elderly or children's play.

All these indicators of spatial injustice make it possible for us to state unequivocally that private vehicles —including electric ones— discriminate against the most vulnerable populations. To begin with, this discrimination against the classes with the least purchasing power comes starkly into view once you calculate all the expenses necessary to buy, use, and maintain a car —even more so in the case of electric cars, which are significantly more expensive. Beyond individual costs, however, there are also unavoidable collective costs that should be taken into account. Estimates show that each private vehicle costs the public coffers nine times what the owner pays. On the other hand, users of public transport pay half the actual cost of each ticket. In the case of active mobility —walking or cycling— the collective cost is significantly lower than the individual cost. In addition, in sparsely populated residential estates —a product of the private automobile, let's not forget— the community costs of services and infrastructure can triple those of compact neighborhoods. Paving streets, providing lighting and sewers, collecting trash, putting out fires, or running ambulances are operations that become significantly more expensive as population density decreases.

On the other hand, it doesn't take much sociological research to deduce that the inhabitants of the housing blocks that flank the highways of any metropolitan periphery are not precisely the richest in the city. Far from espousing the principle of redistribution, the vast amounts of public spending on car infrastructure favor those who are already the most well off. On the other hand, this expenditure could actually contribute to social cohesion if it were devoted to other much-needed areas such as the improvement of public transportation or the expansion of affordable housing stock in *walkable* neighborhoods —which should be highlighted as one of the main infrastructures for fair and sustainable mobility. In Barcelona, the case of the rehabilitation of the Sant Antoni municipal market is a good example of the injustice that usually characterizes public spending on vehicle infrastructure. Although it was accompanied by the creation of a superblock, the renovation of the municipal facility also entailed the construction of an underground parking lot for 500 cars. If the same resources had been invested in building housing for people instead of "houses for cars", it would have helped mitigate the gentrification brought about by the pedestrianization. In the end, we can say, without fear of falling into demagoguery, that "private vehicles" don't exist; all cars are highly subsidized. Subsidized through costly public or private infrastructure —like highways that the government bails out when their concessionaires go under. Subsidized through the privatization of vast amounts of public space, through burdensome incentives for the purchase of new vehicles, or through generous kickbacks for the installation of new car factories. Even the well-intentioned defense of the jobs created by the automotive industry becomes empty rhetoric when we account for the fact that the mass production of all those new cars would require much less labor. Electric motors contain far fewer moving parts than combustion engines, and therefore their production and maintenance would result in inevitable staff reductions, as well as a wave of closures of car repair shops.

But beyond social class, cars also discriminate against the most vulnerable people based on factors such as age, physical ability, and gender. On the one hand, children, people whose vision is impaired, and many elderly people don't have the ability to drive, and their autonomy is greatly diminished in cities that are dependent on cars. On the other hand, the motorized society is profoundly patriarchal. From a statistical point of view, male mobility usually covers longer distances, at higher speeds and with simpler trajectories —from point A to B— whereas female mobility is slower and covers shorter distances but is also much more complex —with several intermediate stops to attend to care tasks and reproductive work, like picking up school-aged children, visiting dependent elders, or stopping by the grocery store. As a result, car-centric cities usually favor men, whereas cities that facilitate travel on foot or by public transport, especially above ground, are more feminist. It is significant that 60% of driver's licenses in Spain are held by men. In terms of public transport, in Barcelona, women make up 67% of bus users and 63% of subway users. In fact, if there is only one car in a traditional family, it usually belongs to the father, and if there are two, the mother's is usually the smaller of the two. Moreover, in neighborhoods with more vehicle traffic and sidewalks that are less frequented by pedestrians, women are more likely to be subject to harassment or assault. Again, there is no indication that replacing gas-powered cars with electric cars will contribute in any way to overcoming these types of discrimination.

ELECTRIFYING FORDISM IS UNFEASIBLE

The third important argument for unmasking the scientific fraud behind electric cars is that their widespread implementation is entirely unfeasible. Fordism has been possible for a short historical period characterized by the exceptional abundance of energy offered to us by oil. But the days of that abundance seem to be numbered. For decades, the unmatched energy density of black gold, combined with the availability of deposits near the surface that made it easy to extract, have normalized intensely wasteful habits like using a one-and-a-half-ton device to move a single person, every day, over dozens of miles, from home to work and back again. However, all signs now indicate that similar eccentricities will soon be out of reach of most of society. This prediction doesn't come from an ideological position or an economic calculation; it's deduced from the laws of thermodynamics. Oil is a finite resource, and it's beginning to show clear signs of running out. According to data published by the International Energy Agency (IEA), scientists like Antonio Turiel claim that the peak of oil —the high point in the global extraction of conventional crude oil— is already behind us, and it occurred in 2005. In the 1960s, for every barrel the world consumed, petroleum explorers found six more; today, seven are burned for every one that is discovered. Since 2014, oil companies' investments in the search for new fields have fallen by 60%, which suggests that supply will soon fall below demand, followed by an inevitable rise in prices. The worst-case scenarios forecasted by the IEA predict a 50% drop in the crude oil supply by 2025. In truth, emergencies like global warming and the health crisis caused by air pollution are already pushing us to stop burning oil as soon as possible. The problem is that there is no real alternative to oil as an energy source if we want to maintain the current rate of consumption. At least, that's what we've heard from Vaclav Smil, who describes the roadmap for an energy transition by 2050 as a "fantasy".

Because the wind isn't always blowing and the sun isn't always shining, wind and solar sources are intermittent. As a result, wind turbines and photovoltaic panels are only productive for one-third of their short useful life, aside from the fact that manufacturing them consumes fossil energy and relies on a complex geopolitical network of rare materials. On the other hand, nuclear power doesn't emit CO_2, but it is vulnerable to uranium depletion. And worst of all, if the ancient Romans had used it, we would still be managing their radioactive waste today. It would take a lot of confidence in the stability of human institutions to defend nuclear energy. In any case, the main limitation of renewables and nuclear power is that they are only used to generate electricity. And electricity accounts for just 20% of the total energy consumed in the world. The remaining 80% is still produced by burning coal, gas or oil in processes that are very difficult to electrify. Given the circumstances, it makes no sense to assume that we will be able to access enough energy to electrify the current fleet of vehicles. Moreover, apart from energy shortages, there are also considerable material obstacles. The minerals needed to produce batteries are also finite, and both their extraction and transport depend on complex geopolitics and operations that rely intensively on fossil fuels. The electrification of all vehicles in the UK alone, scheduled for 2050, would require doubling the global cobalt extraction and buying up half of all copper. On a global scale, with the current rate of lithium production, it would take 175 years to replace all the gas-powered cars in the world with electric vehicles. And that's without taking into account that the size of the global vehicle fleet doubles every 20 years. But the problem goes beyond the availability of energy and materials. It's estimated that 80% of Spanish cars are parked on the street overnight. Expecting the public administration to deploy the infrastructure needed to charge them all is as foolish as it is perverse.

In short, Fordism is hitting bottom. It's possible that electric cars will become accessible to a privileged few, but it's hard to believe they will ever be a mass phenomenon. As a result, it will become less and less economically, energetically and electorally profitable to continue offering cars the protections they have enjoyed until now. And yet, it will take real cultural battle to counteract the propagandistic hegemony of the automobile industry, which is still the sector of the economy that invests the most in advertising. Perhaps that's why the Barcelona City Council, the Catalan government, the Spanish state and the world authorities gathered in Glasgow keep falling into its traps and rolling out the red carpet that has kept it afloat. In truth, it isn't even a question of governments banning cars because they will probably end up collapsing under their own weight. Of course, the collapse may be extremely unfair and painful for everyone who still depends on private vehicles, as was made abundantly clear by the "yellow vests" protests in France. That's why it is both necessary and urgent to begin a truly just transition toward genuinely sustainable mobility —in other words, active or collective mobility. In fact, you don't have to travel to the future to imagine an "electric", "shared", "connected" or "autonomous" car. Nineteenth-century streetcars were all of those things.

However, the design of the city should also account for what Jane Jacobs observed and noted walking through New York's West Village in the 1960s: how the liveliness and livability of the city depended on its density, the diversity of people there, and the events that might happen. This observation, highlighting the irreducibly complex nature of the city, stood in open contrast to the modernist and simplifying ideas that were dominant in those years. Since then, for over half a century, this clash has continued. And, in fact, as is evident in the discussions on the nature and prospects of smart cities, it is still ongoing. The dialectic between density and diversity, in addition to producing urban quality, also creates the necessary conditions for the construction of sustainable and resilient cities. In short, it has become clear that, for the city, there is no urban sustainability without density. And there is no resilience without diversity.

If these are the reasons Jacobs' observations are still valid (indeed, more valid than ever), it should however be added that they are not sufficient as they were formulated at the time. In short, the problem is that Jacobs saw density and diversity as two values to be preserved (the West Village was already a dense and diverse urban environment). Today, however, density and diversity are more often aims to be achieved.[8]

Jane Jacobs sought out and appreciated the variety and openness of the network of interactions in which she found herself immersed. She took an interest in how this complexity of interactions and interdependencies had taken shape, and she looked at how different parts of the city interacted and how they generated a variety of encounters, conversations and social forms. She defended these aspects of the city for many reasons, but perhaps the most important for us here is the following: "Lively, diverse, intense cities contain the seeds of their own regeneration, with energy enough to carry over for problems and needs outside themselves."[9]

When evoking the concept of density in reference to cities, the first image that usually comes to mind is that of vertical density —for which Hong Kong might be the emblem. However, there is also a horizontal density, summarized in the 'low rise-high density' formula, for which

8 Of course, Jane Jacobs was not the only one to defend this characteristic of cities. See, for instance: Lefebvre, 1996; Landry, 2006; Harvey, 2012; Gehl, 2010; and Gehl, 2011.

9 Jacobs, 1992.

many European cities, and Barcelona in particular, could serve as the representation. The horizontal density model does not lead to a single type of city. That said, it certainly implies cities that are not a set of separate and self-contained buildings, but rather an urban fabric made of buildings, courtyards, streets and squares: a potentially dynamic, rich and resilient infrastructure. A city where diversity is favored. Where buildings have communal spaces and where streets and squares are not just infrastructures for mobility, but also public places, the setting for urban social life, which neighborhood communities can take care of.

The density we're referring to here, therefore, is not only represented by the number of people per square kilometer; it is also, and fundamentally, associated with the activities and opportunities for encounters and relationships that the city offers us. Ultimately, the density of a city is given by what we might call the amount of life per square kilometer.[10] We therefore advocate for a dense city, open and full of opportunities, made up of private, semi-private and public places and common property. Despite its apparent obviousness, this choice is actually a first clear stance: a city built in this way stands in opposition to the currently prevailing trends towards dispersed urban environments, which are fragmented into monofunctional areas without any communication with one another and devoid of a holistic articulation within an urban complex.

On the other hand, the life, health and resilience of a city are the result of many elements. First of all, the number and diversity of the entities (both animate and inanimate) that compose it. This has two implications. The first is that diversity is positive and must be cultivated. The second is that, in the face of the tensions that diversity can bring, what needs to be sought is not their integration, understood as homologation (which implies the loss of diversity), but their coexistence. In other words, the different groups must be able to live alongside one another, agonistically addressing conflict as a way to creatively address difference, to enrich sociality through articulated dissent, to reinforce complex community-building and to be able to set common goals.[11] That means having the ability to collaborate. A city where these differences coexist and collaborate will be a rich and resilient ecosystem

10 Manzini, 2022.

11 Paez, Valtchanova, 2021.

12 Sennett, 2018.

13 "The Generic City". See: Koolhaas, 1995.

14 There is extensive literature on the issue of the social resilience of communities in the face of various types of catastrophes. See: Manzini, Thorpe, 2018.

which, in turn, can also recognize and welcome the diversity brought about by non-human and natural agents.

It follows that this city of diversity is best capable of recognizing itself as part of the Earth's natural-cultural ecosystem (to which human beings also belong) —a part that is characterized by a high socio-technical intensity, but which is no less dependent on the presence of the natural substrate on which it is based and which, in fact, makes it possible. Given the difficulties of coexistence between different entities, design should be a medium to actively cultivate them and to regenerate the conditions of their existence and their ability to collaborate.

Richard Sennett, in his most recent work, showed us how urban quality depends on the more or less dialogical or conflicting interaction between two of the city's components: that of a built environment (the *ville*) and that of a lived environment (the *cité*) —which are analogous to the concepts we initially referred to as *urbs* and *civitas.*[12]

This observation by Sennett allows us to better focus on the limits of Jacobs' proposal. For the latter, all attention was focused on the cité, while the ville appeared as a background with a series of characteristics that were not called into question. But the ville plays its own role in urban quality. And this is true not only in new cities, where the ville is being designed and built, but also in existing ones that change over time and, in so doing, can create more or less favorable conditions for the development of the cité. By highlighting these aspects, Sennett makes it clear why social innovation on a molecular level should not be left out of city planning, even on a large scale.

Based on these considerations, Sennett also offers a series of guidelines that make it possible to reclaim Jacobs' proposal, helping it evolve beyond its original limits. It follows that a living and liveable city must be planned to be *open* —which, for Sennett, means that it needs to be synchronic, informal, incomplete, and porous. It needs to be co-produced by its citizens and able to stimulate and nourish its sociality.

Finally, the cities that had characteristics similar to the ones Jacobs described —now subject to processes of gentrification, touristification, and marginalization— are rapidly degrading. They are suffering from a breakdown of their social fabric and a loss of diversity, which, in some

15 See: Rogers, 1998; Rose, 2016; and Rueda, 1997.

16 For Paul Baran's distinction between centralized, decentralized and distributed networks, see: Baran, 1964. As applied to urban planning, see: Dupuy, 2008; Allen, 1999; and Chakrabarti, 2013.

17 Rueda's team at Barcelona's Urban Ecology Agency: www.bcnecologia.es/en.

18 BCNecologia, 2019.

19 *Ibid.*, 4.

cases, takes the form of a real social desertification, leading to what Koolhaas called the "generic city",[13] a kind of branded built environment that stresses the semantic and even political dimension of the urban fabric but misunderstands its civic and cohesive dimension.

With the pandemic and the distancing it has imposed, many have rushed to declare the end of the dense city. But this position is based on a misunderstanding: the density we are referring to does not necessarily imply large gatherings of people. Not only that: it has been shown that the places where people were able to best respond to the pandemic were the ones where there was a social fabric that was dense and dynamic enough to hold up even during the lockdown and the period of social distancing.[14]

Undoubtedly, when it comes to novel approaches to city planning, there is a general agreement in social, economic and urban fields that the kind of urban environment best suited to tackling contemporary challenges is the dense and diverse city.[15] The urban model that offers more hope for successfully tackling environmental and social emergencies is that of a compact, complex, metabolic and socially cohesive city, organized as a distributed network[16] of interrelated yet relatively autonomous units, such as superblocks.

The superblock concept may well be one of the most relevant ideas in recent urban planning. This is so because, although it is an exceedingly simple concept, it holds the promise of radically rethinking consolidated cities. The superblock tackles the epochal question of adaptive reuse of structures at a city-wide level, and thus it provides a stupendous framework for the systemic upgrading of consolidated urban milieux. This approach strongly relates to our proposed 'plug-in' conceptualization for city making projects, which posits design as a regenerative force of pre-existing yet continuously shifting urban realities —both in its hardware (materiality) and its software (relationality).

We owe to Salvador Rueda the contemporary conceptualization of the superblock model. Rueda's team devised a new mobility model that has had an enormous influence not only on transportation, but also on the ecological and social fronts, offering to radically ameliorate air quality, noise pollution, greenery, public space and civic life.[17]

20 The 15 principles are: Compactness vs Dispersion, Decompression vs Compression, Accessibility vs. Private Mobility, Citizen vs. Pedestrian, Habitability in public space, Complexity vs. Simplification, Hyperconnectivity, Green Space vs. Asphalt, Self-sufficiency vs. Dependency, Water self-sufficiency, Reduce, reuse, recycle vs. Waste, Adapting to and mitigating the impact of climate change, Social cohesion vs. Social exclusion, Universal access to housing in more sustainable buildings, and Balanced resources and distribution of facilities. For a summary, see: *ibid.*, 84-85.

The foundation of the superblocks proposal is a reduction in the presence and speed of vehicles, providing more space and safety to pedestrians, turning intersections into liveable squares. But getting rid of cars is only the precondition for a series of other possible developments within the framework of an overall vision that intends to turn superblocks into a "minimum urban ecosystem": a section of the city (around 16-20 ha) where all support services for daily life are available withing walking distance. And where the urban metabolism, in terms of flows of energy and materials, tends to approach self-sufficiency.[18]

Possibly, the most up-to-date conceptual and operative framework for this model is the "Charter for the Ecosystemic Planning of Cities and Metropolises", a working document coordinated by Salvador Rueda that aims to become a new Athens Charter, i.e., a model for articulating debate and best practices when it comes to "designing new urban developments and regenerating existing ones, responding to the current challenges related to social and environmental sustainability in the information and knowledge age".[19]

According to this vision, called 'ecosystemic urbanism', cities are urban ecosystems in which four main axes interrelate: physical (compactness and functionality), systemic (complexity), flows (metabolism) and social (social cohesion). To tackle the transformation of cities from a holistic perspective, all four axes must be considered. Adapting synthetic modelling from ecology's theoretical and methodological framework, ecosystemic urbanism cross-pollinates the four axes to generate 15 principles that serve as guiding criteria for design and evaluation.[20] Within this approach, the superblock is a key concept that serves as the minimum urban ecosystem and the basis of ecosystemic urbanism's functional urban planning model.[21]

The superblock represents the molecular scale of the urban fabric. This idea of regenerating the city starting from its molecular scale has emerged at the same time in several places, sometimes from a spatial and sometimes from a relational point of view.[22] The result is that, everywhere in the world, there have been people who have been busy working in this direction, producing a transformative social innovation[23] that aims to regenerate the social fabric and urban common

21 *Ibid.*, 116.

22 The superblocks are a good example of a spatial-oriented approach, while many social innovation proposals address the city's relational dimension. See, for instance: Bonneau, Jégou, 2015.

23 The expression "transformative social innovation" refers to social innovations generating systemic changes towards environmental and social sustainability. It was introduced in the ambits of the European research project Transit, which ended in 2017. The task was to investigate "transformative social network initiatives and networks in an attempt to understand the process of societal transformation". See: TRANSIT 2017.

goods —and one that has the ability to tackle the major issues hat have emerged in recent years: from the inclusion of migrants to climate change and COVID-19.

Taken together, these initiatives have helped construct a new vision of the city: a collaborative city, made up of people, communities and places, the existence of which is based on a fabric of collaborative projects. Recently, all this has contributed to the idea of a dense and distributed city, in which everything needed for daily life is within walking distance from home. The idea itself is not new: it corresponds to what has been proposed and put into practice in Barcelona with the superblocks. Now, however, in the face of environmental and health catastrophes, this idea has spread and has been proposed for many other cities (including Paris, where the '15-minute city' it is at the center of the current mayor's electoral program).[24]

Design and the City

As we saw earlier, traditionally, urban planners concentrated on the *ville*, and the *cité* was not seen as a problem that needed to be discussed and planned. Today there are several good reasons to argue that this blind spot needs to be overcome. This does not mean that the *ville* should not be considered. On the contrary, what needs to be done is to take both into account, along with their complex relationships: in other words, the mutual interactions between the built environment and the social forms that inhabit it. But that's not all. Today, in the midst of the Anthropocene,[25] the idea of a built city must be extended to include its bioregion (i.e., the physical and biological environment in which it is located). Therefore, the notion of the city must be expanded to include not only the interactions between its inhabitants and their relations with the built city, but also the city's effects on the other living and non-living entities that make up the *urban ecosystem*.[26]

This perspective could be called a relational and ecosystemic approach to the city: "The relational approach," write Ash Amin and Nigel Thrift in *Seeing Like a City*, "delves into the push and pull of competing hybrids of association, explicitly seeking to understand how their traffic, exchanges, and interactions maintain particular orders

24 O'Sullivan, 2020.

25 The Anthropocene is a proposed epoch dating from the commencement of significant human impact on the Earth's geology and ecosystems, including, but not limited to, anthropogenic climate change. On this subject, too, the literature is unlimited. For the fundamental questions, it is useful to read the works of the Stockholm Resilience Centre on the question of the Anthropocene and its limits; and see also: Eriksen, 2016.

26 BCNecologia, *op. cit.*

and hierarchies of power."[27] When adopting this relational and ecosystemic approach, it is necessary to modify the contours of the city, connecting it to a wider network that also includes non-human entities. In doing so, the city becomes an area in this network where human interactions are denser than elsewhere, but which is not to be considered of a different nature, separate from the rest. The city becomes a fabric of non-anthropocentric human interactions, which are intertwined with interactions with the non-human —that is, with the larger web of life, of which the city is a part (a way of seeing things that is founded on the image of Earth as a living entity, where everyone and everything is mutually interdependent).[28]

In other words, to cite Bruno Latour, we should develop a *terrestrial approach to the city.*[29] an approach permitting us, using Latour's terminology, to move "down to earth" —that is, to move inside the city, working to mend it as part of the web of life, taking into account our state of radical interdependence. Looking at the city in this way, the environmental and social crises that affect it appear to us as degenerative processes guided by forms of city making that have led to the breakdown of the web to which the city belongs. On the other hand, social innovation in cities, as a whole, can be seen as an expression of a *regenerative city making*: i.e., city care activities, aimed at healing wounds and forming new connective tissues, among humans, but also between human and non-human agents.

If we want design to have a say in how cities are made, lived in and managed, we need to consider the urban sphere in its full complexity. Where spatial and product design deal primarily with the city's physical-morphological axis (*urbs*), and service, event and interaction design look at its social-relational axis (*civitas*), we should also include the city's political-organizational axis (*polis*) if we are to have a truly complete articulation between design and the city. Indeed, any relevant design practices and outcomes should address, in different ways, all three dimensions of the city.

We argue that design disciplines and the knowledge they generate should be inextricably linked to the urban question in order to envision and enact novel futures with the potential to inform strategy, actions

27 Amin, Thrift 2017, 15, 16 and 30, 31.
28 Puig de la Bellacasa, 2017
29 Latour, 2018a; Latour 2018b.

and policy making. The fundamental challenge is to spark debate and help consolidate networks devoted to thinking and testing design agency to transform the urban milieu toward more environmentally sustainable and socially equitable urban habitats.

DIRECTIONS: FROM THE INSIDE OUT

Josep Bohigas

A couple of years ago, in the context of a workshop organized by "Arquitectxs de Cabecera" (AC), the architect David Bravo invited us to design the city from —and toward— four cardinal directions.

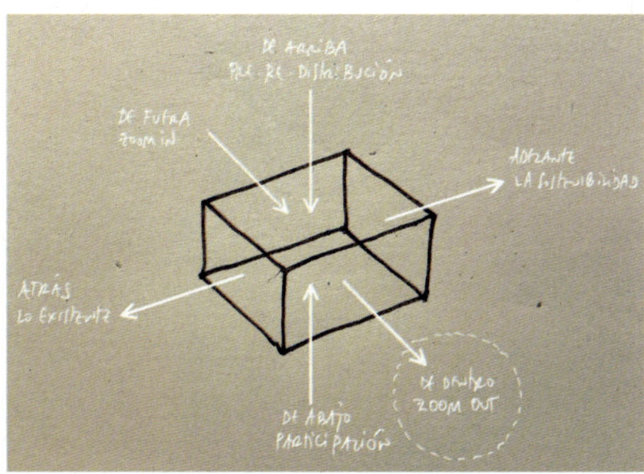

One direction looks *backward*, critically, at history, recognizing what already exists, past experience, what has already been learned, what has been used, etc. as the cultural and material foundation for the present. A vision that assumes the city of the future will be very similar to the city of the past but will need to be adapted and recycled to respond to new challenges, avoiding the pessimism of "back to the drawing board" or the perverse *tabula rasa* that has generated so many false narratives about a supposedly redemptive creative freedom.

Another of the directions runs the opposite way: *forward*. Improving the legacy that we'll be leaving to those who come after us and trying to foresee the social and economic challenges of the future. Looking ahead is especially urgent for the sake of the "future intelligence" demanded by the environmental contingency, calling into question the perverse projection of infinite growth, despite the terms of sustainability in which it may be described.

There's a third direction that goes *from top to bottom*, demanding that designs take into account the urgent need to incorporate policies that conscientiously carry out the pre- and redistributive functions with respect to their benefits, tackling the growing and unjust systemic inequalities of capitalism. Promoting inductive, brave, bold projects that accept both political and technical leadership and responsibilities and that aim to democratize the access to basic resources and improve social cohesion.

And finally, a fourth direction moves *from bottom to top*, proposing actions and projects rooted in participation and activism that combat the abuse of power or clientelism, and that reflect the necessary co-responsibility of an engaged citizenry, articulating new types of participatory governance that allow for visibilizing and constructing new, better and more representative solutions.

David drew this neat diagram on an improvised blackboard that we set up in the middle of the street, in front of a group of students and residents from the Poblenou neighborhood, with whom we were collaborating.

Lecture by David Bravo in Carrer de Poble Nou, as part of the workshop of Arquitecxs de Cabecera

And as a result of the lively debate that ensued, we came up with the idea of completing and three-dimensionalizing the structure by incorporating two new directions that have been and will be fundamental to how the projects are approached: "*from the outside in*", which has been the main strategy of traditional urban planning, and "*from the inside out*", the least common of them all, and which we advocate as a working methodology at AC.

FROM THE BED TO THE STREET

In 2014, I was fortunate enough to curate (along with David Bravo, Anna Vergés, Alex Giménez and Guillen Augé) the exhibition "Piso

Piloto" at the CCCB, where we analyzed and highlighted what was, for us, the greatest pending challenge facing cities: *housing*. We analyzed two cities —Barcelona and Medellín— which, each in their own way, had recently implemented radical changes in their public spaces and facilities and had carried them out with obvious success, which had made them international benchmarks. Yet, both award-winning cities had almost completely forgotten the urgent issue of the right to decent and affordable housing. We've often summed up this paradox using a very apt phrase by Álex Giménez that hits the nail on the head: "If the city were paella, housing would be the rice". And, in Barcelona as well as in Medellín, they had concentrated on "spicing up" the paella with a whole range of brilliant performances in public spaces and with brand new unique public facilities, but, surprisingly, they had forgotten the rice... And you can't make paella without rice, just like you can't have a city without decent and affordable housing.

The exhibition aimed to quantify the dire housing situation through a series of specific themes —the lack of public housing, energy poverty, homelessness, empty buildings, gentrification, new tenancies, slums, evictions, etc.— accepting that the housing problem isn't one single problem, and that there can't be one single solution. It is a multifaceted problem that cannot be solved purely quantitatively, by building new "exemplary" neighborhoods on detached lots on the outskirts of the city, as has been done so many times in the past, with consequences that are still ongoing. The problem also has to be addressed qualitatively, with a consistent project of urban regeneration, compaction and redensification —building new housing, yes, but above all acquiring existing buildings, rehabilitating them and improving people's living conditions. Intervening primarily in places that are already urban, taking advantage of the enormous qualities that the existing city already offers, and adapting it to our current enormous social and environmental challenges.

But to do that, you have to change your strategy and start by getting to know (better and more in depth) the inner workings of people's living spaces, their characteristics, their situations, and the urgent needs of the people who live there. Getting to know the subjects in order to better understand the objects, and from there, deploying new cartographies that can eventually be scaled, incorporating bigger challenges into the buildings, the streets, the neighborhoods and ultimately the city as a whole. From the bed to the street, from the most intimate realm to the most public, instead of only in the opposite direction, as is the case with traditional operations.

I remember how, in the 1980s, when the small squares of pre-Olympic Barcelona were being successfully refurbished, it was naively assumed that the regenerative methodology would work like a reverse metastasis. The City Council began from the outside, choosing a strategic site, regenerating a small public space, with the conviction that the desirable consequences would end up positively "infecting" the entire city, crossing the façades into people's homes. So, new public spaces were created, and the façades were wiped clean in a municipal program meant to make the city "beautiful". But, unfortunately, the plan stopped there, turning the public U (façades and public space) into a mask of luxury that beautified the city without addressing the pressing housing problem.

Today there is still an urgent need to rebuild the city, but now it is time to do it from the inside out to generate that positive metastasis from the heart of the most intimate realm, with the ambition that it will reach out onto the streets to domesticate them, and from there, inspire us to ask ourselves what we want our cities to be.

But to put this qualitative methodology into effect, we need transdisciplinary experts who are well trained and willing to give it their all, and offer solutions from inside people's homes, with and for the people who live in them. Most architecture and design schools continue to train professionals with highly competitive skills, who work tirelessly, locked up in their offices in front of their computers, to then sell their inspired creations to their clients... At AC, we don't deny that this type of expert will continue to exist, but we argue that, today, it is urgent to train armies of experts who understand how to work in transdisciplinary teams, *who know how to listen*, cooperate and create collectively using the clay of reality.

The geographer David Harvey has warned us that the steps we take to free ourselves from one crisis often trigger the next.

An economic crisis is followed by a social crisis, an environmental crisis, an energy crisis... Now, taking on the challenges of post-COVID recovery, we may have a new opportunity to invest huge amounts of resources in implementing fairer measures. Measures that look backward and trust in the experience and opportunities of the past, while also looking forward with an environmental perspective, measures that are more fairly redistributed and that allow for the articulation of participatory strategies. But let us also hope that they will begin from inside our homes, and let's not waste the opportunity to put people at the center, with the conviction that by improving our most intimate living spaces, we can help improve lives that are worth living.

We believe that cities need both city planning and city making. While city planning addresses the physicality of the *ville*, city making addresses the sociality of the *cité*. But both processes should also address the need for a cohesive and political understanding of the urban phenomenon as a whole, therefore assuming its role as *polis*. City planning has consolidated, well-established methodologies, expertise and regulatory frameworks that are constantly being updated. City making, on the other hand, takes a less structured, more flexible, and more fluid approach, both due to its relatively short history and to its nature —as it relies intensively on an open-ended collaboration between organizations and citizens. We define city making as those processes that result in the social and material construction of the city by means of specific projects or initiatives. Design for city making mobilizes disciplines that traditionally have dealt with the city (architecture, urbanism, landscape) but also includes all other design areas (service, product, graphic, interaction) that only recently have begun to consider the city as their natural terrain.

These two approaches are radically complementary and should be used simultaneously. Moreover, we are beginning to have novel conceptual and instrumental frameworks, such as *ecosystemic urbanism*, *superblocks*, or *plug-ins*, that help us (even compel us) to relate city planning with city making to form a richer and more complex approach to the combined physicality, sociality and polity of contemporary cities.

Of course, neither city planning nor city making processes guarantee desirable outcomes per se. Social oversight and scrutiny are necessary. City planning and city making projects have different social and political motivations and implications. They can produce inequalities, segregation and urban commodification, or they can promote equality and create a diversified and vibrant urban fabric. The first kind are driven by the interests of those who consider the city, in all its aspects, as a marketable good. The second, which we espouse, posit the city as a common good. In consequence, we advocate city-making initiatives that are situated practices, in which spatiality in general, and the notion of collective spaces in particular, play a crucial role. Complex and evolving forms of spatiality work to articulate social, political and cultural concerns and ground them in specific hybrid physical and digital milieux where rich urbanity unfolds.

Design is an agent that affects the state of things. By adopting a point of view internal to the system on which it operates, it construes visions, proposes solutions and produces meanings. In other words, it generates transformations that are both symbolic, operative and semantic. In turn, this action on the world can be seen as a process and as a product. In the first case, we are referring to the interactions between a group of people that generate a result. In the second, the result of the action is considered. In turn, the result of the design process can present itself in very different forms: from industrial products and architectural structures to the products of contemporary design, which include services, places, events, communication strategies, digital platforms and applications, and different combinations between them.

It follows that the times and ways in which design participates in city making are also varied and articulated. Nonetheless, they share some common features that derive from the very nature of design: they look at the city from within (i.e., they take the point of view of the actors involved); they connect the built city with the lived city (i.e., they bridge technical-material dimensions with socio-cultural dimensions); and they tend to operate "by projects" (i.e., transversal undertakings collaboratively carried out to achieve a particular aim, which makes it possible to account for the complexity of the city without reducing it). These characteristics of contemporary design make it, for better or for worse, a powerful actor in urban transformation.

In fact, design has many responsibilities in the current evolution of the city towards socially and environmentally unsustainable forms. However, for the same reasons, it can, and indeed should, actively participate to shift these undesirable dynamics in the opposite direction: that is, towards collaboration, resilience and sustainability. We promote an approach to contemporary design that involves discussing its products and how they can help in the ongoing process of city making, and, in particular, how they can act as a bridge between the built city and the lived city.

PLUG-INS AND COMPLEX SYSTEMS

In this book, plug-ins are understood as agents that unveil the multi-layered essence of the city. And by unveiling this essence, they help reflect on the physical, social and political assumptions that cities inherit because of their high complexity. Plug-ins, as active, performative and material intersections of reality, become stepping-stones in the potential re-configuration of the material, relational and semantic assumptions that shape the city.

In a literal sense, a plug-in is “a small device or computer program that is designed to be used with and fits into a larger one” (Cambridge Dictionary). This definition can easily be applied to our discussion: the design outcomes we refer to here (which have been conceived and developed in the Design for City Making platform) are plug-ins because, as anticipated, they are physical, digital and/or relational assemblages designed to fit into an existing system of structures and relationships (the city), changing it in the desired direction.

It seems to us that the image of design as a plug-in is useful because it helps to focus on three very relevant issues: (1) design is a part of a larger system: in this case, the city; (2) design is a subsystem to be used with and fit into a larger system; (3) its raison d’être is to modify the system to which it refers. These three points are important because they offer a guide for designing in complexity. Not only do they remind us of the systemic nature of the reality we are confronted with, they also remind us of our limits and the limits of what can be designed. Moreover, they tell us that, whatever the limitations, there is always something that can be done, something that can be plugged into the system to engender new urban realities.

Additionally, the image of a plug-in highlights the possibility of designing artefacts that are endowed with their own autonomy (definable through a set of features), the actual value of which can only be assessed by observing the change they generate in the larger systems into which they are inserted. In that sense, considering our experiences with design for city making, what are the effects on the urban system that, as a whole, the proposed plug-ins aim to achieve? Is it possible to sketch out the components that make up these plug-ins based on their different operational contexts and the specific effects they pursue?

The plug-ins that were conceived and developed as part of Elisava's Design for City Making platform have a common characteristic: they aim to enrich and strengthen the fabric of both the built and the lived city. In other words, even in the case of a dense city, like Barcelona, it can be useful to work toward increasing its relational density. There are several reasons for this: because the city may be physically dense, but socially deserted; because some relational possibilities cannot be transformed into collaborative practices; because a social fabric may exist but may have degraded; or because the fabric of the built city has become inadequate and needs to be regenerated.

The existence of these different contexts requires different city-making interventions and therefore different design plug-ins. Based on the experiences we have accumulated, we have deduced that every plug-in has three basic components, which we call generator, mediator and identifier. Just as the four basic nucleobases (cytosine, guanine, adenine and thymine) make up DNA molecules that carry genetic instructions for all known organisms, so all design for city making design initiatives are made up of these three basic components. Different proportions of these components correspond to different roles the plug-ins can play in the urban system.

Identifier describes the symbolic, mnemonic or consolidating component of a plug-in. By recognizing, visualizing and labelling spaces and practices that prompt a collaborative city, identifiers contribute to building or maintaining a level of conscious awareness through design for city making initiatives.

Mediator describes the bridging, negotiating or conciliating component of a plug-in. As social condensers that distill existing practices into new relational landscapes, mediators reinforce existing dynamics by producing new relationships that activate the urban system.

Generator describes the creative, transformative or founding component of a plug-in. As game-changers that introduce new elements into a pre-existing context, generators transform the initial conditions by adding another layer into the mix that reshuffles the urban system and opens up new expectations and possibilities.

It is important to clarify that generators, mediators and identifiers are not mutually exclusive taxonomies, but rather dynamic indexes that allow us to characterize, relate and compare all design for city making initiatives.

Let's consider, for example, a group of wooden chair prototypes designed by first-year design students and installed along La Rambla. They act as a generator because they change the normal setup of public space, interrupting the habitual flow of people and offering a space to linger on a highly dynamic street. They also act as a mediator inasmuch as they create opportunities for conversation between residents and tourists, breaking the normality of their mutual indifference. Finally, they act as an identifier because they emphasize both the tourist-local conflict and its potential solution through enhanced interaction, and a design school's contribution to enriching La Rambla's social makeup through a yearly event that ties curricular activity with social impact.

Therefore, the plug-in components overlap with disciplinary niches (space, service, event, product, interaction, etc.) and design tools (triggering, direct action, mapping, concept generation, prototyping, storytelling, etc.). In conclusion, the definition of generators, mediators, and identifiers is an attempt to describe the three different performance poles that articulate any specific contemporary design initiative when applied in design for city making, especially when cities are considered as a mesh of interactions between inanimate and animate natures and between human and more-than-human entities.

FROM THE SOCIETY OF CARE TO THE SOCIETY OF EMPOWERMENT: DESIGN'S ROLE IN VULNERABLE URBAN SITUATIONS

Ruedi Baur

This topic, like all those related to social design (or socio-design, as it should be called), asks a fundamental yet difficult-to-answer question. It concerns the 'doctor-savior attitude'. Though well-intentioned, the doctors' actions almost automatically create an imposing difference between victims waiting to be cared for and carers who are free to act in accordance with their ethics and possibilities. One group symbolically assists the other, who, through this act of benevolence, is automatically disempowered and allocated the status of a being cared for. They can only put their lives into a third party's hands and hope for comfort. With this in mind, this text aims to demonstrate the extent to which two currently fashionable concepts, "care" and "empowerment", are difficult to combine. This reflection picks up the search for a more accurate terminology to describe the justified desire to construct a society that is both more attentive to its environment and offers more responsibility to its citizens. By analyzing design's intervention in so-called vulnerable urban situations, we will see how these ideas stem from different design attitudes and how the response from the "designer-savior" can take away agency from the people involved. But let us begin with our experiences in recent months in order to offer a clearer view of this phenomenon of disempowerment, resulting from a certain type of crisis management led exclusively by the "experts" and their executors.

Recent lockdowns thrust us all into a stark realization of the chasm between these two concepts. They were accompanied in democratically weak countries by pointlessly authoritarian measures facilitated by states of emergency, curfews, and parliamentary votes to severely restrict citizens' freedoms through incessant police repression, for example, or verification of vaccine passports by organizations not intended to carry out this type of task. Of course, the goal here is not to deny the health dangers posed by COVID-19 or to advocate against vaccination, quite the contrary. Instead, the idea is to analyze the difference between a government that calls upon its citizens to show solidarity in a health crisis by entrusting them with responsibilities in the fight against a threat, in accordance with the republican values of dignity and responsibility, and one that shows no trust in the people and tries to solve the problem in an authoritarian fashion, unilaterally defining the rules and each person's actions, as though leading an army. A deep sense of disempowerment and restriction puts citizens into one of three states: either an attitude of indecision or even submission, waiting for orders; resistance, looking for ways to bend the rules; or escape or evasion, for most. Whether consciously or otherwise, the measures were experienced as an attack on the dignity of responsible citizens' and even calling into question the social contract that is founded on electing representatives to act on the people's behalf.

This discrediting of politics and of the social contract that ties us to the democratic system is worrying, given the essential societal changes that are urgently needed to respond to our current environmental and social crises. But returning to the topic at hand, we can link this feeling of removal of rights and freedoms while waiting for decisions from all-powerful "doctor-saviors and politician-saviors" deemed "experts" to the sense of disempowerment felt by the local population when "creator-saviors and adviser-saviors" come to analyze their neighborhoods, considered to be "vulnerable", make a somewhat superficial diagnosis, recommend solutions that may or may not be implemented, and then leave to work on new projects. And all this in spite of the good intentions and the sincerity of those involved.

This preamble seems necessary, since the "society of care" demanded by some, founded on the notion of people's vulnerability, risks putting us all in a position where we are weak and need specialists to take care of us: by orchestrating constant fear; by dictating our actions; controlling, distracting and leading us; giving us bits of information but not the whole picture; maybe even doling out certain sedatives; locking us up when we are deemed to be at risk, etc. Protecting us, in short, by teaching us not to think too much, treating us delicately and seductively when we follow the pre-defined path, but firmly if we dare to become empowered and choose our own way, even if it might be better for the common good. Does that society of care sound like a utopia? It is worth remembering that, not that long ago, a president of the country referred to as the birthplace of Human Rights suggested that preventive medication should be distributed to calm young people who could potentially be anxious, or perhaps just sensitive, in the same way that patients are sedated in psychiatric hospitals. A society of "care" might want to sedate the *gilets jaunes*, or all protesters in general, or political rivals, or the inhabitants of so-called "difficult" neighborhoods: basically, anyone who is dissatisfied, even if they have plenty of reason to be. Incidentally, there are few studies more generously funded today than the ones that aim to understand happiness —or to generate it artificially.

This awful outlook might be considered irrelevant to design if, in 1944, László Moholy-Nagy had not defined the purpose of design as making life —and therefore the state of the world— better. This guiding principle has been taken on board by designers to different degrees since, but it remains a real point of reference. What is clear is that many design projects don't make life better, or they only do so for certain people, namely the project's backers. But it is especially worth noting that certain phases in these various improvements to our lives have taken place without our consent, and without us really wanting what has been presented to us as progress, and often achieved at the expense of others, sometimes even destroying things that should be communal and impossible to privatize. The term *innovation*, which was omnipresent and artificially exaggerated before the pandemic, expresses this autonomization of technology and, more specifically, the digital sector with respect to users' and citizens' real needs. Absurd consumption, incited by advertising and its variants, is not the evidence of desire or of possible improvements to people's quality of life, far from it.

The result of the extended immobilization of hundreds of millions of people across the world and the forced transformation of their everyday lives, as well as the measures that were or were not implemented, has been both a general despondency and a kind of collective awakening. It is as though we have woken up from a dream, suddenly becoming aware of the theatre of power. That ceremonial script in which everyone had accepted their role, sometimes by force, other times through weariness, often simply through blindness. In parallel, the catastrophic effects of what had been imposed on us for decades as supposedly necessary or even critical measures to improve our lives became clear. Neoliberal discourse has fallen apart literally in front of our eyes, without even the need for argument. At the same time, the relativity of the rhetoric surrounding economic impossibility became tangible. From one day to the next, decades of destruction and privatization in the name of ultimately minimal budget reductions were undermined by the sudden appearance, as if by some miracle, of tens or hundreds of millions or billions of euros over the course of this crisis. So, there were reserves all along, and any previous refusals to spend were not out of necessity, but deliberate political choice. Lest we forget the national and European arguments regarding Greece, for example; the pointless attempts to reduce pensions; the absurd privatization of the public sector; the dangerous cuts to the education budget; the closure of viable factories; the insufficient support for environmental causes; the silence and inaction in the face of poverty; and all the micro-improvements refused across the board in the name of savings by an army of neoliberal administrators. All of these past issues were apparently undeserving of the resources deployed to reduce the effects of the pandemic. It is also important to note that these astronomical sums were distributed to nations' central governments, not to cities or regions, which have direct experience of the local social and environmental realities.

We will probably need more distance to judge the lasting mental and behavioral transformations brought about by this crisis. We must analyze what is really broken forever; what will eventually be transformed, after the effects of compensation have passed; what, despite our greater awareness, will begin again, perhaps with more scruples and sometimes even with a clear desire to ignore reality; what will never manage to beguile us again; and what has lost its credibility to the extent that it has been permanently banished to the list of incivilities that must be fought in the public interest.

From now on, we'll realize that certain sirens trying to catch our attention sound out of tune, and that the collective imaginary that formed the foundations of capitalist society, and modernity, is no longer so appealing. A collective narrative has ended, but what comes next has yet to become clear. Despite considerable budgets allocated to brand strategies, some global corporations singled out for actions that fly in the face of the common good are now operating in the shadows, having tried, until recently, to charm us and argue the importance of their no less criminal acts. Their existence seems like it can no longer be justified, given the harm they cause to the Earth. Unfortunately, this increased public awareness will not prevent them from continuing to do harm, though perhaps less visibly, as they are supported by a section of society that includes certain politicians not yet able to see how imaginaries have evolved, who are awaiting a return to things that were accepted in the past, prepared to continue manipulating minds. These submerged machinations are dangerous, not just because of the direct damage they inflict, but because of the harm they do to democracy.

In this difficult context, it is now time to examine the role of design, especially in intervention processes in rapidly deteriorating urban contexts. First of all, this exceptional, transitional time could be considered a new beginning, a reset with better foundations, or what was known as the "Zero Hour" in Germany after the fall of the Nazi regime. This concept paved the way for the creation of the famous Ulm School of Design and enabled German creators, politicians and humanist entrepreneurs to embark on a necessary reconsideration of customs and a redefinition of the social contract. In certain conditions, design can carry out this essential project. It becomes a force for mediation. But like any mediator, it should be independent of the parties involved, which generally creates a contradiction with respect to the contracting party.

Like with a peace treaty, the goal is to reinstate mutual trust, through this symbolic act, so that a new social contract can be defined and implemented in the long term. Our case could be compared to that of an occupied country that needs to be liberated by handing over responsibility to its citizens, who, until now, were considered utterly incapable of managing themselves, or even dangerous. This act of peace must begin with replacing the national police, which all too often behaves in such territories in an abusive, disrespectful, punitive way, outside the bounds of legality. This occupying army must be substituted by a local police force that works side by side with the population and is governed by the area's elected officials. If the idea is to decolonize these neighborhoods made vulnerable by external forces, liberation on its own cannot generate the empowerment and local social contract we are looking for. A host of examples show how difficult it is to implement this process and the risk of it resulting in forms of insecurity or, more commonly, new forms of authoritarianism. The aim is to help the population to take possession of the place where they live, beyond their private homes which, in general and despite financial limitations, tend to be very well kept, proof that they pursue and cultivate wellbeing. Due to its structure and regulations, social housing poses an obstacle to this responsible empowerment of inhabitants or this self-governance that corresponds to other urban structures. If an urban renovation does not include the possibility of residents taking ownership of their shared space, it will be experienced in the same way as the actions of the doctor-savior, who exasperates us with prescriptive measures that are too late in coming. We are given a new living environment that has been designed for us. Following one consultation, no doubt, since designers today are expected to stage some semblance of participation.

The idea of the utopia of proximity is essential here in order to propose an alternative to this way of building the city and managing it via so-called social bodies. The residents of these neighborhoods must be acknowledged as capable of taking control of their community life and their environment. And that applies even if those same citizens seem fearful, exasperated, disillusioned by our society, excessively impatient or pessimistic. Design achieves things through processes of dialogue. It is not built on promises and empty words, but on prototypes that open up imaginations and recreate desires, which must then be brought to life in direct collaboration with the people who expressed them. The idea is not to lure people with the promise of the impossible, but to work gradually towards physical and symbolic transformations based on functions and possibilities. As the goal is to enable the residents of these neighborhoods to take control of their environment, the process must not be expressed through a series of prohibitions and impossibilities. Quite the contrary: while remaining realistic, the objective of the interaction with the designer is to propose new imaginaries through dialogue and represent them so that they can be made tangible and shareable. In this conception process, designers act more like a scribe than a doctor-savior. They can make suggestions in the same way as the authors, give advice and provide tools to allow for outside support, but they do not prescribe or influence and, above all, they do not decide.

Like in any other design process, the starting point is a critical analysis of the existing situation. This must be carried out with the residents, who are experts in the place; without their help, the designer's perspective can only be superficial, and often based on cultural prejudices. At the same time, these experts' habits can sometimes prevent them from imagining possibilities. This is where the creative act comes in, opening up new imaginaries that, of course, must then be approved either orally around a sheet of paper or more tangibly using prototypes based on physical reality and collective experiences. These prototypes are not intended to be recreated exactly. They are meant to serve as the foundation for discussions, even democratic disagreements. The drawing and the beginning of the execution process come afterwards.

By way of example, let's look at the eternal debates around the communal stairways that exist in many buildings in vulnerable neighborhoods. First, we must understand what constitutes the difference between a nice street made up of small plots that connect with public space or a market and these unpleasant, distressing staircases. This example can demonstrate how a process of appropriation can start and shine a light on the conditions needed for it to be successful. The staircase, often reduced to the minimum possible size, obstructed by an elevator that is often out of order, is the place where all design rules are broken. How can it be transformed into a friendly place, full of life? The designer, alongside the architect and with participation from the building's inhabitants, can open up new horizons in this respect. What if balconies, generally designed to be isolated family spaces, overlooked this vertical street, which could be enlarged? How might we imagine an ample intermediate space between the circulation area and the private sphere? What layout would be needed and what habits would have to be transformed so these spaces could be considered central to a community's well-being? The designer should work with the residents to model these new practices, such as vertical gardening, connections between balconies, places for production and exchange. The result could be a series of vertical fab labs, so to speak, managed by the residents and offering occupation, exchange and an informal economy. Prototyping rituals could be put into place, accompanied by a "staircase festival", which would attempt to simulate this collective space and make it more and more real, with the help of more weighty interventions, which the public authority would be well advised to provide.

To conclude, it is worth noting that in such a context and with such aims —geared towards citizen "empowerment" rather than "care"— design must itself be reinvented. If the aim is still to improve people's lives, it should no longer be done "for them", but rather "with them" and even, increasingly, "by them".

→ 295

RECORDAR EL PASADO DEL MOLL DE BARCELONA

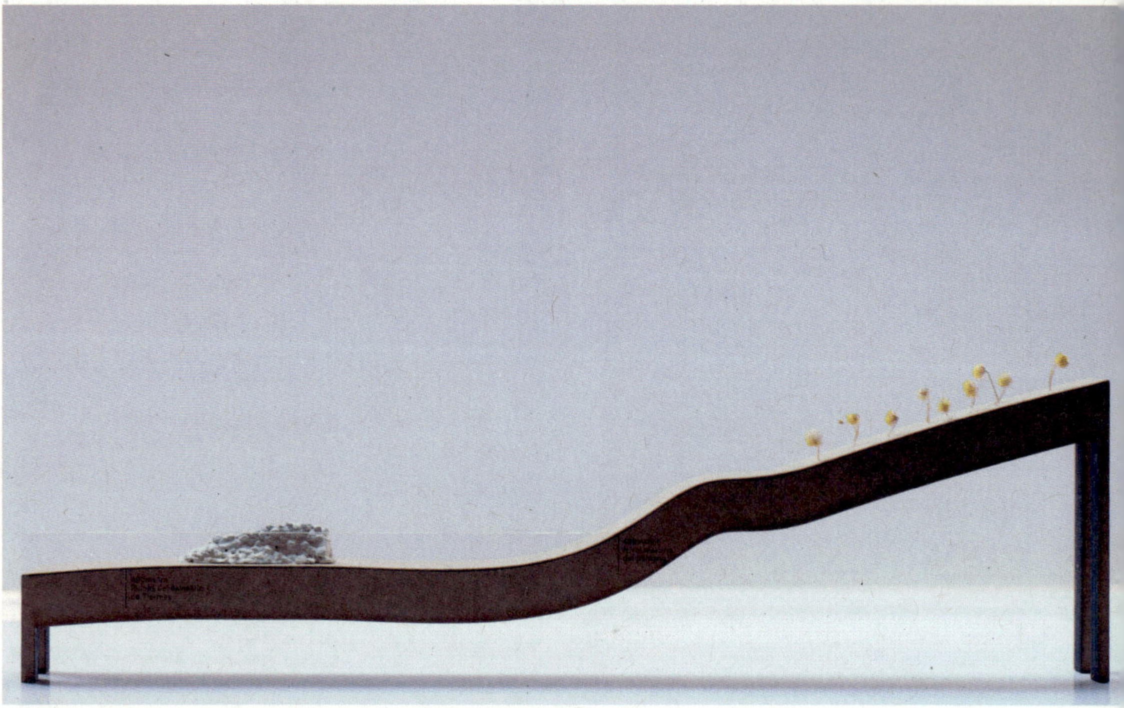

→ 291 EMERGING PLACES FROM NO-PLACES

→ 290

COBOI SOCIAL INNOVATION LAB

POLSER

→ 293 MANIFEST DE L'INVISIBLE

LA PROSTITUCIÓN EN EL RAVAL

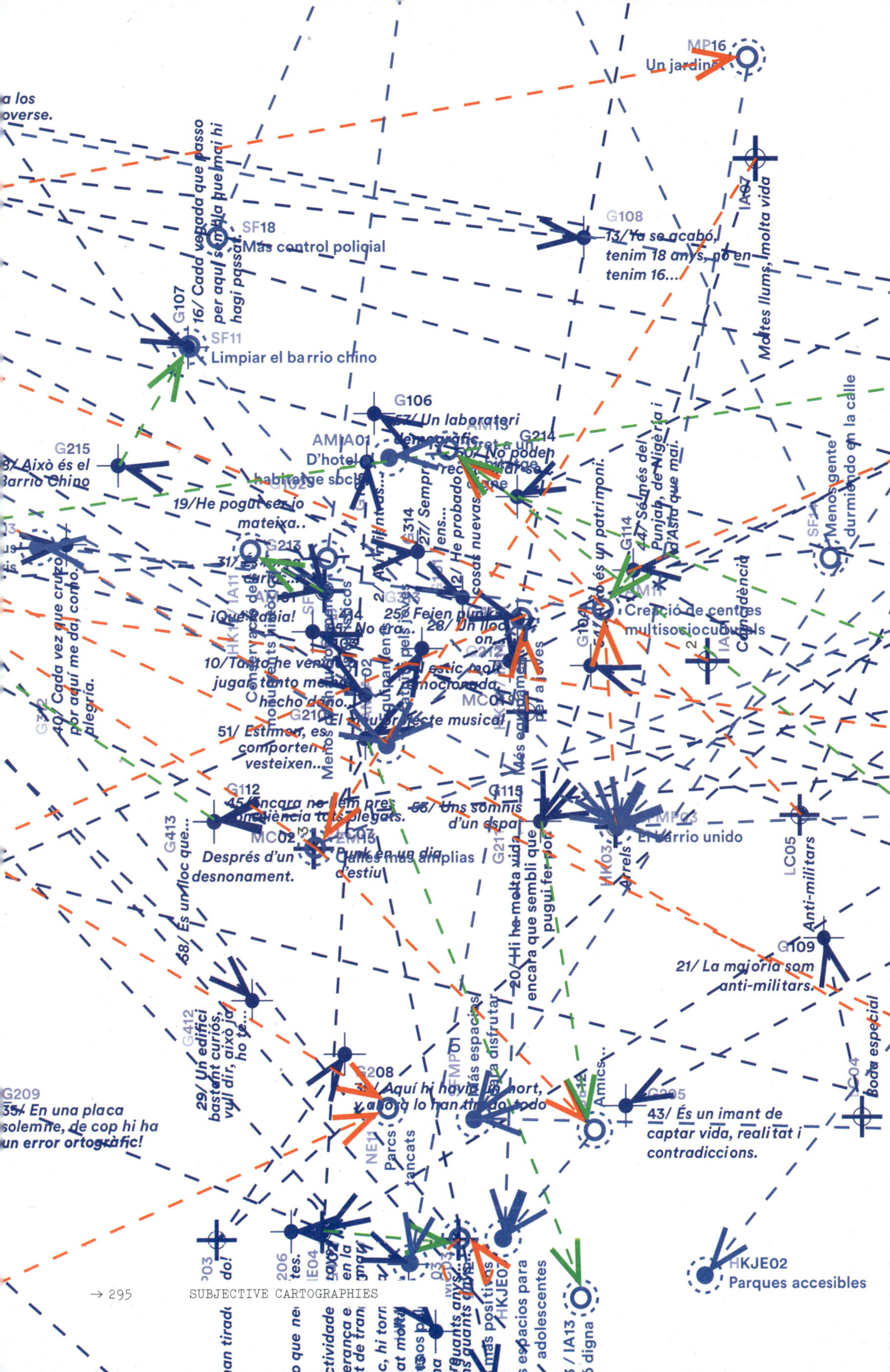

MP16
Un jardín
SF18
Más control policial
G107
16/ Cada vegada que passo per aquí sembla que mai hi hagi passat.
SF11
Limpiar el barrio chino
G108
13/ Ya se acabó, tenim 18 anys, no en tenim 16...
Moltes llums, molta vida
G106
G215
Això és el Barrio Chino
AMIA01
D'hotel a habitatge social
G214
19/ He pogut ser jo mateixa..
Menos gente durmiendo en la calle
¡Qué rabia!
10/ Tanto he venido a jugar, tanto me ha hecho daño.
25/ Feien punk...
Creació de centres multisociocult urals
Convivència
40/ Cada vez que cruzo por aquí me da, como, alegría.
51/ Estimen, es comporten, vesteixen...
G112
45/ Encara no hem près consciència tots plegats.
MC02
Després d'un desnonament.
G115
55/ Uns somnis d'un espai
El barrio unido
Arrels
LC05
Anti-militars
G413
58/ És un lloc que...
G109
21/ La majoria som anti-militars.
20/ Hi ha molta vida encara que sembli que pugui fer por
G412
29/ Un edifici bastant curiós, vull dir, això ja ho te...
G208
Aquí hi havia un hort, y ahora lo han tirado todo
Amics...
43/ És un imant de captar vida, realitat i contradiccions.
Boda especial
G209
35/ En una placa solemne, de cop hi ha un error ortogràfic!
NE11
Parcs tancats
HKJE02
Parques accesibles
Espacios para adolescentes

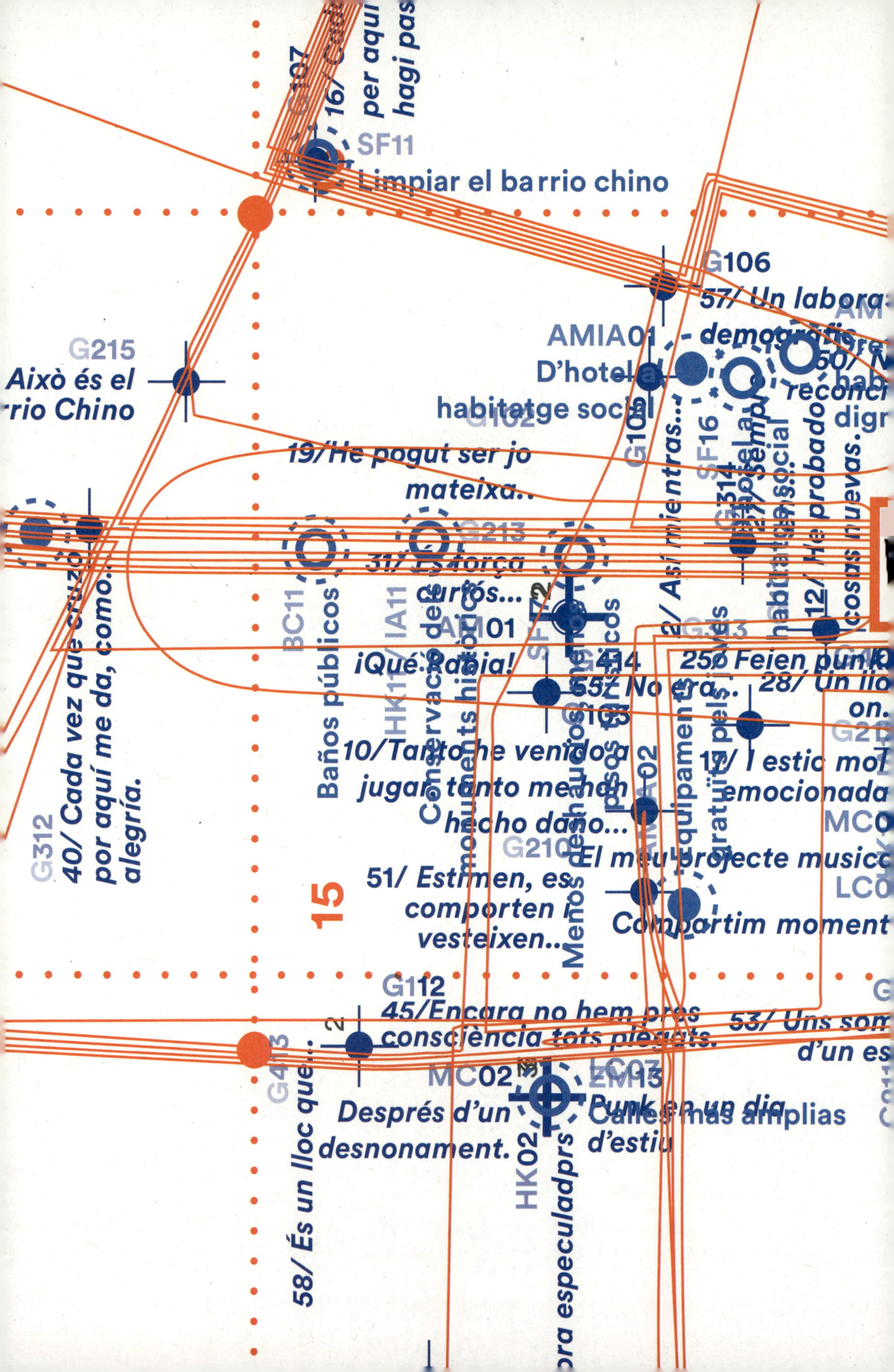

SF11
Limpiar el barrio chino
G106
G215
Això és el
AMIA01
D'hotel a
habitatge social
19/He pogut ser jo
mateixa..
AM01
¡Qué Rabia!
414
55/ No era..
25/ Feien punk
10/Tanto he venido a
jugar, tanto me han
hecho daño...
17/ I estic molt
emocionada
G210
51/ Estimen, es
comporten i
vesteixen...
G112
45/Encara no hem pres
consciència tots plegats.
MC02
Després d'un
desnonament.
LC03
ZM13
Punk en un dia
d'estiu
Calles más amplias
15
40/ Cada vez que cruzo
por aquí me da, como.
alegría.
G312
BC11
Baños públicos
HK11 / IA11
Conservació dels
monuments històrics
Menos desahucios
G413
58/ És un lloc que...
HK02
12/ He probado
cosas nuevas.
SF16
AMIA02
equipaments
gratuïts pels joves

FRANKFURT
DAMM
Frank Frankfurt

BAR

→ 293 MOVING PAPERS

unionpapelera
STAPLES
DIRECTO
MATISSE

SANT LLUC

→ 293

INVISIBLE MAKERS IN CIUTAT VELLA

the City of Things

PART II

THE CITY OF THINGS: COLLECTIVE SPACE AND TEMPORALITY

As we have discussed, environmental and social challenges converge in urban areas worldwide. The city is the world's most relevant human habitat, and any move towards urban sustainability should simultaneously address both ecological and equitability issues. Based on this framework, this chapter addresses design as a city-maker, focusing on a renewed approach that encompasses urbanity, spatiality, and temporality. It does so by positing two basic ideas as groundwork. First, collective spaces are fundamental to sustainable urban milieux. Spatiality is the crucible of urbanity, an overarching and complex condition that goes beyond mere extension and is characterized by an articulation between hybrid physical-digital spaces and situated practices. Second, design needs to embrace temporality to reach its full city-making potential. Introducing the dimension of time into spatial design makes it possible to focus on lived reality and experience, resulting in duration-based situated phenomena with city-making capabilities.

The city is the very place where the private domain can be, and often is, a social domain, just as much as or indeed even more than the public domain. Private buildings as public elements, radiating social meaning and value that extend beyond the actual buildings, embody their urban character. Collective spaces are not strictly public or private, but both simultaneously. These are public spaces that are used for private activities, or private spaces that allow for collective use, and they include the whole spectrum in between.

Manuel de Solà-Morales[30]

The air is thick with anticipation. A few students are dismantling parts of a huge model of a Raval block for safekeeping, before its imminent demise. The model, produced by 28 students of 16 nationalities in the course of an intensive workshop between Elisava (Barcelona) and Balwant Sheth School of Architecture (Mumbai), is so big that it does not fit through the classrooms' otherwise large doors. After a few minutes of debate, a vast majority of the participants decide to ritually destroy it. A final collective action: a few seconds of playful destruction culminate three weeks of intense collaboration. The project, called Community Plug-ins, explores micro-architectures as civic infrastructure to articulate informal, organic and self-managed programs to foster collaboration and social cohesion throughout the district. Given its innovative approach to the city, one that radically incorporates collaboration and temporality, it seems fitting that the video that captures the moment of the final collective fleeting action becomes an integral part of the project's presentation.

Community Plug-ins was developed as a three-week-long collaborative program. During the first two weeks, the Mumbai team identified informal, organic and self-managed collaborative logics among residents of their neighborhood community in the city of Mumbai. The

30 Solà-Morales, 2008, 188.

Barcelona team explored spaces of opportunity in the Raval district where places promoting community life might be designed to effectively improve social cohesion. Mumbai provided programmatic exploration while Barcelona provided the socio-spatial framework. During the third week, both teams jointly worked in a 1:20 physical model of a specific site epitomizing the character of the Raval and used it as a test bed for microarchitectures intended to foster community-building through newly proposed collective spaces. Given their prototypical condition, these solutions could be applied throughout the district, defining a new meaning for the superblock model currently being developed in Barcelona.

The project's topic addresses the community-building potential of collective spaces (i.e., either public or private spaces characterized by a collective use and care), expanding the traditional notion of the urban commons. The notion of 'collectivity' also informs the design approach, one that purposefully explores game-based formats, introducing chance, role play and negotiation to foster a co-design environment. Paradoxically exploring open solutions through precise design decisions, the workshop demonstrates the potential of weak authorship in design and makes a point about collaborative processes yielding concrete (yet radically open) results, thus dismantling the dominant dichotomy between hard and soft approaches to design. The active use of widely accessible IT technologies allows for a type and degree of collaboration between designers and urban stakeholders from all over the world barely imaginable only a few years ago and explores new ways of addressing the articulation between thinking globally and acting locally.

Community Plug-ins' focus on collective space is intentional. Contemporary tendencies such as remote working or cohousing, exacerbated by the COVID-19 crisis, force us to imagine new spatialitics that articulate unforeseen social relations, actively reinventing urbanity beyond the outdated binaries of public versus private, inside versus outside and natural versus artificial. This current condition is greatly reinforced by two tendencies that align with it and feed into it: the generalization of ITs and a shift in authoriality in design as explored through notions of weak or displaced authorship and collaborative models (game-based practices, co-design, self-regulation, emergence, open solutions, scenario planning and so on).[31]

The three plug-in components of this project are clear: first, it actively generates new civic places between the scale of public space and that of the private apartment, which allow for an expanded, lived-in collective space; second, problematizing the limits between traditional housing through the introduction of shared services and spaces, it mediates between segregated groups of residents and opens up the possibility for an expanded notion of community; finally, it identifies specific opportunities present in the built fabric of the city to reinvent its performance without radically changing its physical configuration.

Collective space is not a new concept, and its relevance in the traditional city is represented by the richness of shared spaces (often forced by poor living standards). However, in our current world, collective space takes on a new light, promising a desirable counterweight to hegemonic tendencies towards urban segregation and social isolation.

The Relevance of Space

Space is a complex notion, radically significant across all urban axes. Morphologically speaking, compactness is an essential urban condition. From an ecosystemic point of view, complexity and metabolism are informed by specific spatial configurations, establishing a dynamic relationship between form and function. Finally, from a relational vantage point, social cohesion is (positively or negatively) affected by specific spatial settings, and civic appropriation activates urban spaces in a concrete way.

Spaces can and should be understood as a way to foster and prompt human and more-than-human interaction. Spatial configurations, materiality and temporality generate concrete and specific milieux where social and relational interactions may thrive. We are particularly interested in the ability of space to become place —i.e., a lived space imbued with not only physical but also social, relational, performative and temporal dimensions.

31 Paez, forthcoming.

We have already addressed Sennett's recent re-branding of the *ville-cité* dichotomy, stressing the complex nature of the city, simultaneously made up of physical and relational realities. It is now relevant to swiftly address a few concepts that become operative in this regard, as they touch on the complex spatial-social-political makeup of the city, expand the conceptual and instrumental potential of collective space as well as its emancipatory power, and ultimately influence our conception of design for city making as plug-ins.

Building on the medieval dictum *Stadtluft macht frei* (city air makes you free), Max Weber explains the (Western) city as the social structure enabling unknown people to live together. Thus, 'autonomy' becomes a crucial urban concept. By virtue of the fact that the city breaks down (or at least greatly reduces) legitimate systems of domination (traditional, charismatic, and legal-rational), it becomes an autonomous entity able to sustain new and unexpected freedoms. Weber coins the term "non-legitimate authority" to address this specifically urban form of authority that breaks with the ruler's traditional legitimacy and allows for the appearance of counter-powers of the organized ruled (e.g., *demos, plebs, commune, popolo, coniuratio*).[32] City-dwellers become empowered citizens thanks to the city's autonomous condition at all levels: physical (walls), social (organized community) and political (laws, taxes and war).

Taking Weber's idea of urban autonomy much further, the 'right to the city' states an active (and creative) relationship between city and city-dweller. A concept first proposed by Henri Lefebvre,[33] the right to the city has become very influential in contemporary critical thinking, activism, engaged social movements, and progressive local authorities especially due to David Harvey's more recent revision.[34] Urbanization, worldwide, tends to impose a certain homogenization of lifestyles, applying dominant modes of spatialization and behavior throughout. The right to the city is an aspect of human rights, specifically the right of citizens to collectively co-create and appropriate their urban spaces, breaking free from planning elites and market-imposed solutions. Originally developed as a critique of the functionalist planning of

32 Weber, 1986.
33 Lefebvre, *op. cit.*.
34 Harvey, 2008.

 cities in the mid-20th century, which resulted in a generalized eviction of working class inhabitants from city centers and the construction of isolated housing projects on the peripheries, the right to the city has found a renewed relevance as a critique of the capitalist commodification of cities and urban life. As Harvey states, "The question of what kind of city we want cannot be divorced from that of what kind of social ties, relationship to nature, lifestyles, technologies and aesthetic values we desire. The right to the city is far more than the individual liberty to access urban resources: it is a right to change ourselves by changing the city. It is, moreover, a common rather than an individual right since this transformation inevitably depends upon the exercise of a collective power to reshape the processes of urbanization. The freedom to make and remake our cities and ourselves is [...] one of the most precious yet most neglected of our human rights."[35]

The 'right to the city' implies the idea that space is not a neutral framework for social life, but is actively produced. Through the notion of the 'production of space',[36] Henri Lefebvre presents a radical critique of both the Enlightenment conception of abstract space and the idea of charged space posited by the Modernists.[37] The critique is founded on the understanding of space as a social product. According to Lefebvre, space cannot continue to be conceived of as passive and empty. Space is not a fact of nature or a fact of culture; it is a product of social tensions in relation to the physical environment. By emphasizing that the general framework we inhabit as human beings is a (social) product, Lefebvre redefines the role of spatial design practices. City planning and city making practices are upheld as a political tool for the transformation of reality: "Change life! Change society! These precepts mean nothing without the production of an appropriate space."[38] From the moment that our physical, mental and social reality becomes denaturalized and is understood as produced, all kinds of new proposals for producing the real become possible. In this sense, critical design practices can contribute to the transformation of social space by producing an alternative imagery that promotes the implementation of new social practices and the construction of new realities. The notion of space as a product implies the possibility of producing space. As a result, the traditional

35 Harvey, *ibid.*, 23.

36 Lefebvre, 1991.

37 Rather than the eponymous 1978 performance by Abramovic/Ulay, we are borrowing the term 'charged space' form the Smithsons concept of a 'charged void' (Smithson, 2001, 11), and loosely applying it not only to their understanding of space but also to both Wright's 'fluid space' (Wright, 1960, 285) and Le Corbusier's 'espace indicible' (Le Corbusier, 1957, 25).

notion of space as a neutral and predetermined framework is transformed: space becomes an oriented framework that can be constructed, and the scope of the real is expanded.

Heavily relying on Lefebvre's notion of space, Edward Soja's concept of 'thirdspace'[39] posits the spatiality of human life as a fundamental conceptual axis alongside historicality and sociality. Human life is not only intrinsically historical and social, it is also spatial. Thirdspace adds a level of complexity to the traditional dualistic understanding of space as both a material and mental reality and suggests incorporating a third additional dimension to our conception of space. This third dimension is radically open and explores other forms of spatial awareness that add on to perceived and conceived spaces. Homi Bhabha has further explored the notion of Thirdspace as a space of hybridity, subversion and resistance to dominant cultural politics that develops when different individuals or cultures interact.[40] Thirdspace is a form of spatial awareness beyond the concrete materiality of spatial forms of objective physical space (perceived space or Firstspace) and the mental or cognitive forms of human spatiality of subjectively or collectively imagined space (conceived space or Secondspace). Thirdspace is the site of play and struggle and contains the possibility for social and political transformation as it is constantly expanding to include otherness, thus making it possible to contest and negotiate boundaries of cultural identity and design action. Exploring Thirdspace in practice and finding specific applications "requires a strategic and flexible way of thinking that is guided by a particular motivating project, a set of clear practical objectives and preferred pathways that will help to keep each individual journey on track while still allowing for lateral excursions to other spaces, times, and social situations. If Firstspace is explored primarily through its readable texts and contexts, and Secondspace through its prevailing representational discourses, then the exploration of Thirdspace must be additionally guided by some form of potentially emancipatory praxis, the translation of knowledge into action in a conscious —and consciously spatial— effort to improve the world in some significant way."[41]

38 Lefebvre, *op. cit*, 56.
39 Soja, 1996.
40 Bhabha, 2004.
41 Soja, *op. cit.*, 22.

Taking these crucial notions (urban autonomy, right to the city, production of space and Thirdspace) into account, it is obvious that the conventional division between public and private space is not enough to understand and transform the city's complex spatial articulation between individuals and society. Even in spaces epitomizing individuality and maximum privacy (e.g., the private bedroom), there are aspects of collectiveness (e.g., a flower/a flag on a window, an occasional visitor, a backdrop for digital relationships). However vague it may seem, there is a collective aspect in every urban spatial situation.

We thus propose an understanding of collective spaces at three distinct levels: shared, referring to spaces intimately shared between a few people (e.g., a private apartment); communal, referring to spaces used and actively cared for by a larger collective (e.g., co-living); and public, referring to those spaces belonging to all and used by all (e.g., a public square).

These three levels imply different relational frameworks, and different types of stakeholders and interlocutions, and they mobilize different design tools and actions for the purpose of understanding, designing and transforming them. We need to explore collective spaces in all their complexity, rethinking housing units as shared spaces, reclaiming communal spaces, and reinforcing public space appropriation.

Design has paid a lot of attention to both shared and public spaces —i.e., the individual/familial cell that makes up most of the urban fabric and the public space system that acts as the connective tissue for cities and embodies their narrative. But for several reasons, (Western) cities have lost most of their communal spaces. The contemporary polarization between highly private spaces (my home is my castle) and administration-managed public spaces has resulted in a loss of complexity in the way citizens interact. That has implications in the physical makeup of the city, such as the loss of in-between spaces and urban thresholds, but it also affects the relational setup, oversimplifying our relation towards others and severely curbing our sense of belonging to a community-in-place: either we are isolated in our safe and ultra-connected capsules or we are exposed in public spaces managed by the administration. An intermediate level of communal spaces, shared and cared for collectively, is essential to foster community-building processes in an environmentally and socially sustainable way.

Spaces and Practices

Although there are a number of relevant approaches to addressing collective spaces in our cities, we will discuss just one here: namely, the complex relationship between spaces and practices in design. While spaces define a physical relational framework, practices activate it concretely through time. The distinction and inter-relation between spaces and practices in design is not a new one. In the last 50 years alone, this theme has been addressed by many designers (both theorists and practitioners). We will concentrate on four different approaches relevant to the discussion at hand: disciplinary expansion, design restraint, speculation, and activism.

For some designers, stressing the schism between space and practice displays the impossible articulation between design and use. Fundamentally opposed to functionalist approaches that attempt to directly relate form and function, this line of thought construes design as the imbricated relationship between operations that are both internal and external to its disciplinary core.[42] While design is usually concerned with external phenomena, such as politics, social conditions and cultural values, it addresses them through a constantly expanding disciplinary apparatus. The question, then, is to incorporate external matters of concern into design's internal discipline by mapping, diagramming, scripting, or otherwise formalising informal matters. In consequence, 'external' concerns such as site, narrative or politics come to enlarge design's 'interiority', composed essentially of formal operations that make up design's own internal discourse. What is relevant in the current discussion is the ability to expand design's abilities through the capacity to transcribe any discourse into design operations. However problematic this approach may be in other respects, it offers a way to radically incorporate design processes within design's results. The very decision-making processes, including exploratory, participatory and collaborative work, can thus become an integral part of design's discipli-

42 Eisenman, 1999.

 nary apparatus. That is a crucial point because it offers a way to preclude metaphoric or representational design approaches, fostering engaged and situated design through a constantly updated designers' toolkit —essentially re-situating the questions of 'process vs. result' and 'expert vs. non-expert'. This approach can be seen in Civic Placemaking 2: Kn60Lab / IPSI, where design proposals are developed as toolkits to be creatively developed and transformed by the end 'users'.[43]

Less concerned with design's disciplinary apparatus and more interested in design's political power, other designers posit a radical schism between spaces and practices. Precisely because there cannot be a causal relationship between the spaces defined by cities, buildings, or objects and their uses and meanings, the "disjunction between space and event, together with their inevitable cohabitation" becomes a source of strength, criticality and subversive power.[44] This take on what design can do is very relevant to our current discussion as it introduces the idea that one can never design behavior, but one can design conditions that will affect it —although (and this is a very important caveat) the way spaces are used will always explore paths unforeseen by the designers.[45] A relevant corollary of this position is that when we design, we should be taking into account the radical disjunction between spaces and practices, which inevitably leads to the conclusion that often a good design solution may be not to design (at all, or, more often, not so much).[46] In a nutshell, (designed) spaces should leave space for (un-designed) practices. An example of this restrained attitude is Vora, a prototype to consolidate the temporary public spaces that have occupied streets in response to the COVID-19 crisis. By building a safe boundary between cars and newly pedestrianized spaces, Vora indirectly generates a rich social space between the new boundary and the building façades where users can engage in educational, cultural and leisure activities on their own terms.

Recently, the speculative design approach has offered a third take on the spaces vs. practices dichotomy. Positing design as a problematizing practice (rather than a mere solution provider), speculation displaces design's conventional dependence on the present. Using design's ability to imagine different futures, speculative design uses possible

43 Paez, Valtchanova, 2021a.
44 Tschumi, 1996
45 Manzini, 2015.
46 Price, 2003.

futures "as tools to better understand the present and to discuss the kind of future people want, and, of course, ones people do not want."[47] This approach implies a significant enlarging of design methodologies and tools, including fictional worlds, what-if questions, thought experiments, explorative scenarios, counterfactuals or reduction *ad absurdum* experiments. This poses a very relevant question for our present discussion, i.e., the possibility of displacing the relationship between spaces and practices so that a speculative practice can generate specific spaces with agency in the present world, while a speculative space can prompt novel practices that impact our current lives. A project like SOAP, a collective exercise that uses speculation to navigate the emotionally difficult first months of pandemic lockdown, makes it possible to critically explore different futures in a relatively immediate way. SOAP, originally a tactic used to address psychological distress, quickly became a strategy to identify and outline future design issues.

A fourth approach to the space/practice articulation is that of the activist-designer. From this point of view, both spaces and practices are seen as an integral part of the designer's purview. Working in direct-action formats and putting the designer's body on the line is characteristic from the activist approach. Exploring the rich tradition of engaged design from radical architecture groups,[48] avant-garde theatre and performance arts troupes,[49] art- and design-based interventionist practices,[50] and myriad grassroots initiatives and collaborative social movements, the activist-designer seeks to deepen the relationship between design and social impact, positing design itself as an active social agent. Widely varied in formats, these designs address both spaces (to further practices) and practices (to generate spaces). What is most relevant in our current discussion is that the activist approach considers spaces and practices, equally, as objects of design.[51] On the one hand, spaces are understood as generators, mediators, or identifiers of specific situated practices (often using advanced digital collaborative tools that expand the idea of situated practices well beyond the conventional bounds of physicality). Following performance art methods and aims, on the other hand, practices are assumed as a crucial part of the designer's responsibility and, often, the most evident of design's results. Usually small

47 Dunne and Raby, 2013.

48 E.g., Superstudio, Archizoom, Ant Farm, Haus Rucker Co.

49 E.g., Living Theatre, Odin Teatret, Fura dels Baus.

50 E.g., Vito Aconcci, Francis Alÿs, Assemble Studio, Bik van der Pol, Jordi Colomer, Martí Guixé, Lucy+Jorge Orta, Krzysztof Wodiczko. Refer to Paez, Valtchanova, 2021b.

51 E.g., Raumlabor.

in scale and deeply rooted in local conditions, most activist formats explore the fringes of traditional design, often introducing temporality, duration, and experience as key elements. This should not be surprising, as these marginal pursuits allow levels of freedom that are unheard of in highly codified (and commodified) spatial design formats, as discussed in the next section where the relevance of time in spatial design is addressed. A concrete instance of an activist project is En Mitjons a la Plaça, where design is used as a mediator between neighborhood residents, NGOs, and the public administration, triggering a virtuous cycle of extensive collaboration and civic body empowerment.

The inter-relation between spaces and practices curbs the merely static and formal understanding of the built environment favored by conventional architecture. As stated earlier, while spaces define a physical relational framework, practices activate it concretely through time. The tense connection between the physical and the relational that is triggered through the four approaches discussed above fosters urban complexity and diversity, highlighting the fundamental role of *temporality* to expand the boundaries of how design can promote meaningful transformations in the urban fabric and civic life.

TEMPORALITY

> *Temporality contains the essence of democracy. […] temporary spaces create social knowledge and offer opportunities for active participation.*
>
> Florian Haydn[52]

Overnight, a new element has appeared in a parking area near the entrance to a school. A wooden modular structure defines the new expanded boundary between pedestrians and cars, consolidating a public space that has been tactically pedestrianized during the COVID-19 crisis. A few hours after its unannounced appearance, in November 2020, a formal class takes place in the middle of the street, which

52 Haydn, Temel 2006, 71.

temporarily becomes an educational space. Barely half an hour after the class, the street becomes a playground, allowing children to enjoy games while respecting the compulsory bubble groups imposed by COVID regulations. At the end of the school day, this usually dead place is warmed with activity: children avidly indulge in free play while parents, masks on, socialize barely a meter away from traffic. During a full month, this temporary design allowed the children, staff and parents from the Sagrada Família school in Barcelona to transform what used to be a featureless parking area in a typical Eixample chamfer into an intensively used public space. On weekends and after school hours, this new public space enables all sorts of free appropriations of what had been, until then, a marginal space. Lectures, active classrooms, theatre performances, concerts, free play, informal gatherings, and lingering to read, chat or simply relax, activate a new type of public space, informed mostly through temporality.

The project, called Vora (edge, hem, bank or shore in Catalan), is described as a 'safe occupiable limit for tactical public space extension'. It is a prototype designed by researchers and students at Elisava to consolidate the temporary public spaces that have occupied streets in response to the COVID-19 crisis. It forms a limit that can be played on and appropriated, encouraging new uses for the public spaces that have been expanded by the city council in areas near schools. Vora builds a safe boundary between cars and these new pedestrianized spaces, where users can engage in leisure, educational, and cultural activities.

Although it may look like urban furniture, this design is a system, not a specific object. Its size and layout can be adapted to any site to generate a safe limit that will protect and activate expanded pedestrian space, promoting the appropriation of outdoor public spaces to increase the number of COVID-19 safe spaces. Once the system is installed on the site, Vora's components can be rearranged according to the needs of the site with the addition of slides, steps, benches, or combined playscapes. Temporality permeates the design throughout: it can be set up and dismantled in two hours, allowing it to appear and disappear without a trace. It can be endlessly reconfigured in a matter of minutes allowing it to respond to changing demands, and it prompts temporary activities that currently have no place in the city, turning public space into a terrain for experimentation, open-endedness and improvisation.

The three plug-in components of the project are clear: first, it *generates* a new space of opportunity that did not previously exist by inserting a new element that redefines an edge condition and thus expands the opportunities afforded by tactically pedestrianized public space; second, it *mediates* between diverse communities and between converging or diverging interests (school activities vs. non-school activities, play vs. education, intimate vs. collective actions) that already exist on the site but are only activated through design; finally, it *identifies* and draws attention to socio-relational realities hitherto implicit but hidden from view (positive impact of a school in the surrounding neighborhood, active street reclamation for civic uses, raising awareness of multiple community initiatives, including fringe actions and populations).

Vora's focus on temporality is intentional. Although it may be built in wood, this design's true material is time. All design decisions that went into Vora ultimately addressed time as a lived-in duration, what makes a personal or collective situated experience possible. They also addressed time as the evolving lifespan of a design that constantly changes. They also assumed the active role of chance in the shifting relationships between design and behavior. Finally, they addressed temporality through temporariness, embracing the fleeting existence of reality that confronts us with the value of the here-and-now and dismantles the often-castrating power of grand narratives and permanent certainties. Experience, change, chance and temporariness were taken as positive values to explore through design.

Again, temporality is not a new concept, and its relevance in the traditional city is represented by the preponderance of temporary events over permanent structures (think of how markets were events before they were buildings, or how the socio-spatial impact of urban celebrations marks the passage of time). However, in our current world of hybrid realities and impending *glocal* emergencies, temporality takes on a different hue worth exploring through design.

Temporary is the New Permanent

We live in an increasingly uncertain world, in which temporary is the new permanent. Traditional certainties have dissolved, and change has become commonplace. Change is, perhaps, the only constant in our lives. The flexibility, swiftness, adaptability, responsiveness, reversibility, and resilience allowed by temporary solutions is increasingly being perceived not only as positive but radically necessary. The systemic emergencies we are now living with (social inequality, climate change and pandemics) only reinforce the relevance of temporality in design. Recently, the COVID-19 crisis has fast-tracked the need for a more dynamic approach to city planning and city making, capable of creatively addressing change and finding opportunities to improve the city amid our unpredictable reality. Temporary space design has a crucial role to play in this emerging context, and ephemeral architecture is increasingly being viewed as a serious discipline with a huge social impact, as it helps to adapt to continuous change using few resources and achieving a high level of citizen implication.

ALL THAT IS EPHEMERAL ALSO MELTS INTO AIR (+ AN EPHEMERAL MANIFESTO FOR THE DESIGN-EVENT)

Ramon Faura Coll

The action *Converses a les Rambles* [Conversations on Les Rambles][1] was intended to create spaces to promote dialogue between tourists and residents, which had been interrupted for far too long. The *pretext*, if you will, was to exhibit a series of chairs designed by Elisava students. At the same time, independently of the forms of the different chairs, the space of Les Rambles was filled with places to sit, *free of charge*, and it fostered conversations between passersby who, had they continued on their way, might never have spoken to one another. The students encouraged the residents to express their ideas about the neighborhood. Through orality, they were invited to take back a space, Les Rambles, whose identity many feel has been wiped out by the pressure from tourists.

In a way, *Converses a les Rambles* employed *conditioned chance*. The cooption of public space for tourist uses has ultimately obstructed the relationships between residents and visitors. It has reduced any exchanges to a mere economic transaction and, as a result, it has excluded any local residents who don't have a direct implication in the tourist economy. It's clear that, beyond political decisions, a real exchange between residents and visitors is essential —among other things, to make visitors aware of the fragility of the urban and social fabric. A fragility that has been caused in a large part, albeit involuntarily, by the visitors themselves.

Through their conversations with tourists, residents learn that the tourists are also poorly served by the structures that determine a single fixed way of visiting places. We are witness to the perverse situation highlighted by Günther Anders as early as the 1950s, in which executioners and victims are melded together into a single figure.[2] But beyond the specific case of tourism, which is, of course, central to rethinking public space, *Converses a Les Rambles* restored the idea of public space as a place where two strangers can start a conversation. Beyond Les Rambles, the goal is to break with a narrative of the city based on a wariness of difference, based on fear and suspicion, on an obsession with security —to break with the prevailing dynamic of a public space that is hyperoccupied by connected individuals, each on their own network terminal, but impervious to the physical reality of the place they are connecting from.

Converses a Les Rambles was an ephemeral device, which centered on the event (people's conversations) rather than the object (the specific form of the chairs). The design, above all, was focused on contingency.

CONTINGENCY

A contingent event *may but is not certain to occur*. Paradoxically, although new technologies seem to have created a society immersed in speed and permanent change, those same technologies make it increasingly difficult for unforeseen things to occur. I'll skip over the part about social control and privacy as a commodity. Just by looking at your cell phone, you can find out whether the wind will be blowing this afternoon, if it's going to rain tomorrow, or what the road conditions will be like before you leave the house. The same technology that is casualizing our lives, makes us incapable of embracing any possible contingency.

A text by Isozaki offers some ideas from the standpoint of culture.[3] Whereas, in Japan, public space —that chimera that emerged under the imperative of tourism— is a fleeting entity, not segmented or clearly differentiable from intimate or private space, under continuous transformation. In Europe, the construction of public space is, in essence, just the opposite: it turns provisionality into permanence, whether it is a square, a monument or a stone temple. In contrast with Eastern *indifferentiation*, Western space is segmented into precise functions: pedestrian crossing, market, leisure center, urban garden, parking area, sidewalk, bike lane, loading zone. The specialized segmentation of public space dispels what Westerners can only perceive as disorder: contingency.

In fact, in pre-Western Japan, there were no public squares, and what we call streets were more like our idea of a *path*. Byung-Chul

Han puts it another way: if existence in the West is based on the idea of essence, of "staying in one place,"[4] —in other words, a closed space that is resistant to change[5]— in the East, existence is founded on the idea of walking without leaving a trail, since marking a place entails appropriating it, differentiating it.

With regard to impermanence, it is interesting to look back at the profound meaning Isozaki attributes to architecture and, by extension, design, which ceases to be understood as a thing (a fixed and inert form), to be considered an event. If you'll bear with me, I'll begin a brief *excursus*.

Isozaki sees the roots of this conception in the ancient Shinto shrines, which were *ephemeral*, a place to invite the Gods (*kami*). In Shintoism, the gods reside outside sacred buildings, where they are not given an assigned permanent place like in the Greco-Roman or Christian tradition. In the past, the Shinto ritual consisted of summoning the *kami* using a temporary construction: the *himorogi*, originally just a clearing in the woods, sometimes indicated by a wooden platform. Later, especially in urban settings or palaces, a fence (*tamagaki*) was built around the empty space (*niwa*). During the ritual, a sacred branch (*sakaki*) was placed there, and the *kami* were invited to inhabit it temporarily. The ritual ended when the *visit* was over or, if there hadn't been a visit, when it was accepted that it would not be taking place. This is an important detail: the construction invited the temporary presence of the gods, but it did not ensure their presence.

Whatever the outcome, the *sakaki* was then removed, the *tamagaki* was dismantled, and the provisionally occupied space became once again an undifferentiated part of the forest. The architecture (although they did not use that word) was made meaningful, not as a container for sacredness, but to support a manifestation of the gods in a particular place and during a certain span of time.

I'm interested in one particular idea in all of this. What defines the ephemeral artifact, beyond the obvious fact that is designed to eventually disappear, is the idea of inviting the manifestation of spirits that may, perhaps, reveal themselves. The meaningful ephemeral object, as I understand it, invokes a kind of contingency that is also transcendent. And the space has to be empty because, if it were full, it wouldn't allow for the emergence of anything serendipitous, the advent of any spirit. In our terms, *emptiness is what allows for the participation of others*, and it is therefore contingent. And we call it contingent because, if the presence of the spirits were assured, like in a Christian temple where the idols are always present, the event would no longer be a revelation but merely the confirmation of a predetermined program. It would no longer be revealing a hidden truth but illustrating a dogma. In other words, rather than illustrating a certainty, ephemeral interventions today should reveal an uncertainty and thus encourage critical reflection among everyone involved.

That's the end of the *excursus*, and I'll recap. Ephemeral design for social transformation becomes meaningful when it operates with contingency, when it offers a silence or a void so that participants can express themselves, and when, instead of offering a lesson, it asks questions and fosters critical inquire. When it short-circuits reality and transforms our perception of it: *Converses a Les Rambles*.

IF SOCIAL INNOVATION ISN'T POETIC, IT IS NEITHER NEW NOR SOCIAL

In the project *Revivir* [Revive],[6] the material objective was both indisputable and urgent: reconditioning the space of the refugee camps in Tindouf (Algeria), which are subject to extreme weather (maximums of 57° and minimums of -3°), using recycled plastics. Additionally, the project incorporated a fundamental decision: it had to be possible for members of the refugee community to carry out the construction process themselves. More than an ode to productivity, the aim was to understand how, beyond adversity and discomfort, on a more psychological level, inactivity can affect people's self-esteem and, ultimately, their appetite for life. In that sense, it recalls the projects by Anna Heringer in Rudrapur (Bangladesh), in which the construction is adapted to the technical and material possibilities of the place and its inhabitants. In contrast to the ethnocentric imposition of an opaque technology that generates clients, the implementation of the design is turned into an event. It isn't designed for the users, but in collaboration with them, which makes them into active agents. Offering them an open space to grow and make their voices heard.

Drawing on an ethical implication similar to that of *Revivir*, the project *Manifest de l'Invisible* [Manifesto for the Invisible],[7] works with the non-place conditions of the shacks near the Glòries road interchange, hidden beneath the magnificence of the Agbar tower, the Disseny Hub, the Teatre Nacional and the multi-reflective roofs of the Nous Encants. In the ephemeral and experimental installations that accompany the design (for example, installing shacks under the porches around the Plaça Major in Vic), the intervention is an event insofar as it transforms the spectator. In contrast with the aestheticization of misery or the institutional ugliness of certain leftist movements that are suspicious of aesthetics, *Manifest de l'Invisible* is a poetic action. And not to the detriment of its social intervention —on the contrary. It unveils and uncovers. To put it in Lefebvrian terms, it unmasks the simulacrum —lie of capitalist public space and highlights the underlying conditions of exploitation. It turns us into someone else.

To sum up: *Revivir* and *Manifest de l'invisible* are projects that, beyond the objects they design, do not focus on users. They promote the emergence of active agents who are involved in determining the project. They focus on an event. And they do it by using poetics.

TO COMBAT FORMAL OBSOLESCENCE: RHETORIC

Design interventions focused on social innovation often aim to raise awareness about a problem or a shortcoming. But informing isn't the same as communicating. If the information doesn't become an experience, the information, at best, piles up, but it isn't articulated to become a force for transformation. Wikipedia informs. Dostoevsky and Banksy communicate. In the case of the design-event, form is how the design can turn the (essential) information into knowledge. This is also where the importance of poetics comes into play. The paradoxical use of familiar elements —a chair in the middle of Les Rambles or a strange artefact under the porches around the square in Vic— is what catches our attention and sparks our interest. When we find ourselves asking “What does this mean?”, we become participants as opposed to mere users.

The *design-event* is inevitably discursive. It plays on what we know and what we don't know, because that's the only way it can take us somewhere else and turn us into someone else. While, before, I referred surreptitiously to the poetic act as something that reveals and makes things visible —what lets us form a theory, now I'd like to posit poetic defamiliarization as what catches our attention and incites us to reflect. In poetry, putting a chair in the middle of Les Rambles would be the equivalent of using a word in an unconventional way: a marker of meaning. Counter to the semantic inertia of everyday life (things mean what they seem to mean), poetry plays with the ambivalence of polysemy and metaphor. It pushes us to interpret the world in a lucid way, in contrast with the immobility of a petrified common sense.

Unlike in the literary tradition, in the world of design, the word *rhetoric* is often used in a derogatory way. It refers to a meaningless, capricious form. It designates anything that is arbitrary and superfluous. The design-event, however, insofar as it is discursive, inevitably operates based on rhetoric. In a statement, whether linguistic or in design, information surprises us not because of what we don't know, but because of how what we don't know fits in with what we do know. Rhetoric deals precisely with the order of a statement, the indicators of emphasis, the sequences of ideas, and the formal figures that help us retain concepts.

Rhetoric is consubstantial with the poetic act (revealing a truth), and therefore we should understand it as ground rather than mere form.[8] Barthes explains this very well. Think, for example, about offering condolences to a friend whose father has died. There are a number of ways we can express our regret. While there are formulaic sayings ("My condolences", "I'm sorry for your loss"), those same sayings, when addressed to someone you are close to, may sound meaningless —or even imply their exact opposite, because they are tired tropes. It's important —necessary— for us to become rhetorical, to put poetry into action, to think about how to demonstrate, to share the pain we feel in response to the loss. To choose the terms and design the order of the words so that they convey the truth of what we're feeling. To be rhetorical. If there is one critique we can make of design for social innovation, it is its occasional carelessness regarding the aesthetic and rhetorical side of the work.

There is a related example associated with the "superblock" concept. The controversy surrounding the deployment of tactical urbanism has been, above all, a poetic and aesthetic controversy, not at all frivolous. Of course, some recalcitrant drivers complained about the road space they were losing, but what really got people riled up, fueled memes and filled opinion columns in the newspapers, were the colors, the brutality of the Jersey barriers, the supposed visual disturbances they introduced into the Eixample's gentle grid. We should point out that many criticized the intervention without realizing that it was temporary. In that sense, the tactical urbanism was a success. Our subordination to cars was no longer a neutral piece of information, but an impassioned experience. Whether for or against, hooliganism aside, there was an in-depth debate about the climate crisis, the need to reduce the presence of cars, and the right to the city (when drivers park their cars to head up to their beds, they too become pedestrians). We suddenly realized that we had accepted that it was natural for us to live completely subjugated to the logic of a particular industry.

To sum up: The rhetoric or art of persuasion is, precisely, the technical ability to organize information by adding a meaning that transforms it into experience and knowledge. If the design of ephemeral architecture for social innovation aims to affect its surroundings, it cannot turn a blind eye to rhetoric or poetry. It has to be circumspect in its form, because it is through form that it triggers processes. Form, of course, is not understood as the ultimate goal, but as a catalyst for transformation.

TECHNOLOGY AND SOCIAL INNOVATION

Too often, certain supposedly critical designs take refuge in a kind of neo-Luddism where anything that exudes technology is considered suspicious. Even if it might seem impossible, the challenge should be to take ownership of technology, not renounce it. In a way, it isn't that different from the old idea of taking over the means of production and refusing, by any means, to relinquish them. The *acritical* return to craftsmanship is reactionary and, above all, it turns its back on transforming anything. It settles for alms and appeals to good Samaritanism. Byung-Chul Han talks about something similar in his book about the loss of rituals.[9] Ethical values as an object of consumption or consuming altruism as a new way to appease a bad conscience. If the design-event intends to transform the world, it cannot ignore the technological essence of human beings. Going back to *Australopithecus*, turning our backs on *Homo habilis*, is obviously not a good plan if our goal is to change the conditions for the future. We can only improve the world with technology. Technology is to design what metaphor is to poetry.

This idea isn't mine. Or not entirely. For Marshall McLuhan, metaphor and technology are the same insofar as they transport us somewhere else. After all, that is the etymological meaning of metaphor, from the Greek metapherein ("to transfer"). For McLuhan, technologies, like metaphors, "similarly involve the transformation of the user insofar as they establish new relationships between him and his environments".[10]

Sometimes, in this context, candor, ignorance, fear of conflict, or the absurd veneration for vulnerability that has become fashionable of late, have led certain designs for social innovation to refuse to accept that transforming the world also entails destroying it. The issues that need to be resolved —accommodating refugees with dignity, restoring damaged landscapes, freeing public spaces from imposed external logics— are not natural occurrences. They have been brought about by certain agents for their benefit and, at the very least, that needs to be recognized. Without friction, there can be no possible transformation. That's why the design-event has no choice but to operate technologically. In the words of the mathematician and philosopher Alfred North Whitehead, "The major advances in civilization are processes which all but wreck the societies in which they occur."[11] Metaphor and technology are destroying the world as we understand it today. And this *destruction* is part of any design that aims to change an imperfect present.

EVENT

In *Cartografies Subjectives* [Subjective Cartographies], a series of collaborative workshops held in the Raval neighborhood, design was put into everyone's hands as a useful tool. In this case, it was meant to offer residents a new perspective on their surroundings through the use of mapping. As opposed to the simulation of an understanding of their problems, they were offered participation in a shared code. As Jane Jacobs detected more than half a century ago, the dislocation between languages —technical, normative, cultural, economic, experiential, affective, class-based— favors the construction of a technocratic city that is bereft of any affection: an emotionally stunted city.

From that standpoint, *Cartografies subjectives* is interesting because it puts tools into the hands of city residents. Beyond looking at their neighborhood in a different way (which is no small feat), they are given a means of using codes to which they usually do not have access. It is worth pointing out that such codes are often used for the express purpose of making administrative decisions opaque. The residents were no longer spectators in relation to the design and instead became participants in it. While the action was ephemeral, the effects on the residents were not; they ceased to be passive users and instead became valid interlocutors.

Slavoj Žižek talks about event as "the effect that seems to exceed its causes".[12] From there, Žižek asks a series of questions: "Is an event a change in the way reality appears to us, or is it a shattering transformation of reality itself?" For Žižek, looking at causes means delving into the world of philosophy. For me, it also involves delving into the world of the design-event. Ultimately, and *Cartografies subjectives* is a good example of this, making us look at reality in a different way it is an inevitable part of the design-event.

To sum up: In the design-event the unexpected appearance of something new that weakens any stable design is crucial.[13] I won't repeat the Whitehead quote. The action is ephemeral, its effects are not; that is why I've referred to it as a transcendent action.

THE STOCK MARKET IS ALSO EPHEMERAL

The transformations over the last 20 years have made us sensitive to an uncomfortable truth: all those subversive and liberating proposals that emerged in the 1960s, poised to overturn the sclerotic structures of a reactionary Europe, unjust and dull, ultimately became a perfect blank check for the most savage, barbaric and all-consuming operations of a neoliberalism in permanent revolution. In that sense, the design-event —the heir to happenings and Radical design, to artistic Actionism, to the Human Be-In and to collaborative processes— also participates in this paradox.

The fascination with open form and impermanence, so liberating in the 1960s, is now one of the most distinctive features in the operations of investment funds, land speculation, and the precarization of the labor market. In today's economic, social, work-related, emotional and productive environment, in which the dizzying volatility of every last thing has become the only constant, there are many questions that arise when we think about the values of an ephemeral culture and design that posit innovation (social or otherwise) as their main reason for being. An excerpt from Marshall Berman can be very helpful in fine-tuning this question:

> *Our lives are controlled by a ruling class with vested interests not merely in change but in crisis and chaos. 'Uninterrupted disturbance, everlasting uncertainty and agitation,' instead of subverting this society, actually serve to strengthen it. Catastrophes are transformed into lucrative opportunities for redevelopment and renewal; disintegration works as a mobilizing and hence integrating force. The one specter that really haunts the modern ruling class, and that really endangers the world it has created in its image, is the one thing that traditional elites (and, for that matter, traditional masses) have always yearned for: prolonged solid stability.*[14]

There is a fine line between the design-event and the promotional party. In strictly design-related terms, what are the essential differences between a tent at the end of Les Rambles informing us about the refugee crisis and one promoting a mobile phone brand? Many companies with no goal other than economic gain have adopted the *makeshift* language of protest. Nonconformism is on the rise, and beyond the now distant ad campaigns run by Benetton or Levi's, there is not a single extractive company in the automotive or hydropower industry that hasn't espoused freedom, ecology, feminism or multiculturalism. How can we break free from this circus? How does the design-event transform us while ensuring *solid, long-lasting stability* that can obstruct the excesses of a speculative economy that volatilizes and erodes everything?

In this case, the answer is neither easy nor obvious. However, and with the intention of opening the debate, not closing it, as a final recap I'll point out some of the features that should make the difference between an ephemeral design for social innovation —the design-event— and a mere party that, with or without a moral underpinning, focuses only on the promotion of a product, the spectacularization of our lives, and the masking of exploitative productive relationships.

EVERYTHING IS EPHEMERAL (MANIFESTO)

Design with a desire for social transformation focuses on the event and summons contingency. The contingency summoned by the design-event is transcendent insofar as it leads to changes beyond the scope of the action. The causes disappear but not the effects on how we perceive (i.e., construct) reality.

The form of the design-event is always a medium, not a goal. The form isn't the purpose, but it is the trigger. And that is precisely why it needs to be approached in aesthetic terms.

The design-event short-circuits reality, instead of perpetuating it or fossilizing it. But that forces us to think. It doesn't illustrate a dogma; it lays bare a doubt. The void —whether physical or conceptual— is what allows the user to move on from being a user to become an agent, to formulate doubt. Poetics and rhetoric lend beauty to the design-event: in other words, attractiveness and paradox, which are the prerequisites, the triggers, that push us to ask ourselves about the meaning of things. Conventional beauty isn't beauty because its meaning has been worn out by overuse.

The design-event is always technological because only through technology can we be transported to a new place, become someone else, and see reality from a different angle. Stop valuing reality as an objective given, and instead determine the vectors that generate it, whether conflicting or otherwise, and introduce new ones.

NOTES

1 Converses a Les Rambles: Una acció per facilitar el diàleg entre turistes i residents a Barcelona. Action carried out by first-year students of the BA in Design, 2017-18 academic year, coordinated by Danae Esparza. See the catalog for more information. See Catalogue.

2 According to Anders: "The 'technification' of our being: the fact that today it is possible that unknowingly and indirectly, like screws in a machine, we can be used in actions, the effects of which are beyond the horizon of our eyes and imagination, and of which, could we imagine them, we could not approve - this fact has changed the very foundations of our moral existence. Thus, we can become 'guiltlessly guilty', a condition which had not existed in the technically less advanced times of our fathers. You understand what this has to do with you. After all, you are one of the first ones who have actually been caught in this new sort of guilt, in which everyone of us can be caught today or tomorrow. What could happen to us tomorrow, has actually happened to you. Therefore you are playing for us the great role of a crowning example, yes even that of a predecessor." (Letter 1, Günther Anders to Claude Eatherly, June 3, 1959). See: Anders, 2003.

3 Isozaki, 2006.

4 HAN, 2019, 13.

5 *Ibid.*, 14.

6 Revivir (Tejiendo terreno) by Laura Badia is a Final Degree Project (TFG), directed by Daria de Seta during the 2019-2020 academic year. See: Project Catalogue.

7 Manifest de l'Invisible is a Final Degree Project (TFG) by Judit Tremosa, directed by Daria de Seta during the 2019-2020 academic year. See: Project Catalogue.

8 Barthes, 1983.

9 Han, 2011.

10 McLuhan, 1989, 31-32.

11 McLuhan, 2015, 6.

12 Žižek, 2014, 17.

13 *Ibid.*, 18.

14 Berman, 1982, 95.

At the beginning of the 21st century, ephemeral architecture was perceived as a minor pursuit. Professionally, it was associated with limited commercial or recreational formats such as trade fairs or music festivals. Academically, only a handful of well-established niches such as exhibition design paid any attention to temporality within spatial design practices. Finally, the research component was, with some notable exceptions, all but inexistent. Moreover, despite the huge advances made in the past 20 years, temporary space design is sometimes still perceived as potentially attractive but fundamentally irrelevant.

There are deep-seated reasons that explain why both traditional professional design practices and academic programs pay very little (if any) attention to temporality. This is due to a widespread cultural undercurrent that assumes temporary things are useless, meaningless, gratuitous and essentially futile. This is an extremely relevant issue, as this association is deeply embedded in the dominant branch of Western thought that equates permanence with value, meaning, and, ultimately, with being.

From this point of view, (true) reality is associated with permanence, and so are the categories for describing and exploring this reality: physicality, visibility, identity. A consequence of this interpretation of reality is the difficulty of conceiving and addressing change and becoming (a question already addressed by Aristotle, challenging Plato's stable worldview). Indeed, in today's speech, the verb 'is' is linked to actuality rather than potential, and the dominant understanding of reality is 'that which remains' rather than 'that which becomes'. Although this is not the place to elaborate further on the profound difference between a representational philosophy of 'being' versus a constructivist philosophy of 'becoming', suffice it to say that it has fundamental implications for how we understand the world we live in and the ways in which we can transform it. The conceptual, practical, and political effects of subscribing to a constructivist logic[53] in which experience generates reality are huge—and for us, they are consubstantial with the way we understand time-based design.

Despite the desire for permanence on the part of the state apparatus and its many subsidiaries (i.e., administration, military, technology, finance, economy, etc.), change and uncertainty are unavoidable

53 Glasersfeld, 1984.

aspects of our contemporary societies —perhaps now more than ever, due to globalization. If we are to build a better world for all, learning to creatively address these aspects is of crucial relevance for all facets of society, including design. Specifically, spatial design practices need to expand beyond traditional practices (without abandoning them), addressing temporality to respond to pressing social problems within the framework of globally limited resources and sustainable development goals. Radically incorporating temporality into spatial design's processes and products allows us to cater to human experience, to foster citizen engagement, participation, collaboration, and inter-personal relationships, and to explore spatio-relational potentials that would be unthinkable through conventional permanent means.

The Values of Temporariness

As we explained earlier, in our culture, dominated by a stable understanding of reality, temporariness often has a negative connotation. Counter to this tendency, we defend the value of temporariness as a social activator on every level of urban life (productive, commercial, cultural, educational, recreational, political). In that regard, it is crucial to identify three positive ways of understanding temporariness in the design, use, and maintenance of urban space: urgent temporariness, experimental temporariness and structural temporariness.

First, design mobilizes urgent temporariness when it offers a rapid response to a pressing issue that cannot admit delay, either due to emergency or opportunity. In this case, which we might associate with a patch, to use a sewing metaphor, the intervention is voluntarily acknowledged as temporary, in the sense of short-lived, because its end point is clearly defined from the outset. This condition of programmed obsolescence precludes debates and problematics that, despite their potential relevance, would hinder the speed of implementation or the agility in the transformation of a situation that demands swift action. It is necessary to clarify that the patch, understood literally and without the usual negative connotations, manages —temporarily and urgently— an issue that needs to be resolved. Moreover, it highlights the issue as needing to be addressed, independently of the merits of the solution, which has been offered in a context characterized by limited time, resources, reflection and participation. The urban intervention as a patch, which aims to solve a problem or explore an opportunity in a tactical fashion —rapidly, and with only the available tools, in response to an urgent need, and at a low cost because the intervention is temporary— introduces a highly efficient method of operating in response to a wide range of emergency situations. Due to the context of urgent temporariness, the intervention is conceived and executed as an element that can be modified, disassembled, improved, reversed, or even eliminated. The project Conversations on La Rambla illustrates this type of temporariness.

Second, design mobilizes experimental temporariness when it uses the temporariness of an intervention (in the sense of not definitive) as a testing ground to investigate, assess, examine or explore the behavior of a temporary solution in order to draw conclusions that will inform a future project (which may be temporary or permanent). The experimental value of the design lies precisely in its temporary nature. To return to the sewing metaphor, this type of temporariness can be associated with the idea of basting. Just as basting is used to adjust the fit of a garment so it can be tailored later, experimental temporariness supports a design's ability to anticipate a wide range of situations, whether they are expected or unexpected, typical or unprecedented. Basting allows for taking risks that a permanent intervention could not permit, because it can always be corrected. Because errors can be amended, instead of appearing as problems they become opportunities for improvement. This is an essential point because, as we all know, both in experimental science and in human behavior, we can only improve by learning from our mistakes. In short, experimentation lets us evaluate, testing out materials, situations, and solutions in order to eventually implement the ones that have been deemed satisfactory. The project Teixits Dinàmics illustrates this type of temporariness.

Third, design mobilizes structural temporariness when it works with interventions and projects that always retain a temporary quality at their core; in other words, although they play an ongoing role in the urban milieu, their presence is ephemeral. Whether it is due to intermittence or periodicity (temporary interventions that appear and disappear depending on the calendar), or to versatility and adaptability (permanent interventions that are constantly undergoing transformations), certain urban interventions or situations demonstrate this structural temporariness. The metaphor for this kind of temporariness is the idea of a change of clothes: there are a series of garment types that we wear every day (in that sense, they are permanent and structural), but the individual items are always different (in that sense, they are temporary). This third derivative of temporariness is nothing new, as is evidenced by recurring events such as neighborhood festivals, traditional fairs and travelling markets, or itinerant facilities like bookmobiles or Barcelona's mobile recycling centers. Although there are currently situations in which temporariness is not understood either as a stopgap that responds to an urgent need or as a testing ground to consolidate more permanent solutions after they have been tried out temporarily, we believe that the contemporary urban project should more fully explore designs that incorporate temporariness in a structural way. The project Mercats de Pagès illustrates this type of temporariness.

The rapid pace with which the plug-in logic operates requires celerity in detecting places in the city that demand attention. In that sense, we need smart tools for reading the city and uncovering design opportunities. New urban maps should not be limited to strictly spatial approaches, anchored in permanence, but should incorporate the aspect of temporariness and continuous transformation. In today's world, what we need to understand, above all, is the transformative component of the city. If cities today are to avoid becoming sclerotic and obsolete structures, they need to be designed with an eye to change, adaptation and transformation.

Accordingly, we believe that design understood as city making plug-ins should be contextualized within this triple articulation of temporariness (urgent, experimental and structural). We feel it is necessary to advocate a deeper inclusion of temporality in the design, use and management of collective space. The urban project, as a civic project, cannot be strictly spatial; it needs to incorporate time as a mechanism and as a horizon in order to build a healthier, more just city, the wellspring of a rich and bountiful society.

We posit, therefore, that reinventing the city through design is only possible when there is a combined activation of the spatial conditions of the place, its temporal aspects, and the social dynamics driven by situated relational practices.

Ephemeral Architecture and Social Purpose

We indistinctly use the terms ephemeral architecture or temporary space design to refer to the expanded field of spatial design that radically deals with temporality. It encompasses well-defined formats such as pop-up structures, event design, temporary interventions in public space, and exhibition design, as well as the rich areas of overlap between them, such as emergency architecture, tactical urbanism, flexible habitats, collaborative experiences, or reactive atmospheres. Learning form contemporary art, technology, and sociology, this emerging design discipline uses the flexibility, swiftness, adaptability, responsiveness, reversibility, and resilience allowed by temporary solutions to address precariousness, chance, and uncertainty in order to prompt citizen empowerment and positive social change.

Ephemeral architecture has a huge social and even emancipatory potential —some of it linked to its relatively marginal status within design disciplines. Marginal, here, does not mean inconsequential but fringe. Without dismissing the consolidated center of architectural discipline, it explores and exploits the fluid areas of its edges. Indeed, ephemeral architecture is marginal inasmuch as, devoting itself to happening, change, and becoming, it problematizes permanence, a dominant idea of architecture as epitomized by the second element of the Vitruvian triad, *firmitas,* and a large part of subsequent architectural theory and practice. Less concerned with the structural or objectual aspects of architecture, it focuses on performance and perception. Less concerned with technique per se it focuses on its affects and effects. Less concerned with closure and grand narratives, it focuses on duration and lived experience. Instead of prescribing behavior, it focuses on triggering occurrences. As opposed to conditioning design, it focuses on designing conditions. Rather than defining, it focuses on irrigating, prompting and suggesting. Eschewing specialized authorship, it incorporates the inhabitant/user in the design process—either implicitly or explicitly. Less concerned with optimization, it focuses on exploration.

In addition to its unique conceptual approach, there are also very relevant pragmatic specificities of this emerging design field. Due to its temporal nature, temporary space design usually mobilizes fewer resources (both economic, labor, and material) than permanent architecture. At the same time, its scope and ambition include not only questions of form, structure, and function, but also questions of performance, perception, and action. This combination requires a strategic use of limited resources to achieve maximum results, so that the designer is challenged to 'kill many birds with one stone', so to speak. Practically speaking, this has several implications.

First, one needs to be especially aware of the locative and social place where the project happens, closely reading its make-up and behavior, as the intervention will change its dynamics for a while (perhaps even well after the project's disappearance). The use of operative mapping is a crucial point here.[54] In Civic Placemaking 1: Marianao, carefully mapping the qualities, perception, and uses of a neighborhood informs design decisions to foster community appropriation of a neglected public space.

Second, one needs to be particularly strategic in using material and logistic resources to achieve the desired results. This often implies incorporating the inner logics of these systems into the conceptual core of the project, rather than using technique solely as a solution provider.[55] In REC Pop-UP Space, the lack of material and economic resources coupled with the availability of beer crates drove the design from its conceptualization to its resolution,

Third, one needs to hone the proposal, at all its levels, so that nothing is superfluous, further exploring the idea of design as purpose informed by constraints.[56] In Community Plugins, a gamified set of locational, functional, and material constraints was used to proliferate design proposals that added on to the existing urban fabric to rekindle communal spaces.

Fourth, one needs to take advantage of disciplinary fluidness in order to conceptually, methodologically, and technically expand the field of time-related design.[57] In Chased, a purpose-developed digital

54 Paez, 2019.
55 Numen/For Use, 2016, 126-146.
56 Eames, 1989.

interface allowed students to control public street lamps, subverting their function and temporarily turning them into an animated and responsive environment.

Fifth, one needs to explore and further the critical agency of unplanned, open-ended, improvisational activities and practices usually shunned by planning disciplines.[58] In Slow Down, Stop, and Stay, a shifting choreography of tables interrupted the conventional use of a public square, facilitating unprogrammed events that generated new and unforeseen chemistries.

Finally, one needs to posit the end user as an active agent in the design process.[59] In COVID-19 Niches, the students' own bodies were used as a way to interact with new urban conditions generated by the pandemic and transform them through direct action.

Ephemeral architecture's relatively marginal status within design disciplines affords it a leeway that may be explored with degrees of freedom and scrutiny unlikely in more traditional design areas. Complementing other design approaches, ephemeral architecture caters directly to citizens' actions and desires, focusing on lived reality and experience. It uses its fleeting nature and the lack of many of the technical and cultural hurdles associated with permanent structures "to explore this new freedom aggressively."[60] More profoundly, it insufflates a sense of hope in the human ability to find meaning in life as opposed to in its fixed representation. In that sense, design has a crucial role to play in the current emerging context, defined by a globalized, resource-limited, emergency-ridden, and radically uncertain world.

CODA

The one-two punch of collective spaces and temporality explored in the text above allows us to identify crucial challenges of design as a city-making agent, all of which have a relevant impact on the reinterpretation and redefinition of urban spaces, products, and services. We can summarize them in the two following points.

The first challenge is to embrace the paradoxical spatial scenarios opened up by the collapse of classic binaries such as public/private,

57 Saraceno, 2012.

58 Dell, 2019.

59 Franck and Stevens, 2007; Haydn, Temel, *op. cit.*

60 "Strategy of the Void". See: Koolhaas 1995, 604.

 inside/outside, or natural/artificial. Accepting the loss of stable paradigms and designing under the assumption of a paradoxical reality "is more than an exercise in provocation, it is a possibility to reconcile many variables from reality and thus to assume its complexity".[61] Urban spatiality is undergoing significant changes, exacerbated by the generalization of ITs and the impact of social, environmental, and health emergencies. These new conditions offer a fertile ground for exploring design's agency to spatially situate, socially mediate, and temporally activate the shifting limits that define contemporary cities, giving special attention to collective spaces.

The second challenge is to radically explore temporality in spatial, product, and service design. Embracing impermanence and constant change is a powerful way of updating our relationship with cities in the sense of how we design, use and manage them. In short, boldly exploring the temporal aspect of design lets us investigate multiple alternatives for urban life. Instead of constructing a fixed representation of an idea of the city, we should use design to seek out new urbanities that respond to the current context of globalization, systemic crisis, limited resources, and growing unpredictability. How time-based logics will impact city design in the immediate future is an open question. We claim it will be necessary to understand temporality (designing with time) as a positive value and to incorporate temporariness into the design and use of the city in a structural way. However, rather than temporary in the sense of merely provisional, urban space (from public space to housing) should be temporary in the sense of flexible, adaptable, responsive, and resilient. Most importantly, perhaps a focus on temporality will result in a focus on civic life, situated experience, and new forms of politics and of beauty.

In conclusion, we believe that we should not be working to define a single new city model; rather, we should understand the city as an open-ended project that allows for testing multiple models —accepting, and even desiring, the uncertainty that it entails. Ultimately, we consider that it is time to put urban life ahead of its representation. Exploring new notions of collective space and addressing temporality through design has a big role to play in that task. Rather than striving

61 Muñoz Carabias, 2020, 111-112.

for a single, overarching urban model, we claim contemporary cities should strive for diversity. Given an urban setting characterized by relational and physical density, the abovementioned points are essential to identifying design's multiple roles and potentialities in working towards that open horizon through concrete, specific, and situated practices. Positing design as plug-ins within a larger socio-spatial urban system allows for exploring design as a way of simultaneously *defining* the hardware of products and spaces and the software of relations and interactions, while *enabling* unprogrammed actions, unplanned events and unpredictable appropriations, operatively embracing indeterminacy, uncertainty and chance.

the City of Inter-actions

PART III

THE CITY OF INTERACTIONS: MICRO-INFRASTRUCTURE AND RELATIONAL OBJECTS FOR COMMUNITY BUILDING

In Ersilia, to establish the relationships that sustain the city's life, the inhabitants stretch strings from the corners of the houses, white or black or grey or black-and-white according to whether they mark a relationship of blood, of trade, authority, agency. When the strings become so numerous that you can no longer pass among them, the inhabitants leave: the houses are dismantled; only the strings and their supports remain.

Italo Calvino, *Invisible Cities*. 1972

 Ersilia is the city of interactions: one of the 55 cities that Marco Polo describes to Kublai Khan in Italo Calvino's book *Invisible Cities*. Towards the end of the book, it will be discovered that, in reality, these 55 stories are many different descriptions of the same city, which for Marco Polo is Venice. But for us, it could be any other city.

In fact, each of the stories offers a different way of looking at the city. They each highlight an aspect that can be interesting and relevant. The fact that we have chosen to single out Ersilia is not meant to deny the others. However, in the context of this book, we believe that looking at the city as a network of interactions helps us to recognize some important aspects of its present and its possible futures.

Calvino's Ersilia shows us a continuous effort on the part of its inhabitants to hang strings that represent their interactions —ultimately, what Ersilia is made up of. That is the city we will deal with here. Yet, what differentiates our city from that of Calvino is how this weaving process develops over time. In Ersilia, the spider web continues to grow, to thicken until it makes the city uninhabitable and its inhabitants must abandon it, leaving behind this intertwining of threads. For us, in our reality, although the weavers of these networks still exist, powerful factors are also at work pushing in the opposite direction, cutting the existing threads and making it difficult to create new ones. Or dispersing them into another parallel world: that of digital interactions.

ENCOUNTERS, CONVERSATIONS AND COMMUNITIES

The Festa Major of Sant Antoni, in one of Barcelona's historic neighborhoods, is the most important event of the year for its inhabitants. It is also a time when community bonds are forged, an event in which citizens participate by occupying the streets and squares. This moment, more than any other, highlights how and to what extent the city is a tangle of relationships: between its inhabitants and between them and the place where they live.

But there are some people in Barcelona who, because they are elderly or because they are sick, cannot leave the house and go out into the street to join in the celebration, which can lead to feelings of loneliness and isolation. Could this be avoided? Can this torn social fabric be mended? A group of designers (students in Elisava's MUDIC Master) asked themselves these questions and set out to find ways to reconnect the strings between these homebound people and everything happening outside during the Festa Major and in its preparation. They imagined a group of volunteers could "bring the party into the homes" of these people and vice versa: bring these people to the party using digital means. The project points to a series of micro-events that could make this possible, and it describes the ways in which the group of volunteers could be formed, motivated and coordinated.

This is a precise and localized proposal —it refers to a well-defined group of inhabitants in a specific neighborhood— but it seems emblematic of what we want to discuss here. It clearly shows us the city as a network of interactions: in other words, the lived city, the city of encounters, conversations, and communities. It then shows us how this fabric of relationships can be torn apart, but how it is also possible to imagine plug-ins that, by inserting themselves into the existing system, mend the breakages in the network of relationships that make up the city and help regenerate it.

Taking a step forward in understanding how this can happen, let's take a closer look at the city of interactions. On closer inspection, the network that makes up the city is anything but homogeneous: it is organized into different social forms whose minimum units are *encounters* —that is, interactions with meaning. Paraphrasing Martin Buber, we might say that the social city is ultimately a collection of encounters.[62] Here, we should also note that some encounters, when connected in sequences, produce conversations,[63] and that these conversations, when reiterated over time, give rise to social forms which, by tradition, are given the name *community*. The city of interactions is therefore made up of encounters, conversations, and communities. And its quality is determined by the density and diversity of the encounters and conversations that take place, by the vitality of the communities they generate and, ultimately, by the ability of these communities to produce and reproduce the social city.

62 The original Martin Buber quote says: "All actual life is encounter" (Buber, 1996, 62). See also: Cipolla, 2009, 242.

63 Winograd, 1987-88.

To discuss how this can happen, and whether and how it can be stimulated and supported, it is necessary to pause briefly to delve into the concept of community as we interpret it today. Contemporary communities are in fact very different from those we have known in the past.

Light and Open Communities

Traditional communities, which we might call pre-modern (or non-modern) communities, are relatively closed social forms, connected to a place and characterized by networks of dense, stable and lasting bonds. These communities, where they still exist, are important and we have a lot to learn from them. However, in more modernized parts of contemporary societies, these traditional communities no longer exist or are in serious crisis, leaving room for growing individualization (with all its implications in terms of individual and social loneliness and fragility).

On the other hand, in recent years, as a reaction to this growing individualization, transformative social innovation has produced a variety of new social forms: contemporary communities that are quite different from pre-modern (or non-modern) ones. Unlike pre-modern communities, which were not chosen by their members, contemporary communities exist by choice: they are intentional. At the same time, unlike the intentional communities of the 20th century, which were based on strong ideologies that demanded exclusive affiliation and promised a strong identity, contemporary communities are multiple, non-exclusive and require no special level of commitment. Conversely, very often, they are formed around a theme that acts as a catalyst. We see communities that are built in relation to various topics of interest (for example: food and food networks; music; specific sports or recreational activities; care for people and the environment; and so on).[64] Using the terminology introduced by Bruno Latour, they are a group of people united by a common *matter of concern*.[65]

Another very important characteristic relates to how they are created and how they persist over time: they exist because they are begun and driven by groups of motivated actors who, in fact, operate as designers (designing coalitions). To avoid any misunderstanding, it should be pointed out here that these communities cannot be directly

64 Manzini, 2019.
65 Latour, 1993.

"designed": no one can design human relationships. However, the conditions can be generated for these relationships can emerge and thrive. We will come back to this later.

Here it is useful to focus on an aspect that is particularly important to us: the relationships between these communities and the spaces around them —and, in particular, their ability to generate places.

Communities of Place

Having broken through the constraints of spatial proximity (first due to developments in transportation and then in telecommunications), how communities exist and, consequently, the relationships between people and places, has changed fundamentally. We know the story: actors in modernized societies find themselves living in a context where the possibility for interaction between subjects (and thus the possibility for a community to exist) is no longer limited by the need for spatial proximity between interlocutors. Since it is possible to communicate irrespective of distance, communities are formed in association with places that are not necessarily physical, circumscribed and contiguous. Each of us may be part of a multiplicity of social forms, engaging in conversations with various, widely scattered interlocutors.

The result is that the center of gravity of people's daily lives has shifted, very quickly, towards the digital space. In this context, the COVID-19 crisis, with the lockdown first and the physical distancing after, has forced a large number of people to overcome the inertia and the difficulties of an initial access to digital services and to move many of their activities online. All this has numerous implications, at all levels. The most obvious is related to what these new interactions allow or disallow. In fact, while it is true that there are activities that can be carried out at a distance and online, there are many others that cannot. The case of care, understood in the full spectrum of its meaning, is one clear example.

Looking at caring for the sick, for children, or for the elderly, but also care in the sense of mutual support in times of difficulty, it is evident that, at least for the interactions directly involved in the action of giving, receiving, or exchanging care there has to be a physical dimension. We may be part of numerous online communities, but when we need someone to offer practical support, if those people are not present, we are completely alone and, therefore, left without care.[66]

Something similar can be said for the care of the environment. People who live mainly in digital communities, and therefore in digital environments, tend to reduce their connections with the space where they live to a minimum. In the end, they cannot take care of the space because they are no longer familiar with it. Of course, all this is not solely the result of the rise in online communities. Neglect in peripheral areas of cities and territorial fragility in the face of catastrophic events are also brought about by other socio-economic drivers. However, it is certain that the evolution of people's social lives towards digital forms has contributed to this process of territorial abandonment

To counter this trend, it is necessary to update not only the concept of community (as previously mentioned), but also that of place, and the relations between the two. Today, if we want to have communities connected to places, we must create the conditions for this to happen. In other words, we need communities where interlocutors have reasons to care for the places where they live. In other words, they must be communities whose purpose is to involve people in doing something together in the physical world (sharing spaces, cultivating the same garden, collaborating in the care of children and the elderly). As a result, by taking care of the specific space around them, they contribute to giving it meaning—that is, they transform that space into a place: the place that belongs to the community.

When this happens, it generates what we call *communities of place*: communities whose raison d'être includes the care of the space in which they are located.[67] On the other hand, given that these communities, like all contemporary communities, are open, light and intentional, the same can be said for the places they generate. Contrary to what might have been the case in the past, these places do not exist simply because "they have always existed", but because someone has intentionally done something to make them exist. In other words, intentional communities produce intentional places.

66 Manzini, 2022.
67 Manzini, Politics of..., *op. cit.*

It should be added here that the different nature of these new places is not only their intentionality. Another clear character is their hybrid nature. Up to this point, we have aimed to emphasize the importance of physical places. However, it must be said that, today, they are complementary to the digital places where communities are also formed. In other words, communities of place are increasingly *hybrid* communities of place.

Let us return briefly to the project relating to the Festa Major of Sant Antoni in Barcelona, which gave us our start. It was envisioned as an emblematic intervention in its role as a *generator*, connecting not only people with one another, but also people with the place where they live. In doing so, it collaborates in the construction of a community of place that has the ability, in this case, to include even the most fragile people and those at the highest risk of marginalization. And it does so by operating, precisely, in a hybrid physical-digital space.

Communities of Care

Speaking about the future of services for the elderly in the city, Lluis Torrens, who is the head of the Area of Social Rights at the Barcelona City Council, wrote: "The fundamental idea is what we call the virtual distributed residence: a concept in which a person in their own home receives the same services as they would in a room in a neighborhood residence, on a small enough scale for people with reduced mobility, supplying all the normal services that they would receive in a residential centre."[68] To achieve this, a new service system is required. It must be modeled with a distributed architecture and operate in well-defined areas with equally well-defined groups of residents with care needs.

In practice, this has led to the creation of a Home Care Service (mainly aimed at the elderly who live alone) that has numerous advantages not only in terms of effectiveness, efficiency, and quality of work for the assistants (which is evident because they accumulate less stress and waste less time moving to different parts of the city), but also in terms of the quality of the service they can offer and the role they can play in society. In fact, it has been shown that, when a logistic base is created for the stable group of operators working in each neighbor-

68 Torrens, 2018.

 hood, their presence and their role are more easily recognizable by the inhabitants and local organizations. This allows them to forge connections between the users of the services and the other inhabitants of the neighborhood. In turn, these connections can be seen as the beginning of a new community: a new community of place that is also a community of care that has its ecosystem in the dense and diverse environment of the Superilla.

It should be noted that this community of care is not limited to the professional caregiver-patient relationship. It includes the care provided by people who collaborate with one another, combining different forms of interaction according to their needs and possibilities: from mutual help among family members, friends, and neighbors to help from volunteers and from local shops that often play a social role in supporting lonely and elderly people.

All this tells us how and to what extent the city of interactions determines, and is in turn determined by, its capability for caring. Commenting on their projects, Lluis Torrens and his team write, "The common denominator of these practices is the idea of proximity." And they continue, "It is based on the hypothesis that in order to coordinate social care programs and services in a more subtle way, it is necessary to take territorial scale into account. Spatial proximity would be essential in economic and ecological terms, from the perspective of democratic governance, management and service quality at a social-community level."[69]

Several projects developed at Elisava in the framework of the D×CM program also began from the same foundations, developing a series of proposals in coherence with and in support of those the City Council is already pursuing. A constellation of initiatives emerged in relation, for instance, to the use of bars or other shops as social sensors (Radars) or as places for intergenerational encounters (Connectats —Caring Communties).

These initiatives are very different in the themes they address and in how they proceed; however, careful observation shows us that they have two underlying common features: they include in the system on which and in which they operate actors and places that, normally, are not considered or not connected (system reframing). Additionally, they

69 Torrens, Retort, Juan, 2020.
70 Puig de la Bellacasa, *op. cit.*

tend to produce relational qualities, at the core of which there is an (explicit or implicit) idea of care.[70]

Given that all the care-related activities happen in different places (institutions such as medical centers and hospitals, but also other private and public sites where such encounters can occur), all together these places form an *ecosystem of care*: the ecosystem where a community of care lives. This ecosystem, like the care community that inhabits it, has a hybrid nature that also includes a more or less extensive digital component.

SOCIAL SUPERBLOCKS: A NEW SOCIAL DESIGN

Lluís Torrens

Social or care superblocks are an adaptation of the idea of mobility superblocks to the creation of small areas where the city is divided up into intervention units of the various local social policies, run by the authorities on their own or in collaboration with citizens and organizations. Tasks in social superblocks are taken on in small teams and allow transitions between home and neighborhood. Unlike mobility superblocks, social superblocks do not have predefined physical boundaries although they are intended to fit together. A more detailed explanation can be found in Torrens (2019 and 2020).[1,2]

SOCIAL SUPERBLOCKS AS A RESPONSE TO NEW CHALLENGES

William Baumol, a North American economist who died in 2017, described the paradox of the costs of public services: the sector's productivity may not grow as fast as that of the rest of the economy, but its workers' wages certainly do.[3] So, if healthcare and care services require an interaction between social-healthcare staff and patients-users in a ratio of dedication (in hours of time) that is more or less constant in the long-term, their productivity advances less than that of other services that can be automated by technologies or that of agricultural or industrial services able to use robots or machinery. The consequence is that the wages in the sectors that increase their productivity can go up without having an impact on costs, whereas if we wish to keep doctors or nurses on a certain pay equity with other productive sectors, their wages ought to rise and so will the costs of the associated services.

The increase in the costs of those services in which productivity hardly increases at all —for example, educational services or music quartet performances (the example used by Baumol)— implies that society must allocate an increasingly large part of its total production to the payment of those services. Does this mean there is an ever-decreasing portion of production for other consumers? This leads to a paradox: as productivity rises, the remaining production available in absolute terms in reality is not reduced, only its relative participation in the total is reduced. Where is the problem? In the fact that many of the services where productivity grows less are public or non-market services (their productivity is actually measured by the wages they pay), and the divergence in productivity implies that society has to allocate an increasingly large percentage of its resources to the payment of those public or non-market services. And that means an increase in the need to collect more taxes to finance them. Looking at the trend over the last few decades, it seems that society does not wish to accept that they must pay (even) more taxes to adapt to this new situation. Therefore, a technological divergence leads to a problem with the social distribution of resources.

Let's add to Baumol's analysis the fact that the socio-demographic structure in which the Welfare State was created in the middle of the last century —in response, first, to the Great Depression of the 1930s and later to the aftermath of the Second World War and the rise of communism— is no longer the same today, resulting in new big public-spending packages that were not previously contemplated in the original design.

First, life expectancy has grown and the demographic pyramid has been inverted. In 1960, when Jane Jacobs was writing her book on the vitality of cities,[4] 9.5% of Barcelona's total residential population was over the age of 65 and only 3% aged 75 or over, whereas 28.5% was under the age of 20. By the beginning of 2020, the percentage of the overall population over the age of 65 had more than doubled (21.1%) and that of people 75 or over had almost quadrupled (11.3%), whereas the percentage of people under the age of 20 had dropped twelve points (16.5%). Since 1975, the life expectancy for people aged 65 has risen from 15 to 22 years. One of the consequences is that healthcare spending has shifted towards treatments for chronic illnesses and multiple medical diseases associated with an aging population.

A second decisive change has been the mass incorporation of women into the labor market. In 1960, 35% of women in Barcelona aged between 20 and 64 were employed; by the beginning of 2020 that percentage had more than doubled (76%).

These two changes alone represent essential transformations that have had a deep impact on living in the city and revealed the limitations of the current welfare models. More than 350,000 people over the age of 65 live in Barcelona, and 90,000 of them live alone. However, there are only 13,000 spaces in public care homes for the elderly, with a waiting list of 6,000 at the end of 2019. Most people obviously will not have access to a public care home unless their situation of dependence or illness makes it absolutely necessary for them to be admitted. It should also be added that the overwhelming majority of elderly people do not want to leave their homes, and that, increasingly, the need for care is lasting longer and has to be shared between fewer relatives. If current gender inequalities in care work are not reversed, and given the decreasing size of households and the disappearance of extended families, this situation implies an excessive physical and psychological burden on an increasingly smaller number of women in the family circle.

The lack of available spaces in public care homes implies that most people with support needs for everyday life activities (more than 100,000 people in the city, more than 40,000 of whom have a recognized degree of dependence and receive some type of non-residential support) have to receive such support at home or be accompanied to day centers to receive it. Furthermore, a significant percentage of elderly people (partly coinciding with the same group) experiences loneliness (48% of people over the age of 80).

This is where Baumol comes in: because the public cost of attending to people is monetarily cheaper at home than in a care home, limited public resources should tend to favor home services. But with a difference: the social cost is enormous either for family caregivers (as they sometimes make up for the welfare state's shortcomings with "slave" dedication) or for the persons cared for, who receive less assistance than they require.

The second focus has to do with women entering the labor market. Far from the discriminatory situation of 60 years ago, when 75% of women did not work outside the home and their Spanish ID cards stated their profession as "housewife", 76% of women were active members of the workforce in 2020. And yet, in Barcelona, care services for children ages 0 to 2 (in Spain, this type of care is non-compulsory and is not subject to free universal coverage) do not even reach 50% of minors in this age group. Low-income families cannot afford the cost of private day care and are thus faced with the problem of not knowing where to leave their children for care. Add to this two facts —on the one hand, working hours in Spain, especially in a city like Barcelona, are dominated by the retail and tourism services, which are not at all childcare friendly; and, on the other, public subsidies for families and aids to access affordable housing are scarce— and we will have found some explanation as to why Spain, and Barcelona in particular, has one of the lowest birth rates in the world.

Back to Baumol: since the public cost of creating and maintaining new day care centers is prohibitive, the limited public resources force lower income families to care for their own children —or to be more precise, and taking into account gender inequality, this task falls primarily to mothers and grandmothers. In the case of mothers, the social cost is enormous because they give up their professional careers or the possibility of promotion, while children tend to perform more poorly than those with earlier schooling. This is another huge social cost.

Both cases are examples of how a city like Barcelona needs to develop not only in the diversity of its inhabitants' origins (the percentage of residents born abroad has risen from 3% to 28% over the last 30 years) but also in generational and social diversity. The challenge is how to tackle this and maintain the value of diversity through an equity approach.

Thus, just as it is unreasonable and undesirable to create ghettos according to origins, so it is to confine elderly people (or the mentally ill) in institutions, or to "confine" women by forcing them to spend most of their time caring for children or the elderly or to double or triple their unpaid working hours.

The thesis of the social superblocks is, therefore, aimed at achieving a more diverse and balanced city in the use of time and reproductive work for all its members, in which care work, both for those who receive it and those who give it, is more equally distributed.

SOCIAL SUPERBLOCKS, HOW ARE THEY CREATED?

The idea of social superblocks in Barcelona, one of the densest cities in the world, arose from the convergence of, on the one hand, the need to change the inadequate institutional model for caring for an aging population whose family care network has diminished, and, on the other hand, the need to improve the public system for providing home assistance, which employs 4,000 family workers (90% of whom are women) who travel from home to home throughout the city.

The pilot projects began in four areas of the city in 2017. Family workers in self-managing teams attended to service users concentrated in a small area. These experiences rapidly became the cornerstone for building the social superblocks. In the coming years, most of the city will be rolling out this home-assistance model and, as it expands, new services will gradually be added that will reach most city residents. One of the advantages of this now tried-and-tested model is that the new way of working can be learned quickly and it spreads "virally", since the original teams train the new ones.

The new services can be provided by the city council itself or co-produced with citizens. The necessary connection between existing requirements and the public and private resources for designing and implementing new services, or coordinating existing ones, creates the need for new professional roles that can channel these needs while also generating a new leap forward in improving resident-assistance quality.

HOW DO THEY OPERATE? A NEW CITY SOCIAL MODEL

Given that each superblock is different, there is no one standard deployment process; rather, there are common features that we believe ought to guide the new social superblocks in their development:

- *Co-responsibility and co-production*. All superblock members must be concerned with the well-being of their neighbors. No one is just a problem who needs support, and no one is just a resource who contributes. Each superblock has its own specific assets and liabilities, which is why there are no single solutions, only solutions adapted to each situation. Co-responsibility and co-production entail co-governance in designing and implementing solutions.
- *Proximity and friendliness*. The idea of the 15-minute city does not have to be solely linked to the issue of reducing transportation needs and associated contamination from emissions. It can also include the idea of five-minute home-care or, in other words, the idea of a distributed care home, where any residence with a dependent person in it is under five minutes' walking distance from a carer who can come over to help them. The idea is not just to promote access to the function of care (in dedicated facilities), but also to ensure that the function of care can access homes.
- *Focus and personalization*. There are no longer aggregate statistics, there are detailed lists with the names and surnames of the people who need assistance and posters in those people's homes showing the photographs of the teams assisting them. The ultimate goal is for all of us to be on both sides as far as we can, which means being on lists and posters as care generators and beneficiaries. It is the public authority's duty to ensure no one is left out involuntarily.
- *Overlapping and synergies*. Social superblocks are rolled out in layers of new services with effects that are incremental as they accumulate in the area. They harness and maximize existing resources as a result of greater coordination. New roles are created to facilitate the onset of these advantages: facilitators, points of reference, connectors, and so on.
- *Social recovery of common spaces*. Social superblocks occupy and cross sidewalks, roads, parks, and public and private facilities (such as roof terraces) in order to expand living spaces for people subject to constraints (elderly people who

cannot go out for a walk for fear of getting sick or lost, children who cannot play on the street, subletters of rooms without access to a private kitchen, etc.). Common spaces may become an extension of private spaces or, more importantly, the forum where transactions between individual needs and community offers can be carried out.

The COVID crisis has ushered in exceptional times, in which long-term trends have revealed unforeseen problems and new, unexpected problems have suddenly emerged, which need to be tackled along with existing ones. Both challenges represent the core of social innovation, and the social superblock offers a basic framework for addressing them.

NOTES

1 Torrens, 2018.
2 Torrens, 2020.
3 Baumol, 2012.
4 Jacobs, 1993.

Communities of places, communities of care, and their ecosystems are fundamental components in the making of the city of interactions, but the opposite is also true: the shape of cities is crucial in generating communities of place, communities of care, and their proper functioning.[71]

Given this condition, what conclusions can we draw regarding how (or if) the city of interaction can be designed?

Over 15 years of experience in design for social innovation tells us that communities, like the encounters and the conversations on which they are built, cannot be directly designed. But it also tells us that a lot can be done to encourage their birth, their capability to last over time, and their orientation towards the production of social and environmental values.[72] In other words, a lot can be done in terms of *Infrastructuring*: an expression introduced years ago by Leigh Star[73] and later taken up by Pelle Ehn and his colleagues at Malmö University.[74] For them, infrastructuring means designing artefacts that are "sunk into" sociomaterial structures, thereby making several other activities possible.

When it comes to generating the city of interactions, infrastructuring indicates every design initiative that creates favorable conditions for a variety of encounters, collaborations, and community-building processes.[75] Here we must add that although, traditionally, the term infrastructure calls up images of basic facilities (resulting from large top-down projects), more recently we have recognized the infrastructural role of other artefacts that, during their lifetime, support a range of activities that were not defined, or even imagined, from the outset.

When this happens, we call it *micro-infrastructuring*.[76]

Plug-Ins as Micro-Infrastructure

In a previous paragraph, we talked about the Home Care Service. We have seen how, by creating logistical hubs in each district, it becomes possible to create a stable base of connections between the users of the services and other residents of the same neighborhoods. Now we can add that, once put into practice, this systems can also support other types of interactions and social forms. In other words, by locating and producing

71 Manzini, *Livable...*, *op. cit.*

72 Manzini, *Design When...*, *op. cit.*

73 Star, Ruhleder, 1996, 111-134; Star, Bowker, 2006, 151–162.

74 Pelle Ehn presents the traditional idea of infrastructure in this way: "An infrastructure, like railroad tracks or the Internet is not reinvented every time, but is 'sunk into' other sociomaterial structures." See: Ehn, 2008.

75 Björgvinsson, Ehn, Hillgren, 2010.

76 Manzini, Thorpe, *op. cit.*

care communities, the service becomes a micro-infrastructure of the city that can also be used in other ways that were not initially foreseen.

To reinforce this statement, let us now consider another example, again in the field of care relationships. More often than not, a person in need of care will interact with a variety of informal and professional caregivers: family members, but also friends and neighbors, on the one hand; and any number of employees from the public health service and social services, on the other. Each of them will play a part, in different ways and with different roles —and often with a certain difficulty. And there are always difficulties with regard to coordination. In view of all this, a digital platform was proposed with the goal of making coordination and mutual support easier for caregivers and, ultimately, making the process smoother and safer for the recipients of care. The project, called Care Sharing, was conceived and developed by Elisava students in collaboration with the Social Rights Area of the Barcelona City Council.

The main intent was to increase both the effectiveness of the service and the well-being of people in need of care, but also to support professional and informal caregivers (especially family members), while also raising issues such as the dignity of assistance and gender equity in caregiving. However, it is clear that, once implemented, this platform can also have other and unexpected uses, including uncovering previously unforeseen caregivers (such as, for example, the shopkeepers in the Radar project or the young people in the Connectats project) and thus acting as an infrastructure for other types of social activities.

In other words, as these cases involving communities of care shows us, the network of encounters, conversations, and collaborative practices that makes up the city of interactions can exist because it is supported by an enabling infrastructure. In turn, this infrastructure consists of a multiplicity of tangible and intangible artefacts: from basic structures (such as energy, water, mobility, internet, and social media) to dedicated structures (such as public spaces in a particular neighborhood or digital platforms for a determined set of services) capable of supporting existing communities and fostering new encounters. All these are different types of plug-ins which, operating as infrastructures, play the role of generators that bring about meetings and activities that, otherwise, would not have existed.[77]

It follows that, when it comes to making the city of interaction, the infrastructural role of the large facilities designed and built from the top down must be joined by a bottom-up infrastructure made up of products and services originally designed with specific purposes but which, over time, can evolve in their role and collaborate toward forming networks from which unforeseen opportunities can emerge.

Plug-Ins as Relational Objects

In the city of interactions, encounters and conversations not only need to be practically possible, they also need to be stimulated. In fact, to start a conversation, and therefore to start any type of collaborative activity, it is not enough for people to be given the material possibilities. They also need a topic to discuss and to gather around.

In other words, if infrastructuring means designing to make conversations possible (and therefore, to make possible the collaborative activities that may follow), it is also necessary to design another type of artefacts, which, by virtue of their relational nature, can serve as new conversation themes: plug-ins that, in this case, will play the role of *mediators and identifiers.*

For instance, let's look at a digital platform that supports meetings between seniors and young people, with the letter helping the former to access online services, as in (Connectats - Caring Community). In addition to the service it offers, the platform also stimulates meetings and conversations that otherwise would not have occurred. Another example is a craft workshop imagined as an opportunity for local artisans and immigrants to work together (Migrants Workshops Project): beyond offering a work opportunity, it can serve as the trigger for better mutual understanding. A third example: new architectural features (such as stairs, elevators, communal spaces, bathrooms, shared kitchens, etc.) can be added to existing buildings to create micro-infrastructures that can offer increased livability/usability (Slow Down, Stop, and Stay or Community Plugins), but they can also stimulate new conversations about the city and, in doing so, generate new communities of place.

77 Manzini, Thorpe, *op. cit.*

In conclusion, these different initiatives share the fact of being plug-ins endowed with a very special ability: they activate social conversations and catalyze urban regeneration processes. And they can do it because their insertion into the pre-existing system helps to connect otherwise remote and separate interlocutors (in this they operate as mediators), and because they are capable of pinpointing solutions and catalyzing energies (operating as identifiers).

In other words, they uncover common matters of concern and, equally importantly, they create the conditions in which trust, cooperation, mutual respect, and empathy among the interlocutors can appear. In consequence, we can also define them as *relational objects*:[78] artefacts with the ability to trigger and encourage what is needed to start a conversation.

In conclusion: the quality of the city of interactions can be (re) generated by designing plug-ins that play different infrastructural and relational roles, interacting with their context, modifying it and, in this way, making something that is desired come to pass. Their relevance, therefore, should not be assessed in terms of their size, but by observing what they generate in the larger systems into which they are introduced. In other words, their role in city making is not a question of their scale, but of their capacity for transformation.

78 The notion of a "relational object" is very similar, but not coincident, with the idea of "boundary objects" introduced by Susan Leigh Star and James R. Griesemer. See: Star, Griesemer, 1989.

→ 290 THE CITY OF INTERACTIONS

un CAP

→ 291 EN MITJONS A LA PLAÇA

→ 290

COMMUNITY PLUG-INS

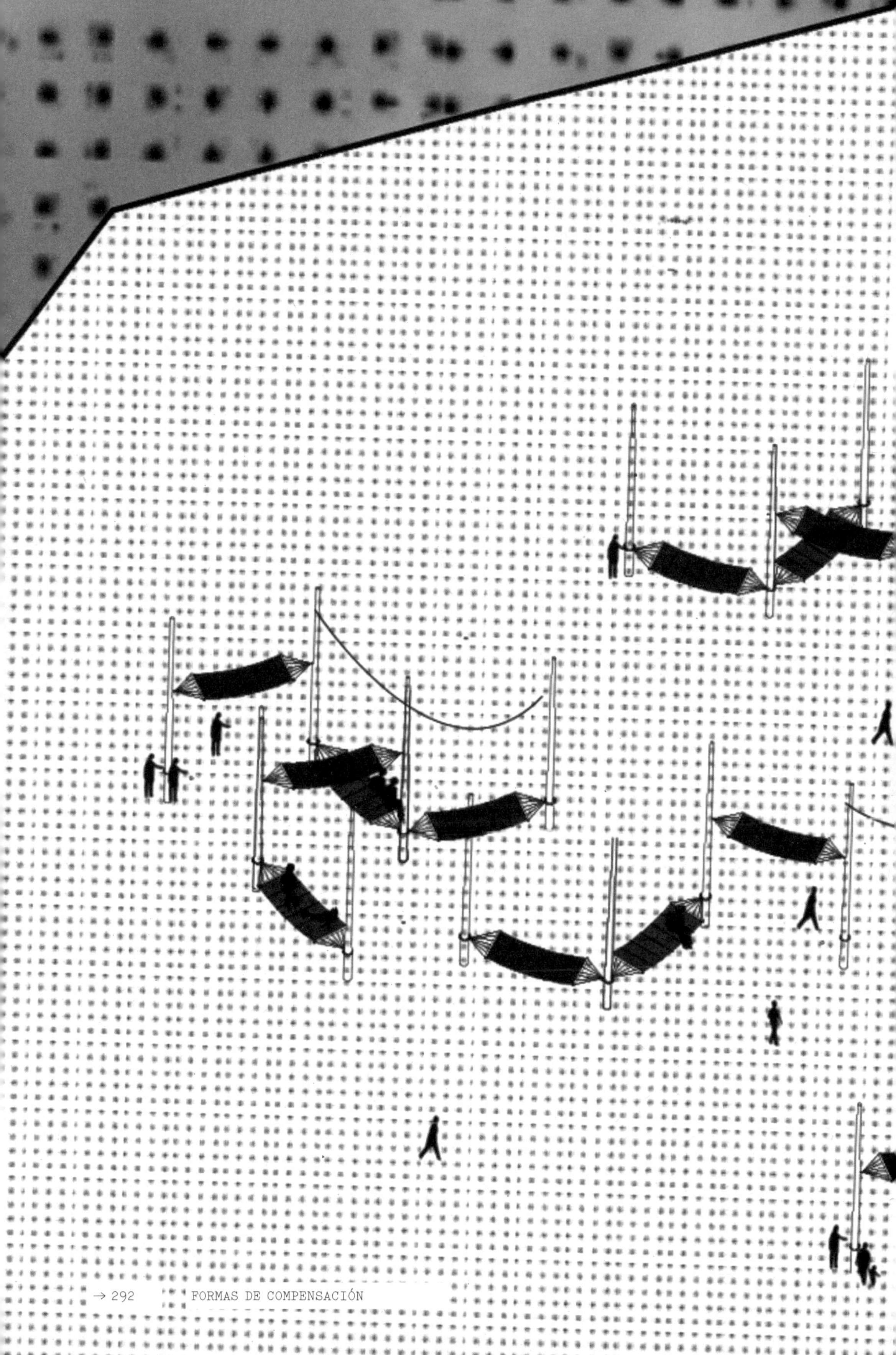

→ 292 FORMAS DE COMPENSACIÓN

→ 295 REVIVIR

G101

→ 292 FAR AWAY, SO CLOSE

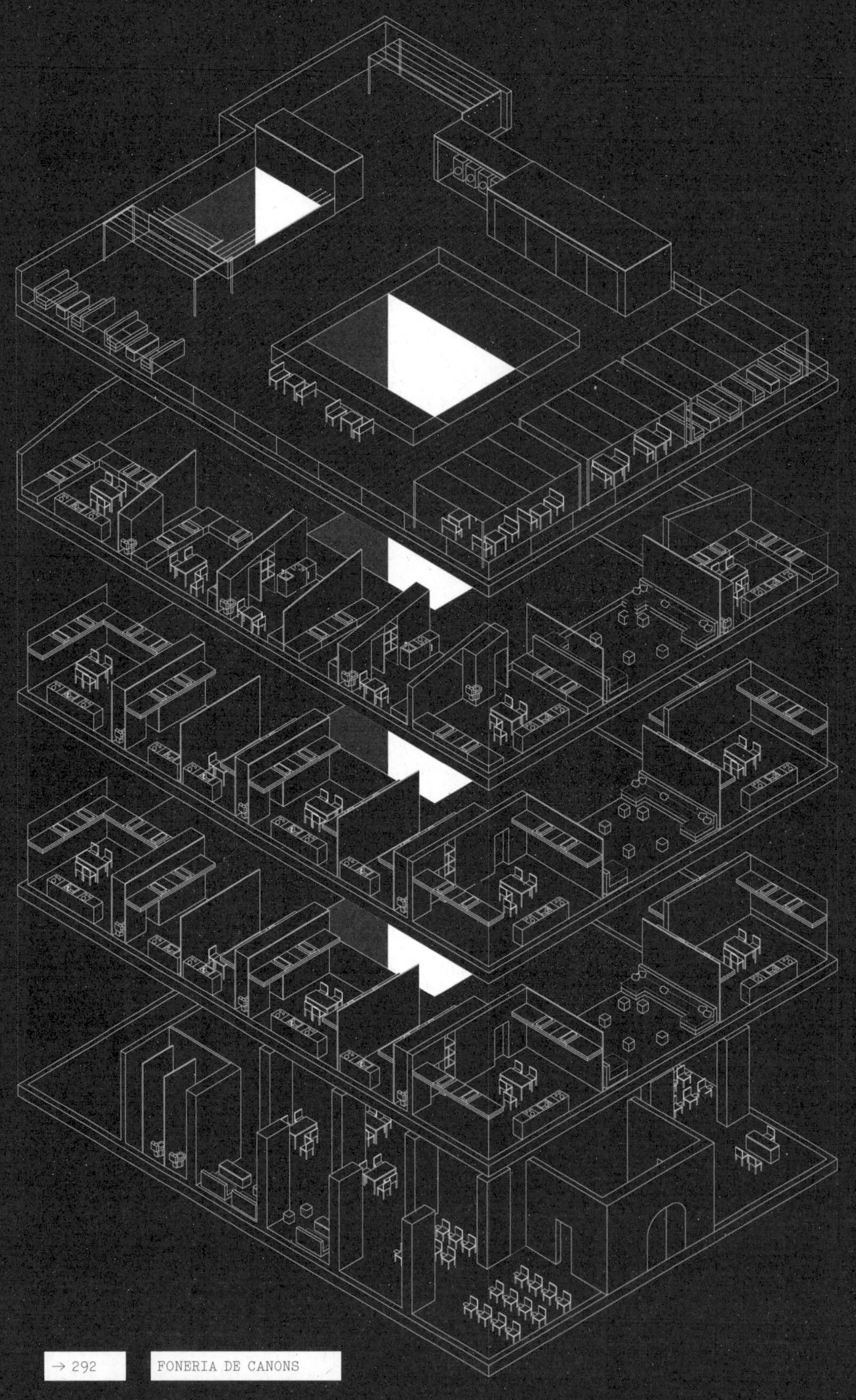

→ 292

FONERIA DE CANONS

→ 289 A LA PLAÇA

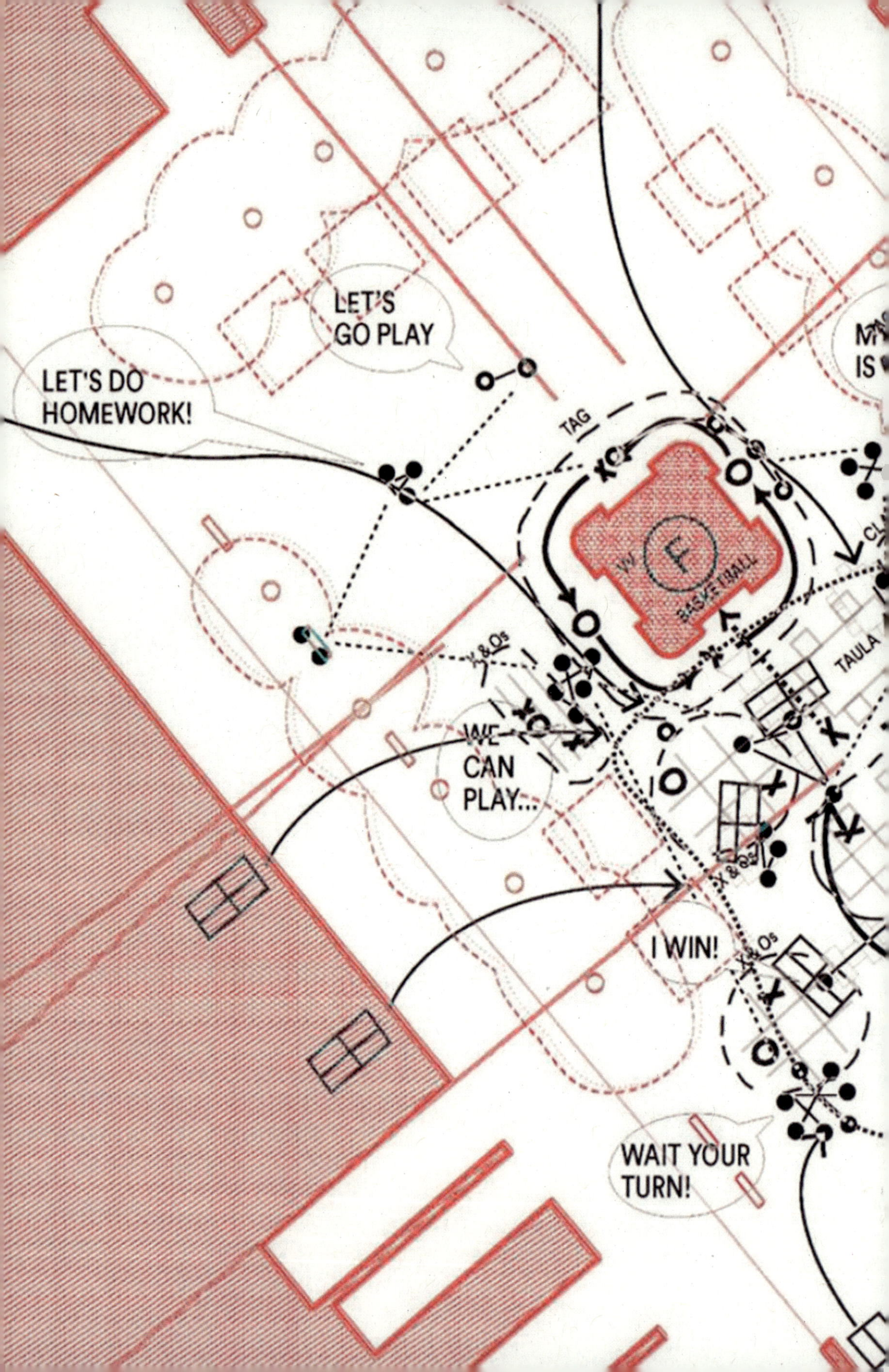
LET'S GO PLAY
LET'S DO HOMEWORK!
TAG
F
BASKETBALL
X & Os
TAULA
WE CAN PLAY...
X & Os
I WIN!
X & Os
WAIT YOUR TURN!

→ 292

INTERVENCIÓ O ACCIDENT

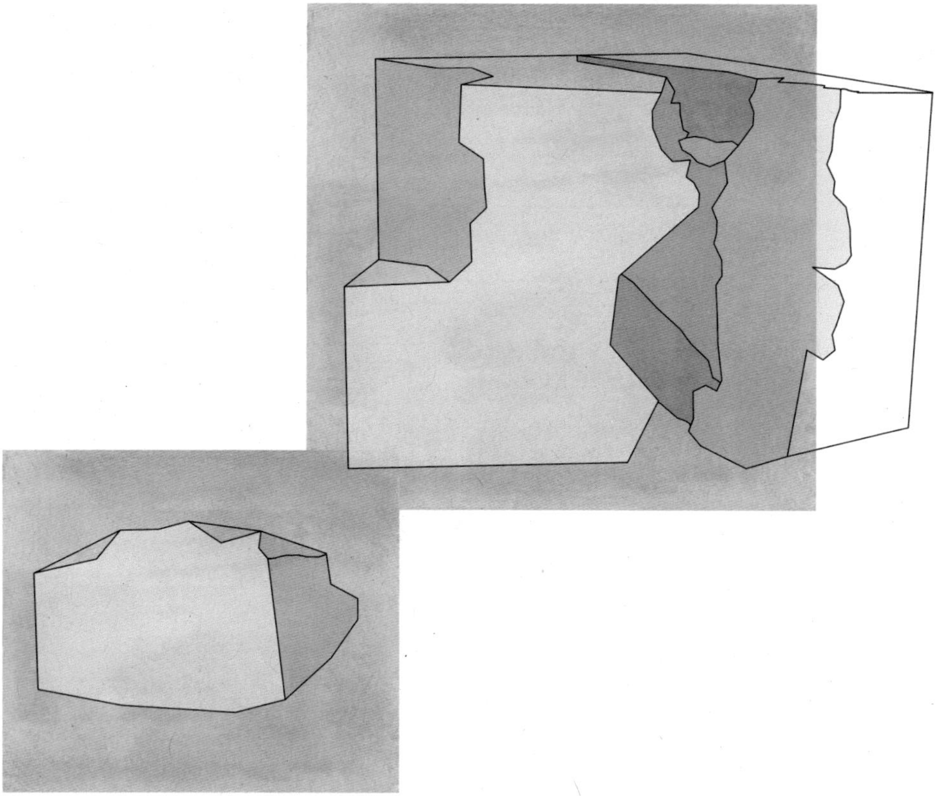

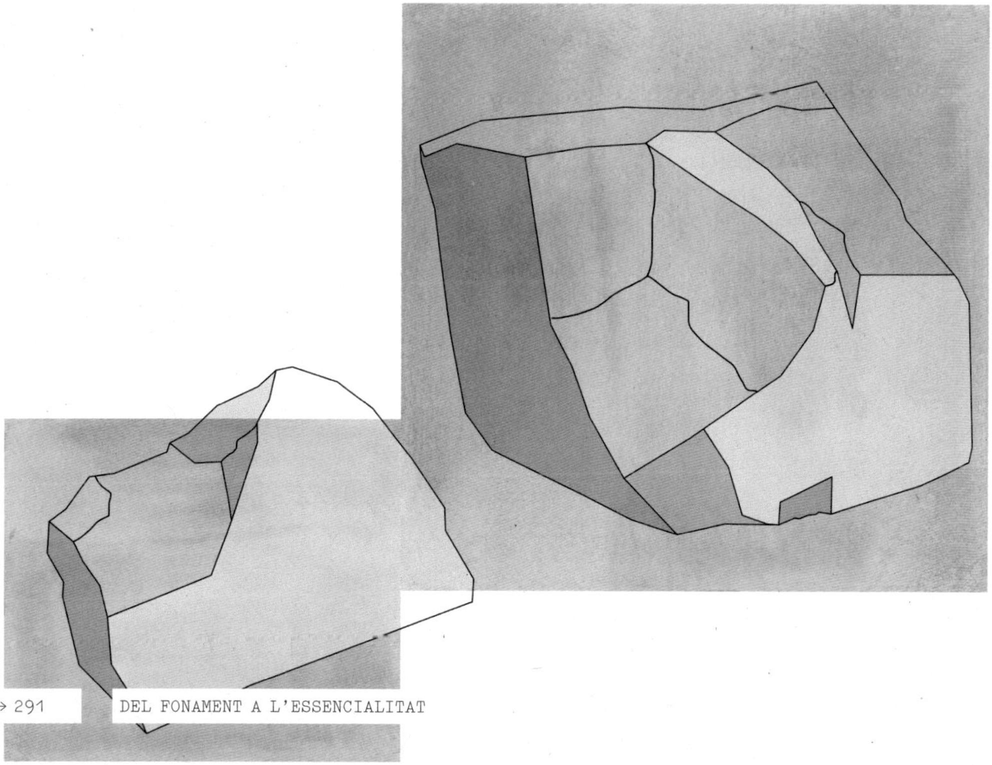

→ 291 DEL FONAMENT A L'ESSENCIALITAT

APP
APP
APP
APP
A&G
A&G
FTW
DIY
14:00

→ 290 CITY AND MAKER CULTURE

→ 293 LA LUZ DE LAS INVISIBLES

→ 295 SLOW DOWN, STOP AND STAY

→ 294 PARADISE NOW

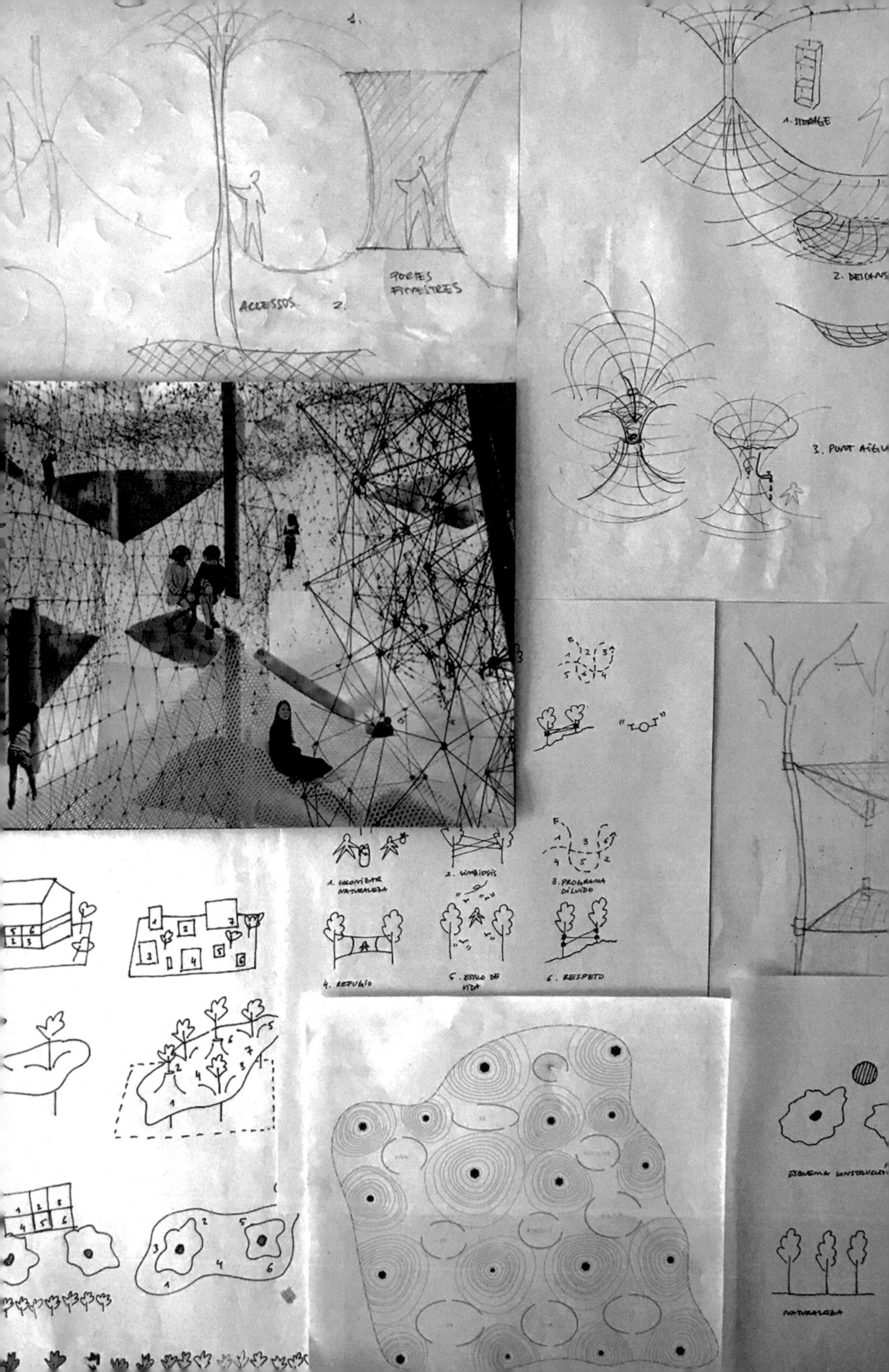

ACCESSOS 2.
PORTES FINESTRES
1. STORAGE
1. COLONIZAR NATURALEZA
2. SIMBIOSIS
3. PROGRAMA DILUIDO
4. REFUGIO
5. ESTILO DE VIDA
6. RESPETO
NATURALEZA

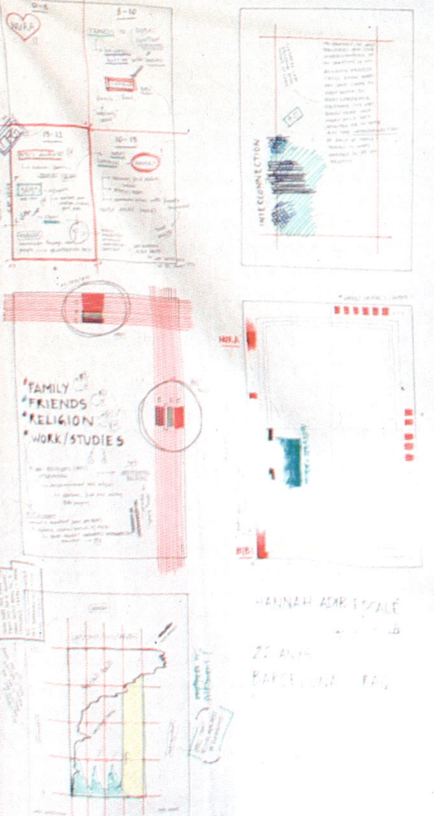

→ 293 SISTEMA RETICULAR PER A LA MATERIALITZACIÓ D'IDENTITATS MULTICULTURALS

CAFETÍN DE BUENOS AIRES
MARRUECOS

the City of Meanings

PART IV

THE CITY OF MEANINGS: MATERIALITY AND IDENTITY

MATERIALITY

The Assumed Primacy of the Built Environment

A series of movable chairs have been set up in the middle of La Rambla, Barcelona's most popular boulevard. People are sitting on them, some just resting, others excitedly engaged in warm conversation. Some people are taking pictures of the moment; others are discussing the relevance and quality of the form. Still others are commenting on the firmness of the chairs and their distribution. Slight nervous signals in the faces of the young people gathered nearby reveal this is part of an academic project. Students and professors are taking part in the event with a clear academic purpose. But family members, local residents, tourists, members of the city's government, and even journalists have gathered with clearly different expectations. The event began a few years ago as an open air showcase of the results of an exercise on sitting, involving formal, material, and technical criteria. But in recent years, it has evolved to become a more reflective and explorative exercise on the potential of design in making meaning at an urban level. Any change to the chairs' features (if they were fixed to the ground, harder or softer to the touch, if their finishes were natural wood or painted electric blue, if they were designed with armrests or with decorations mixed in with the structure) would introduce a series of nuances that would affect not only the functional dimension of sitting. By changing these features, the whole experience of being on the site would be altered. And, through these formal and material differences, a reflection on the semantic understanding of the relationships between human beings and the built environment could potentially be raised. Undoubtedly, the materiality, the colors, the forms and the distribution of the chairs in the middle of La Rambla affect the design outcomes, which are not limited to small and circumstantial events and decisions, but embody design's capacity to build meaning. As a result, design as a discipline that operates through both processes and physical products is reinforced in its capacity to participate in the identity of the city as much as any urban plan.

As stated in the introductory chapter, cities are complex networks of economic, social, and environmental relations. Due to this complexity, their foundation and development have been historically related to institutions that have controlled resources, trade, religion, or military power. The representative and symbolic dimensions of these complex systems have been entrusted traditionally to urban planning and architecture. Certain buildings (temples, palaces, city halls, markets) and public spaces (squares, parks, boulevards) have commonly been used to define the identity of the city, and they have played a central role in concentrating the sense-making apparently needed to maintain a cohesive and legislated human collective. When planned, the sites of ordinary life have been conceived as a continuum of civil buildings designed in keeping with certain pragmatic building techniques and more or less influenced by regulatory laws —as seen in many examples from Western culture (e.g., Raffaello's housing for Rome, Hausmann's plan for Paris, or Cerdà's Eixample in Barcelona). According to this logic, the built environment —the so-called shape of the city in both its visual and built presentations— has commonly been understood as fundamentally conceived from a mindset that upholds planning as the foundation for urban identity. On this basis, the city's main symbolic dimension is derived from the expression of architecture and urban form.[79]

The epitome of this conception of the formal dimension of the city as a means to create meaning and identity is the monument. The monument, a conceptual node between architecture and urban planning,

79 For examples that support this mindset, see: Benevolo, L. 1975-76; Rossi, 1966; Kostoff, 1991; and De Landa, 1997.

80 Perhaps the first attempt to conceptualize this effect and its links with gentrification are: McNeill, 2000, 473-494; and Plaza, 2000, 264-274.

81 Koolhaas, 1995.

82 As is clearly stated in the most popular ranking of livable cities: Mercer, n.d. or Best Cities, n.d.

83 Sennett, 1994.

84 Rilke, 1910.

85 Aragon, 1926.

becomes the ultimate tool to summarize and perform the many underlying forces implicit in urban complexity. Both the classic examples from Renaissance and Baroque city planning (e.g., Rome, Washington, or Karlsruhe) and Modernist proposals (e.g., Le Corbusier's Plan Voisin for Paris, Soviet Moscow, or Niemeyer's Brasilia) reveal a neat assumption of the monumental nodes of the city as key agents in combining and harmonizing the diverse and complex systems intertwined in its fabric. The market-based transformation of cities in recent decades has concentrated the monumental dimension of symbolic buildings and urban form. This unprecedented process, described by some researchers as the "Guggenheim effect",[80] takes root through strong links to global investment phenomena and mass tourism. It has reinforced the commodification of the city and its reliance on key monumental nodes to sustain its identity city. The market-based processes of city planning —most often associated with strategic processes such as Universal Exhibitions, Olympic Games or International Trade Centers— result in an identity attached to icons to be featured on postcards, in guides, and on social media[81] and a conception of the city as a place for tourism, leisure or business.[82]

In the shadow of this overpowering idea, almost nothing remains of the lived city, of the concrete experience of its inhabitants, the embodied connection of humans to their environment, in which memory and perception build identities. A breach has cracked any possible connection between the lived city and the symbolic one, at least in modern Western societies. Several authors from diverse fields have explored the origins, limits, and depth of this breach at the turn of the 20th century.[83] Literature evidenced this gap, as the transformation of cities and architecture advanced at a speed that seemed to leave behind the attention, and even care, for the inhabitants. Many texts expressed and reflected on the links between human beings and the built environment in the modern city. In Rilke's famous passage about a party wall, the vision of a demolished building sparks the young protagonist's awareness of the hidden layers the modern city has covered up in its race for change.[84] With an analogous precision, Louis Aragon reveals the "thousand divine concretions"[85] unleashed in a modern city like Paris on an inhabitant

86 In line with the guiding principles of Marinetti's *Futurist Manifesto* or Le Corbusier's writings, this sense of nostalgia, decadence, and even illness is made explicit in: Cacciari, 1981; or Tafuri, Dal Co, 1976

87 Rossi, *op. cit.*

88 Seeing as the book was written in 1971, the city was not yet affected by digital media, yet Leroi-Gourhan has a clear awareness of the impact of audiovisual media, and his analysis can easily be applied to the increasing impact digital technologies have produced along the same lines.See: Leroi-Gourhan, 1993, 361.

who is a peasant. Both examples capture an intense and concrete experience, aiming for a kind of recognition and identity that 20th century urban processes seemed to dismiss. Many of the main theorists of modern architecture criticized these expressions as reservoirs of nostalgia, as the products of a decadent bourgeois society.[86] It seemed that, to protect modernist and rationalistic architecture's position in fueling the unprecedented growth of contemporary cities, no trace of the human dimension of the urban phenomenon could be permitted to remain.

Nevertheless, coming from the field of urban theory, Aldo Rossi stressed the tension between the abstract understanding of architecture and its concrete expression. Rossi stated that "the architecture of the city is the concrete sign of [human] biography".[87] To counterbalance, and even question, a symbolic construction of the identity of a city deployed with a disdain for its inhabitants as agents of this identity, Rossi suggested an understanding of the city as something constructed over time and an assemblage. This diverse and promising approach to the urban process, which Rossi took partially from Claude Lévi-Strauss, was further developed in the same period by the anthropologist André Leroi-Gourhan. In *Gesture and Speech,* Leroi-Gourhan constructs a global reflection on the relationships between human beings, the material environment and symbolism in fields as diverse as biology, crafts, or urban history. In a chapter summarizing the processes fueling the transformation of cities, the author offers a precise critique of the measure to which the contemporary city is leading societies and individuals to apparently lose "one of the specific attributes of *Homo sapiens,* the capacity of the body, hand, and brain to exercise the individual privilege of material and symbolic creation".[88]

IMAGINING EMERGENT FUTURES FOR CITIES AND THEIR BIOREGIONS

Tomás Díez

The major problems in the world are the result of the difference between how nature works and the way people think.

Gregory Batson

Cities have become a 21st-century obsession. For generations, architects, designers, urban planners, engineers, sociologists, economists, politicians and organizations like the United Nations have been focusing our energies on imagining and creating a "new model" for the city, as though it were a scientific exercise, where a theory is tested through experiments aimed at proving or refuting it. However, the failed efforts throughout history, which relied on demonstrating that there is only one way to create a city, on attempting to understand its rules and wanting to control it as though it were a patient in a hospital, invite us to explore new kinds of city making based on the complexity of the nature of the city as a system of systems in constant evolution —like human beings, who are not only our bodies but also our thoughts, ideas, and knowledge, our families or our geographical contexts, and our emotions. The idea of the city as an object leads us to assume that it is controllable, malleable, and manipulable —something we can design like a chair, while exploring function and form within a given discipline. The urbanism of the spectacle arrived in our cities in the form of branded museums, sculpture-buildings, and large renovation plans in emerging districts with huge real estate operations behind them. We have moved toward "form and function follow the market" —or a state in which the form of the construction of the city, and its functions, have been (and are) dictated by the market— and disciplines such as architecture or design have given over their efforts toward complying with the real or fictitious demands of the invisible hand that supposedly regulates that market. Not only does the real estate market play an important role in this configuration, which is devastating for the construction of the city, but the political market and the rise of populism have also led urbanism and architecture to become instruments at their service, either through processes of transforming neighborhoods into new focal points for innovation promoted by companies, and the consequent reclassification of land uses, or through the spread of participatory processes such that citizens can be used to justify decisions that have already been made in political and economic spheres. The micropolitics of neighborhoods have not been alien to the processes that occur at the national level, such as political polarization, the growth of disinformation or the rise of neo-nationalisms, since it is in cities where ideological battles are fought —sometimes literally in the form of occupying public space for protest, and in some cases in the manifestation of institutionalized violence, be it public or private.

Given the city's complexity, it cannot be considered an object of scientific study like dissecting a frog in a laboratory. As with nature, and the phenomena of which we become a part when we participate in them, like traffic, we must realize that individuals and communities are part of the city and contribute to making it, as opposed to conceiving it as an object that is removed from the logics with which we operate on the same scales. That is why when we decide to use public transportation, we are making the city —or when we decide to buy what we need from a multinational digital platform, or when we order takeout on a rainy day. Each and every one of us is constructing the city with our actions, our attitudes as passive consumers who follow along with the established rules of the game, and who function according to operating logics that are rooted in a relatively recent history, connected with the appropriation of natural resources and distribution channels through multiple processes of colonization. When the micro-actions of each individual or community are aggregated using digital platforms that allow businesses to scale up by organizing information to turn orders into products sent out to people's homes, the impact generated by this way of inhabiting the city of consuming the resources that reach it through local, metropolitan, regional, national, continental, and global supply chains —is also scaled up. The extraction and processing of natural resources to meet consumer demand on a rainy day when we call for takeout, or the purchase of extremely complex electronic devices at ridiculously low prices, including 24-hour shipping, takes on an enormous planetary scale, which turns entire territories into mines for the continuous exploitation of resources, which will eventually end up in landfills once they reach the end of their useful lives, or which will become micro-particles in the air or in our global water systems.

As a result of our micro-actions and macro-interventions in the territory —like deforestation or the creation of open pit mines —human beings have become agents of geological transformation on a planetary scale through widespread interventions in the movement of sediments, manipulation of natural systems, and the construction of infrastructures that require an intense consumption of resources and energy to perform their function.[1] The relationship between engineering and design has given the human species the ability to change the morphology of natural environments and their relationships using technologies for the domination and manipulation of those systems, which sustain human life in the city and in urbanized rural environments. Providing today's urban settlements with the supplies and utilities they need requires complex infrastructures, which have not only been built using extractive and linear principles in terms of their material ecologies, but which also operate according to those same principles, putting at risk the natural systems that preserve the necessary balance of life on a planetary scale. The current rhythm and demand for the consumption of products, energy, natural resources like water, the use of soil for agriculture, or the mining that makes our technological devices like smartphones possible, depend on natural logics that interfere with human beings' coexistence with other species. And those species are participants in the provision of food, raw materials, and the climate balance that supports the planetary cycles necessary for the existence of life —which evolved over thousands of years of natural innovation without the intervention of the human species. The model of consumption based on extractive and linear industrial production has been constructed artificially, usually in association with purely economic logics,[2] leaving behind the cultural and biological principles of the sites where cities have grown up over the last 4,000 years.[3] These logics of consumption —accentuated especially from the 15th century onward, following the European occupation of the East and West Indies and the consequent appropriation of natural resources and imposition of European culture —have led us to turn the planet into an industrial mine fueled by artificially cheap oil, with supply and distribution chains controlled through militarization, and the existence of new forms of slavery to guarantee fictitiously cheap labor.[4] Access to a vast source of new natural resources, extracted from local native communities to meet growing consumer demand, led Europe into one of the richest periods in its history, opening the doors to the Renaissance, and then to the Industrial Revolution.

Paradoxically, the processes of conquest and technological advances also brought about internal disruptions in Europe. Whereas artisans in medieval cities and towns once worked and lived in the same place, machines drastically transformed production processes, and then the practice of craftsmanship and design itself. The printing press was followed by the steam engine, the steam engine was followed by wireless communications, assembly lines, and a new source of energy and materials in the early 20th century: oil. Oil energy and advances in the military industry were followed by computers connected on a global scale through the Internet. Most recently, digital technologies have changed almost everything we do, combining ones and zeros to encode messages, videos, pictures, tweets, bank transfers and physical objects, transforming design again. Combining physical and digital realities, design plays a fundamental role in changing how we live, work and play in cities. Current urbanism is leaning towards big data, the internet of things and new forms of control in cities, as we have seen with some of the interpretations of the Smart City, while maintaining the principle of understanding the city as an object. However, there is one aspect of the digital sphere that can dramatically transform today's urban dynamics, and which has not been examined sufficiently: digital fabrication. Just like we can produce texts and videos, and capture and share images, digital fabrication lets us transform bits of information into atoms that can form part of the physical world; in other words, with these new production processes, people and communities can access a means of production that will make it possible for them to design and create the reality they inhabit. Because digital manufacturing builds on the two previous digital revolutions in communication and computing, it is possible to share the designs of physical objects like chairs, shoes, houses, or computers in the same way that we share photos or spreadsheets via email or on digital platforms. Bits are easier to transport than atoms. If we conceptualize digital manufacturing as a new infrastructure in the form of fab labs, flexible factories, materials libraries, and material flows that operate on an urban scale, we could intervene in the city to develop the capacity to produce (on demand) any product or tool using local supply chains, and thus recalibrate the global economy. Imagining emerging futures for productive cities that can retain atoms on the city level and move bits of information on a planetary scale also means enabling processes through which urbanization can become restorative, regenerative and productive in order to reshape the relationships between all the species that inhabit our planet Earth.

MULTIPLE CONVERGENCES

We're currently living through a time of accelerated change, in which new economic, environmental and social paradigms are challenging the status quo of the industrial society built up over the course of more than 200 years since the Industrial Revolution. The biosphere, financial markets, family structures and society as a whole are being challenged and transformed in one of the most important transition periods in human history. Although the Industrial Revolution contributed countless benefits for society, we are now faced with a plethora of complex and interconnected problems that are calling into question our productive model: climate change, the curtailment of civil rights, and the centralization of wealth and power, to name just a few. Now is the time for us to ask new questions about how we organize production and consumption in cities and their relationships with the natural environment. It is time for technology to redefine its role in society so it will no longer be a tool for perpetuating a linear and extractive model that exploits people and natural systems in the pursuit of fictitious economic growth. It is time to imagine and create emerging futures for our cities that will help us to transform the way we live, and how we generate and distribute value within our society.[5] To make that possible, we need to understand that this transition period will entail profound transformations, and that it will present a series of unprecedented urban, technological, ecological, social, and economic challenges, but that we can rely on the combination of technological and scientific capacities to respond to those challenges, so long as we are capable of constructing accords based on a series of common goals, as a species on a planet where other natural systems have the same rights as we do, and fomenting fundamental values that go beyond religion or nationalist dogmas —which, for the moment, may seem like a utopia.

One of the characteristics of this transition period centers on the fact that most of our current challenges are characterized by an interdependence and a complexity that makes them "wicked problems", which adds a new level of difficulty to this moment of convergence of various crises and technological capacity. Wicked problems run the risk of becoming permanent aspirations, and being turned into utopian promises, since the number of actors and factors that are implicated make them practically impossible to solve. Those problems might include reducing ocean pollution, microplastics in food, poverty, or terrorism. Because these are systemic problems, they require systemic solutions, built up slowly in complementary layers. These kinds of problems need to be addressed from a multidisciplinary and collaborative perspective, with a transversal and multidisciplinary vision that allows for the design and implementation of interventions on multiple scales at the same time, through iterative and aggregative processes that can help us understand new social, cultural, biological, and technological geographies to resolve short-term challenges while maintaining a long-term vision and conception. One still common, but increasingly obsolete response to these complex problems is to seek out "moonshots" and short-term magic solutions; they will never be sufficient to remedy problems created by decades or centuries of human action, which affect the natural design of our ecosystems created over millennia. In contrast, small-scale interventions can help us to address large-scale challenges in a systemic way, given an understanding of the necessary interrelationship between scales, actors and complementary systems that can help us break up those same "wicked problems" *(and to be able to scale those interventions using the power of digital networks and the agility of today's society in adapting to transformations)*.

At the same time, traditional industry is being disrupted not only by the climate crisis, but also by the growth of an emerging production paradigm supported by advanced manufacturing technologies, new forms of synthetic intelligence, new materials science, and connected systems, which offer endless opportunities for calibrating the negative effects of activities created by human beings on a planetary scale.[6] Some of these emerging technologies —such as digital manufacturing, synthetic biology, artificial intelligence, and blockchain, to name just a few —are already disrupting the established mechanisms through which our production model operates, and they are bringing about massive cultural transformations in society. Where the machine age aimed to shape the human habitat by creating interfaces with natural resources through science and technology, the ubiquitous nature of digital technologies will require the rapid articulation and synchronization of both biological and synthetic systems at different scales. The emergence of these new tools and technologies demands that we formulate new questions about how we relate to our environment, and it prompts us to come up with new ways of assigning value to effort or work. In addition, in a scenario where the automation of processes frees human beings from tasks that previously required their effort, for which they were provided remuneration, there is room to ask ourselves even more profound questions about our species' individual and collective purpose *(which invites us to envision outcomes that are different from the ones we already know and to design possible futures for (human and non-human) life so it can thrive on this planet).*

CITIES, PRODUCTION, AND DIGITAL REVOLUTIONS

Over the last two centuries, humanity developed a globalized industrial model that has reached its peak in recent decades, producing a constant flow of contaminants into our hydrological systems and polluting soils, disrupting the planet's natural cycles associated with temperature and biodiversity, and leading to an unprecedented increase in CO_2 levels. During that time, we have perfected the systems for the movement of atoms on a planetary scale in the form of raw materials, using energy sources associated with fossil fuels to transform those materials into consumer goods (food or products) through industrial processes that generate high levels of emissions and large amounts of waste and tabulate labor at competitive prices in a global market that is increasingly concentrated in the hands of corporations and authoritarian governments. Thanks to innovation in the aeronautical, automotive, and engineering industries for the construction of large infrastructures the movement of goods, it is possible to transport materials and products around the world with fictitiously cheap production and distribution costs, in keeping with the rules of a global economy that feeds into the model based on competition and economies of scale. This economic model is founded on infinite growth, access to infinite natural resources, and prioritizing economic benefits over caring for biological and social systems. In reality, the labor, energy and raw materials associated with most of the products we consume are not cheap, and their social and environmental externalities are not calculated as part of the real costs of any product or company. These impacts are taken on by future generations like a mortgage they never chose to sign.

Under this linear economic model, the morphology and urban dynamics of cities have developed around infrastructures for the movement of atoms: airports, ports, highways, along with technologies such as cars, trucks, trains and planes, and largely neoliberal economic logics. That seems logical enough given that we have seen that most of the knowledge development and advances of the 20th century have focused on those technologies. However, the urban development model of the last century is currently in crisis, not only in cities but on a global scale, due to the pressure that cities exert on non-urban environments, and their dependence on natural systems associated with their consumption needs. As we know, cities are responsible for the majority of CO_2 emissions and the largest concentrations of population on the planet. These impacts will continue to increase, which means we need to devise and implement an economic model for cities that is regenerative with respect to the systems they depend on; a model that permits cultural diversity in relation to the generation and circulation of value on a local scale; with principles that contain logics of care for all the natural systems that interact in the city, including the people within them; and that provides for the integration of technologies at the service of those forms of life that interact in the city and its bioregions, and not the other way around. The starting point for the Fab City global initiative, born between Barcelona and Boston, is implementing a model that will prevent atoms from traveling thousands of kilometers from city to city to arrive in our hands and stomachs. Instead, they will circulate on a local scale, and bits of information will be the ones to travel thousands of kilometers around the planet. This will be made possible through the digital revolution in computing, communications (Internet) and manufacturing, understood as key infrastructures for developing an urban model, over the coming decades, focused on the development of productive cities and bioregions.

Digital fabrication means that computers are connected to machines to make and produce (almost) anything, turning bits into atoms and atoms into bits. 3D printers and scanners, laser cutters, precise computer-controlled machines are some of the examples of processes that allow the information contained in a computer to be transformed into a product manufactured by a machine in a matter of minutes, or a few hours.[7] These technologies have existed for decades in industry. What has been really disruptive is the process, which has been taking place over the past ten years, of democratizing access to these technologies, and which has made it possible for people and communities to share designs digitally on a global scale while manufacturing or producing locally. As part of this new digital revolution, combined with the revolutions in computing and communications, communities and people acquire knowledge that allows them to create new tools and technology to interact with their environment and to improve quality of life for humankind and other species. That is how manufacturing and production in cities can help increase citizens' resilience and give us back the ability to meet the needs of our communities at the local level, by introducing technologies that can help:

- Promote the production of a large amount of food near urban centers, reducing energy consumption in transportation, improving the nutritional quality of food, and supporting transparency in supply chains.
- Transform the model of energy production at the local scale, using different complementary technologies of microgeneration and distribution.
- Increase the use of new raw materials made from materials that were once considered waste, in association with an increased demand on the part of the existing industrial capacity in cities and peri-urban areas.
- Reduce the transport of materials on a global scale and the excess of production, since cities can produce what they need on demand, using mainly local materials.
- Rethink the urban infrastructure needed to provide cities with the capacity to be productive, with infrastructure for urban metabolism, including biodigesters, materials libraries, flexible factories on a large scale, and fab labs as centers for learning and prototyping.
- Develop repositories of designs and new open source technologies for the regeneration of vital natural systems in cities and their bioregions.
- Increase the technological sovereignty of cities thanks to the increase in infrastructure and knowledge to support a local innovation model, connected to knowledge networks on a global scale.

Where the rapid urbanization of the 20th century was made possible by the Industrial Revolution and the assembly line —which enabled the rapid reproduction and replication of infrastructure, products and repetitive urban patterns in cities around the world —the urbanization of the 21st century needs to look at how cities will produce (almost) everything they need to consume within their bioregional limits and through new principles of interdependence between territories on a global scale. Urban morphology and urban dynamics have produced standardized patterns and ways of living over the last two centuries. At the same time, and in keeping with the linear economy, today's cities consume most of the world's resources and generate most of the world's waste (according to the United Nations). Nonetheless, the exponential growth of digital technologies (computing, communication, manufacturing) offers the opportunity to begin a transition toward a spiral economy (an open circular economy approach), in which data (and knowledge) flow globally and materials flow locally: from logistics networks that move atoms, to information networks that move bits. The cities of the future must be smarter and be equipped with multiple technological layers that support the provision of services to citizens. We also need to rethink the principles behind the development of the Smart City model, which has shown some weaknesses in terms of social and ecological sustainability. Social stability is at risk, since Smart Cities have not yet resolved how to protect citizens' digital rights against economic and political interests in manipulating their decisions (Facebook, Cambridge Analytica). Ecological stability is an issue in terms of the resources that cities need to consume to function and meet the demands of their inhabitants. That is why the future of cities is dependent on a profound transformation of the productive and economic model, and digital manufacturing can play a fundamental role in providing the skills, abilities and technologies necessary to reinvent our cities based on new ecological and human perspectives.

Fab Labs, maker spaces, and other community-based or individual open innovation platforms can become the source of regenerative technology production in cities, towns, and bioregions. Fab Labs have the potential to profoundly impact the way we live, work and play. However, they need better tools for governance, assessment and value sharing to incentivize impact within the network and in their local surroundings. Nonetheless, the main values and missions of the Fab Lab community can be understood as follows:

- *Collaborative community*: Over the past 15 years, the Fab Lab network has been meeting in a different country each year for an annual Fab Conference. Leveraging tools that support global collaboration, such as GitLab, GitHub, fablabs.io, WhatsApp, and Slack, Fab Labs are organized into regional networks, with the most consolidated examples found in Latin America, Asia, and Europe. The networks collaborate on educational programs such as the Fab Academy, the Textile Academy, and the Bio Academy.
- *Open source philosophy*: Thanks to digital manufacturing technologies, the open source movement is shifting from software to hardware as Fab Labs exchange code, files, and instructions to design and produce things anywhere in the world, without the need for shipping any materials. By its nature, open source software lacks incentive mechanisms, but that is not the case when it comes to hardware. All the content from the Fab Lab network is publicly available online: inventory, educational curricula, video lessons, project designs, platform source codes, and online tools.
- *Circular economy and open innovation*: The ultimate goal of Fab Labs is to bring to life the vision of the Fab City project. According to this mission, data —not things —will be sent around the world, making it possible for objects to be manufactured locally. The circular economy is not based on

managing materials, but on creating value from waste products and their ability to be reintroduced into the supply chain at a local level. This ambitious goal requires open innovation at its heart, a core value of the Fab Lab network.

- *Social impact*: Neil Gershenfeld, director of the MIT Center for Bits and Atoms, stated in 2005 that the network's aim was to encourage hands-on activities and invention by bringing science and technology to peripheral and marginalized communities. We're seeing that in action today, as people at Fab Labs around the world are taking on the challenge of stepping out of the comfort zone of the empowered, self-satisfied geek, and using their knowledge to help their local communities, and then measuring and documenting the impact. Digital fabrication has the potential to provide solutions to address specific needs anywhere in the world, especially for communities that lack access to water, power or communications. One example of this is the Vigyam Ashram Fab Lab in rural India, which has implemented successful solutions such as LED lighting, precision farming control devices, and a sanitary incinerator. Fab Labs are physical spaces that have the potential for social inclusion, empowering like-minded people (individual and collective agency), and encouraging their capabilities. Digital empowerment takes on another dimension when bits and atoms are connected, and when people and communities can meet their local needs through access to new means of production.
- *Access to digital manufacturing tools*: The primary goal of the Fab Lab network is to democratize access to digital fabrication tools by developing educational programs and facilities for communities around the world. There are a growing number of Fab Labs developed by the public and private sectors that provide free access to spaces and machines. However, this access is not limited to equipment: the goal is to provide citizens with the knowledge and tools to expand the network's potential on a global level.
- *Development of educational programs*: Individual Fab Labs, regional networks, and the global community have been developing and implementing new educational programs worldwide, including certified programs like the Fab Academy or Bio Academy, as well as STEAM (science, technology, engineering, arts, and mathematics) programs in schools. These new educational programs teach the next generation skills that are necessary in today's digital economy and are in demand at large companies, startups, and innovation organizations when it comes time to hire new staff. Fab educational programs stimulate the entrepreneurial spirit:

a large number of Fab Labs have been founded by alumni as start-ups, along with the development and creation of new products.

- *Development of new economic models based on new urban industries*: Fab Labs supports the Fab City vision, which aims to transform urban dynamics and space through an industrialization based on clean technologies, on-demand production, the circular economy and citizen innovation. Fab Labs have the potential to articulate a transition towards a new production model in cities, capable of providing access to tools, promoting new skillsets, and offering a new type of services and products that can challenge the 150-year-old industrial model.
- *Catalyst for a new model of distributed production*: Fab Labs will not replace industry, but they will speed the transition toward a new manufacturing model at different scales within cities and regions. They can help provide necessary services and products in cities without compromising the planet's resources or exploiting workers. Fab Labs are places where ideas become reality; prototypes are designed and tested with users, and business models are developed, while connections are forged with larger manufacturing ecosystems on a city and regional scale. For example, the approach taken by the Make Works database of open access factories is complementary within the worldwide Fab Lab network, since it includes industry-scale manufacturers and suppliers across cities and regions.

FROM FAB LABS TO FAB CITIES

Fab City brings the impact of Fab Lab digital technology to cities by connecting distributed networks of hyperlocal and productive ecosystems, which support the mass distribution of goods and resources worldwide. By embracing the Fab City challenge, cities can radically transform how production and consumption take place within their metropolitan regions, replacing standardization with intelligent personalization, focusing on interconnected processes rather than isolated products, and, more importantly, empowering citizens and communities while reducing environmental impact and the side effects of urbanization. The Fab City Global Initiative is an action plan for cities to make this change possible while incrementing their resilience by relocating the production of energy, food and products. It supports the articulation of global communities of designers, creators and thinkers who can amplify and multiply the scale of this important transformation in conjunction with civil society, government and industry. Fab City is not just a concept, it is rooted in the fact that it is possible to reduce the movement of atoms that travel around the world to provide products to cities. Over more than 10 years, the network of digital fabrication laboratories (Fab Labs) has grown exponentially. A Fab Lab is a place where you can do (almost) anything. There are machines that help people turn ideas into reality, where people can learn not just to be users of technology, but to create it. If we can create technology, then we can rethink how our mobility systems work, or how we filter water, or how we produce food in urban areas, to name just a few examples. Fab Labs provide access to digital manufacturing infrastructure and serve as spaces for learning and creating prototypes, where a cultural transformation can take place around manufacturing. These labs let us imagine that fundamental changes in our production systems can be derived from citizen inventions on a local level and open source knowledge exchange on a global scale.

The Fab City global initiative has put together a 40-year roadmap that began in Barcelona in 2014, when the city's then mayor challenged other world leaders to develop a new urban model: cities that produce everything they consume locally, while sharing knowledge globally. That challenge has been taken up by 37 other cities, regions and countries, including: Detroit, Amsterdam, Bhutan, Shenzhen, Ekurhuleni, Santiago de Chile, Boston, Paris, São Paulo, Seoul, Hamburg and Rennes, among others. Fab City is now an ongoing project articulated by a distributed network of urban planners, designers, creators, innovators, artists, developers, engineers and other professionals and enthusiasts around the world, representing institutions such as the Danish Design Centre, the Royal College of Arts and Design, Waag Society, Parkhuis de Zwijger, Metabolic, Materiom, Open Dot Milano, Fab Lab Berlin, Fab Lab Santiago, Fab Lab Barcelona, Green Lab London, Fab City Grand Paris Association, Politecnico di Milano, Incite Focus Detroit, Dark Matter Labs, and Fab Lab Bhutan, to name a few. The Global Fab City Initiative is made up of three parts:

- *Fab City Collective*: the group of people (urban planners, designers, creators, innovators, artists, developers, engineers and other professionals and enthusiasts from all over the world) who contribute to the development of different projects at the local level, with the support of organizations, governments and other actors. This group participates in different projects worldwide —concentrated largely in Europe at the moment, but movement is picking up in Asia and America.
- *The Fab City Network*: A network of cities that have joined Fab City since 2014; there are currently 34 members. This network operates at the other end of the network of Fab Labs (nearly 2,000 in number), making it possible to articulate public policy and build up a more institutional layer for Fab City

locally in each city. The current list includes Barcelona, Zagreb, Thimphu (Bhutan), Shenzhen, Georgia, Curitiba, Occitanie Region, Puebla, Mexico City, Auvergne-Rhône-Alpes, Amsterdam, Cambridge, Kerala, Sacramento, Plymouth, Hamburg, Yucatán Region, Belo-Horizonte, Ekurhuleni, Brest, Boston, Toulouse, Paris, Santiago, Velsen, Seoul, Oakland, Somerville, Detroit, Kamakura, Sorocaba, Rennes, São Paulo, Recife.
- *The Fab City Foundation*: We recently saw the need to generate a certain organizational structure, which is why we launched the Fab City Foundation. The foundation was established as a legal and organizational structure in Estonia to support the location-independent work of the globally distributed Fab City community. It is enabled by Estonia's e-Residency program, which allows people and organizations to function seamlessly across borders and bureaucratic boundaries.

THE FAB CITY FULL STACK

Full Stack: "In computing, a solution stack or software stack is a set of subsystems or software components needed to create a complete platform such that no additional software is needed to support applications. Applications are said to 'run on' or 'run on top of' the resulting platform." —Wikipedia

We are currently facing a fundamental transformation of our 100-year-old urban model, which must take on highly complex problems. Fab City has developed a strategy based on an analogy with software development: full stack. That means that we think of cities as platforms with complex internal networks, and they need different parts, actors, technologies and strategies to help them function. It is true that the city is much more complex than software, and that at the same time it is a living element; it has a life of its own and cannot be controlled. But it is possible to exert an influence on cities in order to generate the conditions for the necessary innovation in transforming the model of production and consumption by which they operate. Our strategy incorporates the following layers:

- *Network of bioregions*: Shared metrics to assess progress towards local production in cities and their bioregions. Formulation of policy, regulations, and planning for regenerative urbanization.
- *Platform ecosystem to meet local needs*: Repositories of projects for urban transformation. Distributed and decentralized repositories and mechanisms of value exchange for global collaboration. Fab Chain, the blockchain project to support distributed design and manufacturing within the Fab City.

- *Shared strategies adapted to local needs*: Global urban transformation programs related to the local production and processing of food, energy, water, information or other production systems. Implementation and deployment strategies on the part of the Fab City Collective. Fab City prototypes.
- *Distributed incubation for urban innovation*: Programs to support innovation in regenerative technologies, taking advantage of the power of Fab Labs, as a distributed knowledge network, to visualize, design and create open source technology for urban transformation.
- *New ways of learning*: Creation of distributed programs that offer opportunities for the development of 'learning to learn' skills and learning-by-doing, a foundation for lifelong learning. The Academy of Almost Anything (Fab Academy, Bio Academy, Fabricademy), STEAM education and career training.
- *Distributed infrastructure for innovation in digital manufacturing*: People, communities, spaces (Fab Labs, Makerspaces, Hackerspaces), equipment, tools, flexible factories, installed industrial capacity, and materials libraries. There are already thousands of spaces and communities in all major and mid-sized cities across the world.

The Full Stack strategy lets us divide up the Fab City's biggest challenge into smaller parts, which helps us make the strategies for the development of technologies for urban regeneration more operational. The challenge we're facing is not only technical, political, social or economic; it is the sum of all those things operating at the same time, within a system that feeds back into itself. On the other hand, the scale of the challenge is not nation versus city, or centralization versus decentralization; it is based on a complementarity of scales and strategies that can provide for the construction of more resilient, inclusive and regenerative natural, social and cultural systems. In the same way, the duality of the local versus the global becomes an element of acceleration in the transition towards a model of productive cities based on regenerative principles, since it allows for stimulating diversity, while also drawing from other communities and individuals who are working on similar challenges with a shared purpose, and who are able to share the knowledge they generate through digital platforms. We recently saw examples of this in the response from the world of open innovation to the crisis of ventilators and masks to protect patients and medical professionals at the beginning of the COVID-19 crisis. Thanks to citizen connection through digital platforms, access to digital manufacturing technologies such as 3D printing and CNC machines, and the altruism of designers, engineers, makers, and ordinary citizens who shared their knowledge in digital repositories, it was possible respond to a local and global crisis like a pandemic at much faster speeds than any government or company could have managed.

FAB CITIES AND BIOREGION DESIGN

In the current context of transformation of the climate and the territory as a result of human activity, it is crucial to coordinate efforts toward the configuration of bioregions. Territorial organization around bioregions requires a new attitude in relation to the natural systems that surround us and the development of a caring economy that goes beyond anthropocentric visions of sustainable development. Bioregions are defined by cultural relationships and by natural systems in a given territory. Bioregions let us operate on a territorial scale large enough that we can understand cities beyond their artificial physical or political limits. At the same time, bioregions operate within global logics, such as climate change, the interdependence of aquifer systems, the transport of microorganisms through the air, or the influence of natural or artificial phenomena on temperature changes at a local scale. Because of the human impact on the ecosystems that make up the bioregions, it is impossible not to tie in this relationship between biological and synthetic elements with their spatial and cultural dimensions.

The challenge is not only to achieve the sustainability of the material world we depend on today, but to use regenerative logics to recover a large part of the biodiversity that has been sacrificed for the sake of economic and industrial development. In that sense, it is essential to reshape our relationship with the living systems that help us satisfy the energy needs of the human species, in terms of electricity or the food that serves cities and rural populations. In order to take on such an enormous challenge, we must be able to generate spaces for learning and cultural exchange between various species, in areas that combine political, cultural and biological dimensions, and that can serve as the foundation for research projects and programs focused on immediate action and the application of existing methodologies, tools, and skills in both local and global environments. That will involve generating networks with other bioregions, cities, towns, communities, and individuals who share the goal of transforming and evolving how urban life functions today. Only by articulating our efforts in a connected way and in the form of a global network will it be possible to take on the difficult task of addressing the wicked problems that always exist in cities. Replacing colonial logics based on scarcity, competition, extraction and exploitation with new logics that we can identify and discover through experimentation in cities, bioregions and human settlements is one possible challenge amid the ongoing efforts currently being pursued by multiple organizations, networks, communities and agents on a global scale. The potential of distributed learning and innovation networks, such as the Fab Labs network, supports the construction of complementary layers for combining our efforts on a small scale. In the same way that the negative impacts of the daily actions of today's urban life generate problems on a global scale, we can imagine that the articulation of small efforts through collaboration, open source code, and experimentation can help us develop new responses to the new questions we will be asking ourselves about that great perpetual object of desire, the city.

NOTES

1 Phillips, 1997.
2 Papanek, 1972,
3 Van Newkirk, 1975.
4 Patel and Moore, 2017.
5 Díez and Tomico, 2020.
6 Díez, 2012.
7 Gershenfeld, 2017.

The aforementioned examples point to the possibility of questioning the secondary role to which contemporary urban processes have relegated human beings. And, by doing so, they defend the need to displace architecture and urban planning from their leading role in the construction of urban identity and the need to explore knowledges and practices that counterbalance the modernist breach between interior-private space and exterior-public space, where the latter is given primacy in shaping the city. Urban planning and architecture have saturated the public dimension of cities, where any individual or collective outcome is openly criticized, legally criminalized, and consequently banished to the private sphere.

Materiality emerges as a major, profound concept to be developed here. The awareness of our environment in its material dimension leads directly to the understanding of ourselves as bodies, and all the processes and systems intertwined between the two —body and environment. Given this understanding, the human-environment interaction can no longer be abstract (i.e., distant and supposedly objective) but becomes concrete, based on a particular experience and context. The sociologist Manuel de Landa has drawn on Deleuze's and Guattari's concept of *assemblage* to suggest a new social ontology. The assemblage is, for Deleuze and Guattari, a key agent to trigger both the process of content and its expression, and that of territorialization and deterritorialization. Most importantly, through these two processes, the assemblage allows a third process to happen: that of codification and decodification, which fundamentally conforms human understanding of the world.[89] De Landa highlights the importance of matter in this tension between content and expression, and promotes the material relationship between human beings and their environment as central to sense-making. By recovering the concept of assemblage and stressing the importance of matter, De Landa aims to displace language from the core of the social phenomena and to force a balance between semantics and other factors in a new ontology. He writes, "A component part of an assemblage may be detached from it and plugged into a different assemblage in which its interactions are different."[90] The relative autonomy of the individ-

89 The authors offer a wonderful metaphor for this understanding, citing Leroi-Gourhan, who refers to the importance of the duality of mouth-hand, and consequently gesture and word, in developing this processes of codification and deterritorialization. See; Deleuze, Guattari, 1987, 88.

90 De Landa, 2006, 10.

 ual in relation to the structure reveals a materialistic approach, which assumes that sense-making may arise from the concrete relationship between individuals and their environment, rather than only from linguistic structures.

Many design projects in recent decades have been developed according to this materialistic turn in the human ontology, aiming to explore the boundaries of the semantic construction of the world through concrete experience. A simple set of pottery, apparently to heat and serve Senegalese food and drinks, condenses the main characteristics of this turn. This set, called Barada and Casilooroo, was designed by Julia Claveria as part of the project *Lugares dialécticos* [Dialectic Places], an open process carried out by students and professors from Elisava together with migrant collectives in Barcelona. Migrants can be held back by social prejudices and therefore may end up working at the lowest levels of hierarchical societies and on the margins of regulated labor. In this case, the designer's approach was to undertake a series of actions that helped promote shared understanding, which ultimately led to the design of the set of pottery. Like other relevant projects from the last decade,[91] the project highlighted certain dimensions that are commonly dismissed in modern design. The set of pottery made no semantic assumption regarding the roles of anyone involved in its design. In addition to its basic function of heating, the product acts as a plug-in that generates unexpected urban situations to promote the construction of a new identity by generating new meaning from the actions of individuals in a particular context. Barada and Casilooroo raises awareness of the importance of materiality and explicitly assumes that materiality not only defines our attitudes or actions but also promotes a reflection and transformation of our conception of the world and the semantic connections that structure it. On a deeper level, the project enhances the key role of gesture and body movements in human interactions with the environment.

Early 20th-century French anthropologists, like Jousse or Mauss, suggested that all social or cultural constructions are rooted in our embodied dimension.[92] A new understanding of human relationships with the environment was suggested, paving the way to break with the

91 To name just a few: Gamper, M. 100 Chairs; Claret, C. T300; Armengol, M.- Santomà, G. *Furniture for the exhibition Digital meditation through virtual reality.*

92 Jousse, 1974; Mauss, 1935.

Cartesian primacy of mind in the construction of human knowledge. The phenomenological turn explores the same discussion, suggesting a primacy of human experience in the construction of meaning. This phenomenological approach has led to a reflection on the assumed primacy of language and lived experience. Especially fruitful in the field of the performing arts,[93] an embodied understanding of human interaction with the world and, therefore, of human knowledge, has attributed new importance to human experience. And, by doing so, it has repositioned the layers and hierarchies related to certain practices that were once understood as subsidiaries of linguistics. In that vein, design —as a practice that actively relates human beings with their environment— has come forward to question the construction of knowledge and design's own role in relation to other disciplines.

The set of pottery referred to above should be understood as a generator of a certain interaction between individuals, and between individuals and their environment. This generative nature of design is not just an anecdote strictly related to a particular action or moment; rather, it confirms the potential of gestural practices as a path to sense-making. As Jürgen Streeck states, gestures are conceived as "human *practices*: not as a code or symbolic system or (part of) language, but as a constantly evolving set of largely improvised, heterogeneous, partly conventional, partly idiosyncratic and partly culture-specific, partly universal practices of using hands to produce situated understandings".[94] Gesture and movement provide a disclosure of the world, apart from what is revealed by sight, and they promote the questioning and construction of meanings in our immediate environment. Along similar lines, *The Materialization of Multicultural Identities*, by Hannah Adib, assumes design processes and outcomes to be a fundamental tool for rethinking and redefining hybrid and critical identities in a first-person approach. In her project, reflection, conversation and gestures are channeled through a specific protocol into rugs that become a visual and material support for consolidating and rethinking individual identity in relation to the environment. Examples like the T300 metal tripod, the heater, or the rugs suggest a multilayered dimension of design, which, far from being dominated by the primacy of linguistics, demonstrates

93 Sheets-Johnston, 1999; Perez Galí, 2015.
94 Streek, 2009, 5.

 a clear capacity to reflect on the status quo and define identities in any human context.

Curiously enough, in De Landa's process of reflecting on social categories by taking individual experience as the starting point, the design outcomes are only expressed in architecture. The discourse progresses directly from conversations and routines, as the first level of human expressions in the environment, to building elements, architecture and urban planning. A different breach, related to the one between human beings and the urban built environment that developed during modernism, seems to be maintained here —a breach that separates the construction of the meaningful world from direct and immediate human experience. Although this gap seems to be abiding and unsolvable, two examples developed in Barcelona in the last century show the power of apparently simple, material and contextual objects when it comes to uncovering sense-making and even identity in the city. A small concrete tile and a stone slope are radical examples of how a simple and relatively cheap design can respond to multiple demands and reveal a deep understanding of what a city should be. The first example is a small sidewalk paving tile, measuring just 20 × 20 × 4 cm and manufactured using a simple and cheap material: cement. It was first designed in 1906 for a small area of the city, but later spread throughout all of Barcelona's streets, from the city center to the suburbs, from bourgeois neighborhoods to working class housing estates. It became a continuous pavement that connected the entire city. Moreover, in addition to its more basic function of providing a safe and clean paving surface, it also helped all citizens recognize the common and essential role of the street and public space in generating urban identity.

The second example is a stone slope (1991), a radically simple design that connects the street level with the sidewalks. This urban device, originally intended for one particular boulevard, was eventually implemented everywhere to serve as an urban threshold, allowing all citizens —young, old, disabled, whatever their means— to move freely along the streets under equal conditions. Both these examples express the capacity of design to combine social, cultural and functional aspects using relatively simple forms and materials. In another sense, they confirm the capacity of material expression —to use Deleuze and De Landa's terms— to qualify the environment, encouraging people to behave with freedom and respect, and raising awareness of the need to express the complexity of the city using precise forms. These two examples also reveal the strength of concretion in design, the capacity to generate outcomes that are relevant to a specific environment but that can be easily replicated —devices that not only relate to function and aesthetics but that also engage in inquiry and a construction of semantics and meaning.

IDENTITY

Design as a Sense-making Practice

De Landa's oversight regarding this initial step of human interaction with the environment can be explained by the common assumption that places design as a part of mass media and consumer goods, which centers on the professional designer as a sense-maker through industrial production.[95] An anthropological approach developed through the 1970s and 80s revealed fundamental insights on the role of goods in societies, which was especially relevant for a Western society overwhelmed by objects.[96] Nevertheless, a collateral effect of this approach was that objects and elements of communication were relegated to the back-end, as the final step in economic mass production. There, the role of individuals is almost passive in the process of the production of identities. Occasionally, the examples highlighted in these studies revealed a problematic relationship between individual goods (including their arrangement in the private habitat) and the more homogeneous urban and social planning. Yet they did not suggest the opportunity of expanding this sense-making to the urban environment as a whole.

Not surprisingly, Jan Gehl's studies on the human scale of urban design reveal a similar dismissal of this first step in the human relationship with urban environment. In Gehl's multiple and careful examples used to suggest paths for designing cities that place human wellbeing at the center, there is a clear attention to buildings and streets, but no detailed reflection on the objectual world, apart from some raw sketches

95 Barthes, 1957; Baudrillard, 1968.
96 Douglas, Isherwood, 1979; Appadurai, 1986; De Certeau, 1990.

of urban furniture. Gehl assumes the importance of dimensions and relative distances in city design (as a clear legacy of E.T. Hall's work) and raises awareness of the need to define the interactions between human beings and their environment. Nevertheless, this conception of space is presented as if it were only a question of measures and proportions, with apparently no attention to matter, expression and content.[97] Again the clash between individuals, as inhabitants with concrete experiences, and urban planning, as the result of professional decisions, is evidenced by the void —the aforementioned breach— created in this crucial layer of the urban fabric. In a way, projects like *Intervenció o Accident*, developed during the initial lockdown in response to the COVID-19 pandemic, explored this capacity of design and promoted a series of observations, actions and scenarios to reflect on the potential relations between individuals and the urban fabric. Following the thread opened by Koolhaas in *Delirious New York*,[98] accident and narrative are key factors in harnessing a wide range of design experiences to perform possible realities.

As stated previously, materiality can be the path to bridge this gap and to begin a process of identification that forges a meaningful connection between human beings and the city. In recent decades, post-phenomenological approaches have suggested new avenues in our understanding of the built environment. New materialism has brought back the importance of matter in the structures that define our world, while adding the semiotic dimension in a non-logocentric understanding of knowledge.[99] This dialectic process permits a constant reflection on the identities and boundaries in the urban fabric, in an assemblage that posits human's and objects' agency on the same level. Moreover, it promotes a performative understanding of the process of sense-making, which aims to break with the primacy of language that still dominates the semiotic interpretation of the city.[100]

One thread in this philosophical understanding of matter and the objectual world has also led to a critique of the abstract understanding of production in the 20th century, which, focusing on economic management, failed to consider the concrete environmental, social and ethical particularities in which it was taking place. The concept of situated knowledge[101] forces a deeper approach to the production of objects

97 Gehl, *Cities for…, op. cit.*

98 Koolhaas, 1978.

99 Latour, *We have…, op. cit.*; 1991; Verbeek, 2005; Harman, 2010; Dollphijn, Van der Tuin, 2012.

100 As stated in the secular work by Floch, J-M. *Sémiotique, marketing et communication: sous les signes, les strategies*. See: Floch, 1990.

101 Haraway, 1988.

and their unquestionable and relevant relations with the context, while assuming the non-neutral nature of any design action. This approach was fundamental in a research project developed as part of a third-year mandatory subject at Elisava, in which students from the BA in Design actively researched Invisible Makers in the Poblenou neighborhood. The selection of the context was not random and was intended to force the narrative of Poblenou as a digital innovation hub, within the framework of the 22@ plan developed by the Barcelona City Council. The goal was to look for "makers" outside the confines of start-up myth. They could be associated with traditional crafts, which were overshadowed by the semantic framing of the urban policies developed for the neighborhood. The research project uncovered more than 100 spots, which promoted a new understanding of the context and design opportunities on two levels.

On a first level, it put designers into a real interaction with productive citizens. The unforeseen outcome of the process would arise from this meaningful interaction, which would provide both agents with extraordinarily relevant knowledge. On a second level, by using mapping as a key tool, this random and open research was carried over into a symbolic dimension, building a visual identification of the space that could interact with the one promoted by the municipality —and strongly supported by public communication campaigns. The interactive digital platform and the magazines designed by the students pursued the clear aim of counterbalancing the existing narrative and pushing for a new, more inclusive, less mythologized one. Mapping and design were clear identifiers of unexpected realities that were plugged into the context, aiming to transform the neighborhood's dominating narrative structured by municipal policy and digital business strategies.

As a spinoff of the same project, fourth-year students from the BA in Industrial Design selected one of the 100 invisible makers identified during the first phase and worked with them to reposition or transform their craft to help them face future challenges. Students developed a strong process of shared recognition and understanding, to be able to to "design with" the craftspeople (to borrow the terminology used by Ron Wakkary following Donna Haraway).[102] Reflecting on a wide range

102 Wakkary, 2020.

 of dimensions, from materials to communication, from form to digital technologies, the project unleashed unexpected avenues for the future transformation of the neighborhood's productive tissue. Collected under the common name City and Maker Culture, the academic initiative suggested design processes to perform as plug-ins by breaking the semantic assumptions that conditioned the craftspeople's work and their ties to the city. As a result, the design outcomes promoted a rediscovery of the positions of these agents, both from the standpoint of their individual capabilities and in their connections with the urban context. They deployed a process of assemblage so that the constructive development could be achieved while respecting the need for awareness of the symbolic dimension of any human practice as a means for identity building and sense-making.

Furthermore, by assuming the material and embodied dimension of our relationship with our environment (as opposed to a merely visual one prioritized by market-based strategies) the Invisible Makers+Maker Culture projects led to a problematization of the myth of innovation.

Innovation, which has been associated with a contemporary conception of design over the past three decades, especially in the English-speaking world, promotes clean and even abstract design processes, commonly pushed by business models, and with little or no ties to the concrete experience of the people involved. In this mindset, human experience is framed by the term "user", in a role that seems to be limited to feeding data into the consumption process for a better performance in the market. Running contrary to this myth of innovation, certain studios are paying increasing attention to the concept of maintenance, rooted in the world of do-it-yourself and repair work. This focus on maintenance processes suggests a radical transformation of the role of design in human experience. As stated by Martin Tironi, in contrast with innovation, maintenance "is a mode of exploring new narratives for the city, incorporating care and experimentation as central elements, allowing the frictions of the city to (in)form new possibilities on the composition of the urban life".[103]

Projects designed by MEATS such as Slow Down, Stop and Stay or those developed for the LlumBCN Festival in Barcelona, such as Alice, Anima and Llacuna, suggest how the exploration of our built environ-

103 Strebel, Bovet, Sormani, 2019.

ment through design outcomes can offer new insights into the idea of the city. Through modular furniture, lighting devices or abstract objects, these projects reveal a profound understanding of the role of individuals and collectives as active stakeholders in urban development. This approach was also explored by Sara Torres, a student in the BA in Design, in the project Formas de compensación [Forms of Compensation], as part of the collaboration with CoBoi, a Social Innovation hub in Sant Boi de Llobregat, Barcelona.

The design outcomes presented here aim to highlight design's capabilities with regard to sense-making. This capacity can be developed by identifiers —relating to remembrance, legacy or fairness— or by generators —recovering spots, environments, and individuals, or collectives that should be recognized for their role in creating urban identities. The reflection on the design examples detailed in this chapter, following the arguments of Rossi, Leroi-Gourhan, Deleuze and De Landa, promote reducing the primacy of the visual sphere and that of architecture in reinforcing the symbolic dimension of cities. They all share a focus on embodied practices, gesture and materiality as powerful tools not only for transformation and innovation, but for care and maintenance. They suggest individual, collective and design-based tools to break down the semantic links that lead only to a certain kind of city, and to re-open other possible avenues toward a desired urban environment.

→ 294

PAISAJES DE LA MEMORIA

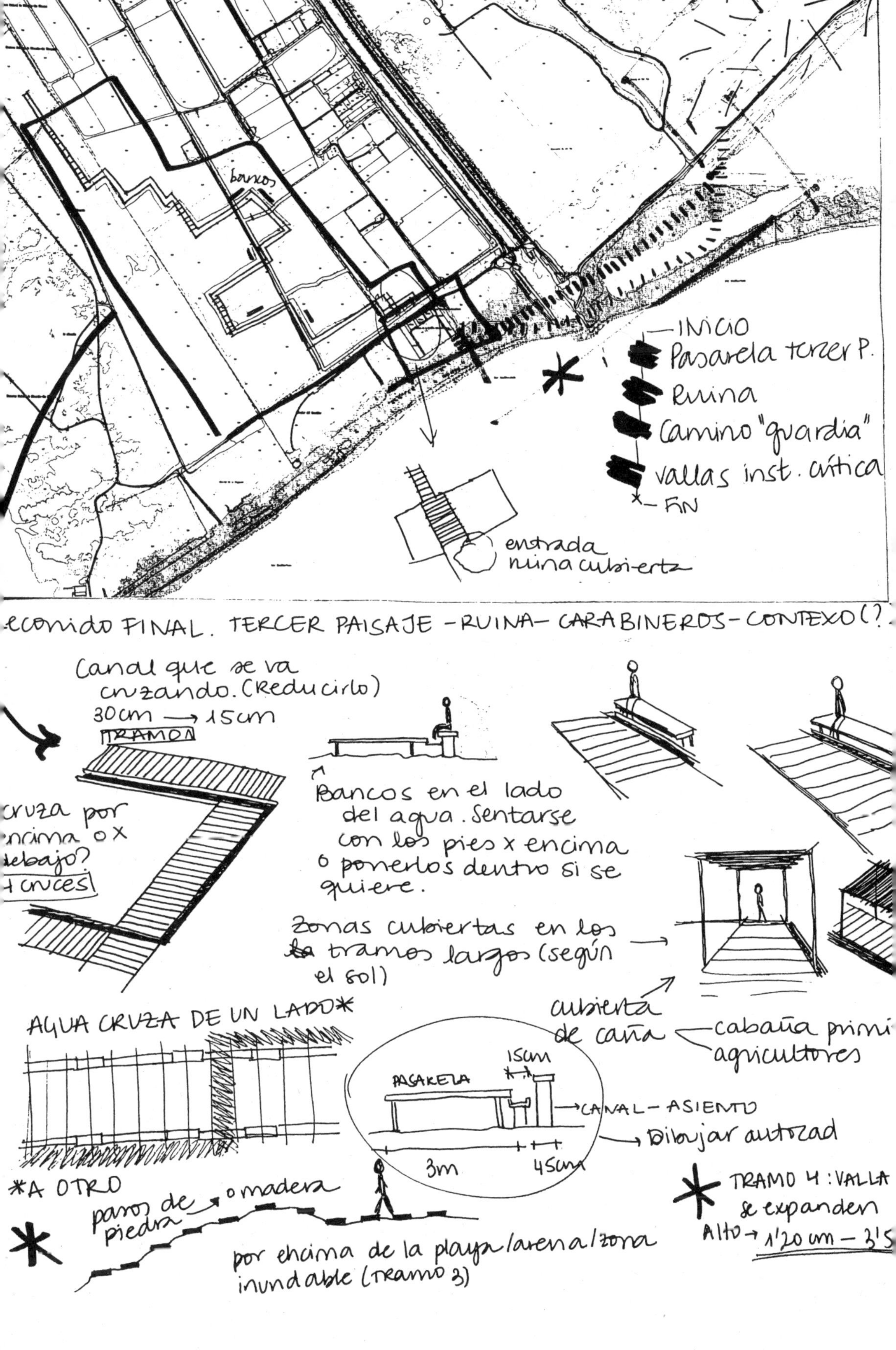

bancos
INICIO
Pasarela tercer P.
Ruina
Camino "guardia"
vallas inst. crítica
FIN
entrada ruina cubierta
ecorrido FINAL. TERCER PAISAJE –RUINA– CARABINEROS– CONTEXO(?.
Canal que se va cruzando. (Reducirlo)
30cm → 15cm
cruza por encima o x debajo?
+ cruces
Bancos en el lado del agua. Sentarse con los pies x encima o ponerlos dentro si se quiere.
Zonas cubiertas en los tramos largos (según el sol)
cubierta de caña
cabaña primi agricultores
AGUA CRUZA DE UN LADO*
*A OTRO
PASARELA
15cm
CANAL – ASIENTO
Dibujar autocad
3m
45cm
pasos de piedra → o madera
por encima de la playa/arena/zona inundable (TRAMO 3)
TRAMO 4: VALLA se expanden
Alto → 1'20 cm – 3'5

→ 289

ALICE

→ 293

MI REALIDAD

A veces logramos escapar.

→ 290

COBOI 2.0 / CENTRE D'INNOVACIÓ SOCIAL

→ 292

THE HUMAN FLAG

→ 296

WHAT MONEY CANNOT BUY

→ 296

VORA

CNDH53
SOCCER
ADVENTURE

→ 293 LE DAMOS LA VUELTA

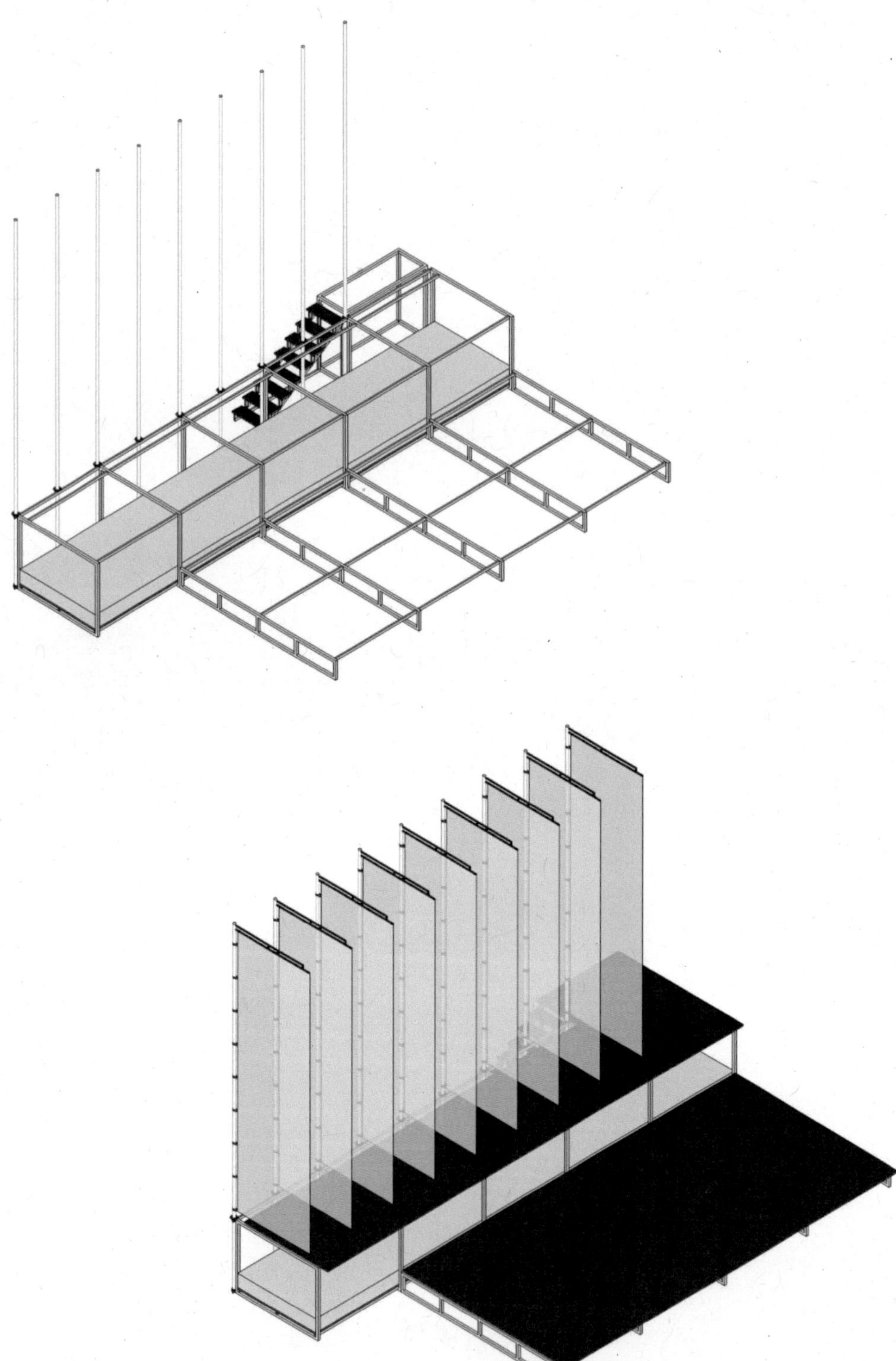

→ 289 CAN GUINEU

→ 289
ANIMA

→ 296

URBAN DOORS

→ 293

MATÈRIA FORA DE LLOC

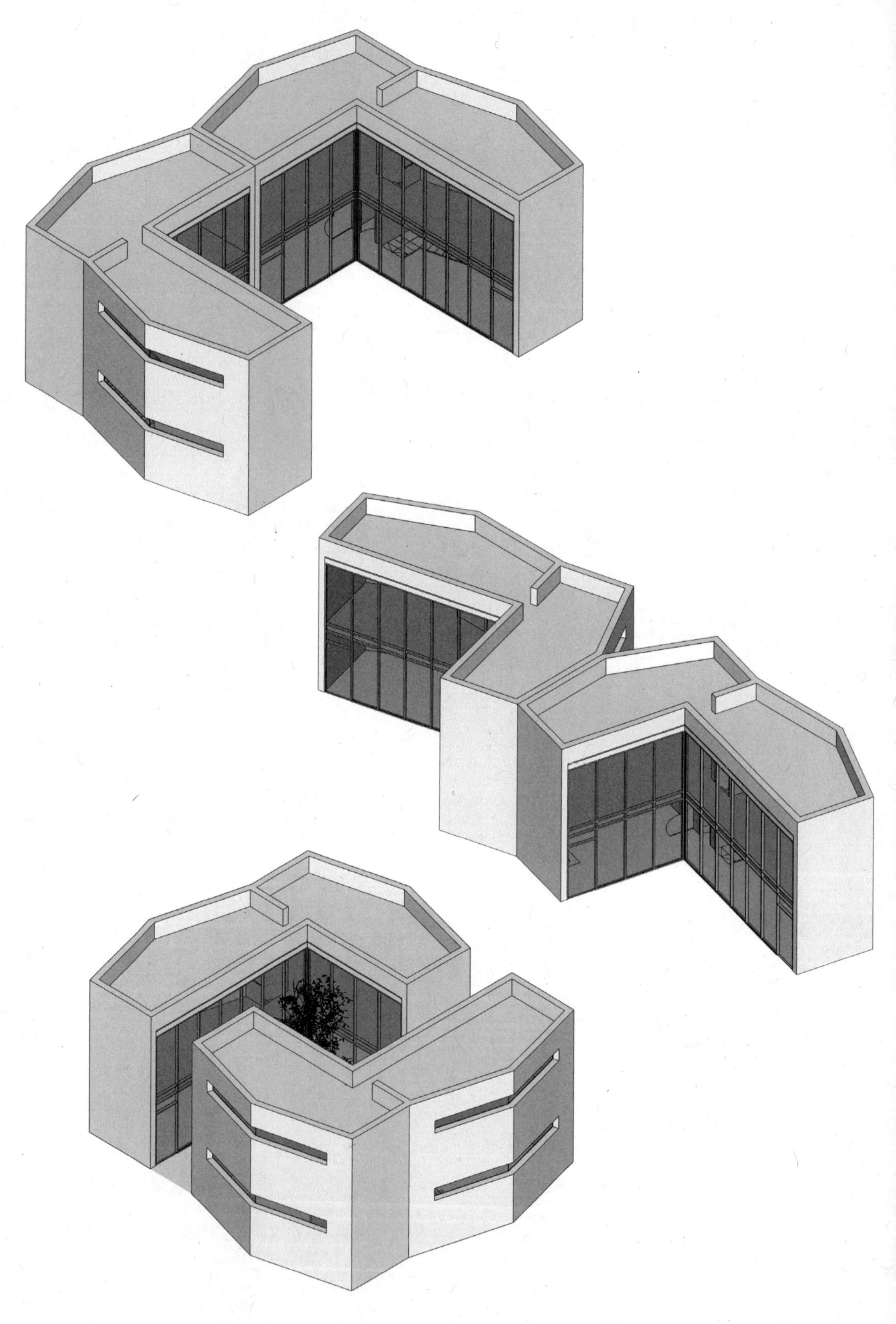

→ 293 LLACUNA

→ 290 CHASED

Navigating Complexity

PART V

NAVIGATING COMPLEXITY

Cities are hyper-complex natural-social-technical systems —certainly, the most complex systems that humans have helped to generate, and the ones whose evolution has the greatest implications not only for their inhabitants, but for the entire planet. At the same time, the pandemic and the climate crisis have shown us that it is precisely in cities where the greatest problems are created, and where the ideas and practices to deal with those problems can emerge. In other words, cities are a crucial arena to learn how to navigate complexity to arrive at sustainable ways of life. Undoubtedly, cities today are home to the most diverse and challenging technological productions of human beings in terms of infrastructure, resources and management, and they also seem to increasingly define the key aspects of human relations with the environment, political trends and cultural leadership.

Traditionally, control has been the underlying constant of any design process related to the city. To tackle randomness, unexpectedness and the fear of undetermined outcomes, modern urban planning and architecture have mostly been wielded as deterministic devices to reduce this uncertainty. In doing so, their design processes have successfully addressed key human needs (such as hygiene, food, and education), but they have also become one of the fundamental ways in which top-down urban policies have been imposed on citizens.

This book suggests a needed shift in this common mind-set, which can be summarized in a single sentence: understanding design for city making as plug-ins in complex urban systems.

This book and the Barcelona-based platform Design for City Making on which it is based are a contribution to this necessary learning process. The following notes, retracing the previous chapters, indicate some generalizable reflections that this experience has brought up for us.

ENGENDERING PRACTICES

Over the last century, the dominant approach to complexity has been to reduce it. In practice, that has meant adopting reading models and control tools to help us eliminate the randomness, uncertainty and contradictions that complexity brings into our lives and projects. In this spirit, city planning traditionally developed models of interpretation whose purpose was to try to control the evolutionary processes that characterize the city as a complex phenomenon. However, since complex systems and their evolutionary processes, by their very nature, cannot be controlled, this approach has shown its limits and, ultimately, it has contributed to the critical situation (in social, environmental and ethical terms) we are experiencing today.

This book advocates a radical change in this approach: extending the meaning of the traditional city planning to the one of *city making*, avoiding mechanistic and simplifying representations of the city and exploring urban visions and practices that recognize its complexity and try to critically navigate it.

To move in this direction, the first step is an act of modesty: to fully recognize the complexity of the systems we are dealing with, and of which we are a part, and therefore recognize that, since we cannot control them, we cannot totally control the final effects of our actions. The reason for this is to be found in the fact that, within a complex system, each agent interacts with the other agents in an unpredictable way. Recognizing complexity therefore means recognizing that we cannot actually "produce results", but only contribute to their cogeneration. Bruno Latour proposes the word "engendering" to characterize design activity when taking into account the network of interdependencies in which its action is inserted and therefore on which the final result depends. He writes, "To speak of engendering is to establish a distinction between the act of producing —which attributes the undertaking and the central role to the human agent— and the act of contributing to the generation —which shifts the center of gravity onto other modes of action."[104]

Unlike the anthropocentric idea of production that we often use in our contemporary Western or Westernized societies, when we refer to "engendering practices" we see ourselves as part of a larger process over which we have no global control, because we are just one of many agents that interact with others and, together, form the web of life.

Taking this position does not at all mean being overwhelmed by complexity and letting things go as they are without taking responsibility for intervening. On the contrary, it means taking responsibility for acting while accepting and understanding the limits of our actions. And, precisely for this reason —precisely because our starting point is a more appropriate model of reality— this can give us more chances of coming closer to reaching our desired goals.

URBAN SYSTEMS AND PLUG-INS

Many cases presented in this book can be seen as engendering practices: actions that generate transformations in the urban ecosystem, with the intention of giving what one would like to see happen a greater chance of existing, thriving and lasting over time.

While city planning relies on top-down design forced onto a complex and shifting reality, city making introduces subsystems into the urban ecosystem that are capable of generating changes. Design for city making strives to devise these subsystems in such a way that what emerges from them is likely to resemble the city we desire.

As mentioned earlier, we call these subsystems *plug-ins*, and we claim they are a solid yet supple conceptual framework for rethinking design's agency in the city. We understand plug-ins as design outcomes that, when inserted into a larger system, generate new configurations of the whole. They are subsystems we have a certain degree of control over (meaning we can design and implement them) that activate a systemic change we do not fully control. In our opinion, the heart of design in

104 Latour, 2018a.

 complexity, and therefore of design for city making, lies in the relationship between what we can actually produce through our actions and what emerges from the intricate play of interdependencies that characterizes urban habitats.

The nature and function of plug-ins express, in no uncertain terms, the contradictory condition of the designer, who, when faced with complexity, must accept it without being overwhelmed by it. Designers must take a stand and act accordingly, knowing that their ideas, and how they translate them into practice, are introducing a designed element —a plug-in— into the tangle of interactions that constitutes the web of urban life.

RECENTERING TERRITORIAL DESIGN: REDISTRIBUTION AS A SPATIAL PRACTICE

Adrià Carbonell

It is a rare occasion that a design brief lands on an empty desk in the form of a fixed and certain commission. On the contrary, the practice of architecture and urban design increasingly requires the active engagement of the designer in defining what the actual design endeavor will be. More and more, the first stage of a design process consists, precisely, in composing the design brief itself. What is the research question, the frame and angle given to the theme, the scope and reach of the project, the program, the externalities, the social benefits, the environmental impact, etc.? All these questions have come to be part of architectural design, where architecture is understood as a spatial practice that spans various scales and integrates abilities and knowledge spanning from the material to the environmental, from the social to the economic. In this light, Design for City Making is, no doubt, an open-ended question, and even more so today, at a time characterized by rapid change and indeterminacy. Dealing with indeterminate factors is a common thing in most —if not all— variants of design. Those indeterminacies, though, can grow when it comes to dealing with *the city*, a notion that in recent years has seemed to be on shaky ground. Because the city, as a study subject and a as design object, is under continuous scrutiny. From its multiple aspects and layers to its very definition and historical evolution, the city is permanently being rethought, rewritten and remade.

And yet, this is by no means an oddity. As a complex system, the city evolves and transforms; as a social, economic, political or material system, it is by its very nature in constant change, and so is its definition. In fact, the urban system can hardly be considered a system, insofar as it encompasses a number of other systems in a sort of system of systems. Accordingly, in this short essay I will draw on an understanding of the city that overcomes its limits as a finite structure or, to be more precise, that situates the city —as an artefact, as a social body and as a type of space— within a much broader framework for analysis, which operates on a territorial scale. This is the framework we work with in the collaborative group Aside, with the aim of forging new paths for both urban research and practice in what we have called *territorial design*. In this context, design can be approached not so much as a problem-solving discipline but as a practice concerned with the transformation of the everyday. To do so, it must synthesize a variety of kinds of knowledge, acknowledge that the city is an entanglement of material and immaterial forces, and invest in the formulation of questions and capacities encompassing human and more-than-human agents. In short, what I will propose in this essay is the transgression of disciplinary boundaries and scales in order to respond to key challenges in contemporary cities, and by doing so address the question of how architecture and urbanism can operate as tools for spatial redistribution.

REDISTRIBUTION OR RECOGNITION? A SPATIAL PROBLEM

Redistribution is a term largely used in politics and economics, mostly associated with redistributive policies and incremental tax systems. In recent history, one of the most compelling examples of redistribution was implemented by the social-democratic political project subjacent to the creation of the so-called Welfare States, particularly in Europe. However, the problem of economic distribution so essential to the modern political economy throughout the 20th century, has been paired, in recent decades, with that of social recognition. The critique of power structures and institutional forms of control promoted by post-structuralism, together with the emergence of social movements and grassroots organizations, have confronted structural asymmetries and endemic inequalities in a struggle over difference and identity. Race, gender and sexuality, as well as indigenous claims, ethnic and religious minorities' rights, and other forms of struggle over forms of misrecognition and oppression have seemed to relegate the social-democratic principle of redistribution behind that of recognition.

The issues at stake, as well as the philosophical problems that arise when thinking about *redistribution* and *recognition* have been thoroughly interrogated by Nancy Fraser and Axel Honneth in an excellent political-philosophical exchange.[1] Regardless of Fraser and Honneth's shared concern and political sympathy, their respective positions diverge to a seemingly irreconcilable point when it comes to locating recognition in a philosophical-political system. While Honneth conceives recognition as a moral category and seeks to subsume the problematic of redistribution within it (encompassing both "recognition of rights" and "cultural appreciation"), Fraser presents both categories as "co-fundamental and mutually irreducible dimensions of justice". The major contribution proposed by Fraser makes a shift in the discussion about recognition and relocates it to the realm of justice, against Honneth's moral category, hence reframing the question of both redistribution and recognition through a democratic-egalitarian lens.

Nonetheless, redistribution cannot be thought about or practiced without a frame of reference that builds a paradigm for justice. Equally, redistribution can hardly be approached theoretically or applied through policies, laws and normative frameworks unless the issue of the social body in which it is being applied is clearly defined. In other words, a theory of redistribution cannot skip the question of its beneficiaries: who is entitled, who has the right to claim fair access to limited resources? How is a just distribution measured, and thus, enforced? It is in this regard that Nancy Fraser turns to the principles of redistributive justice to guarantee equal access and treatment within a body politic as a whole. However, the multi-layered and multi-scalar nature of the current asymmetries and the advent of new forms of dispossession (from urban to planetary, from economic to environmental) demand an urgent revision of the concept of redistribution that may spill across several layers and align along different axes.

In this context, to address both redistribution and recognition in spatial practices may be seen as an unavoidable dual imperative to foster more just and equitable ways forward. Reconnecting the practice of architecture and urbanism with that of critique and social theory —which too often stand in apparent opposition, thus neglecting the potential mutual benefits which could result from a closer dialogue— may be part of this endeavor. Hence, beyond the political-economic analysis, addressing redistributive claims spatially may cast new light in the study of pressing issues in contemporary cities. On the one hand, the exponential growth of cities has fostered internal urban inequalities in a continuous process of *metropolization*, where urban features are increasingly embedded and interconnected in larger territories. On the other, the rapid urbanization has increased the pressure on urban externalities thus triggering a dramatic exploitation of natural resources and causing major alterations in global hinterlands. This dual process of urban concentration and expansion —a dialectic of implosion/explosion, to use Henri Lefebvre's expression— has accelerated multiple polarizations and triggered conflicting scenarios. In this light, the question of the redistribution of wealth, services and resources that decades of neoliberal hegemony had swept under the rug of market competition and individual freedom is making its way back into public debates and global political agendas in the form of urgent challenges, if not threats.

In the fields of architecture and urbanism, an echoing parallelism can be found between two major traditions that run all the way throughout the history of modern urbanism, between design conceived as an instrument for social reform and a conception that privileges the artistic autonomy of the discipline. Whereas the former would be primarily interested in questions of redistribution, the latter would essentially gravitate toward questions of representation. These disputing approaches, despite having a much longer history, arose as central to the disciplinary controversies that marked the maturation of Postmodernism in architecture. Where Modernist architecture and urbanism pursued a political agenda and explicitly participated in redistributive plans –for instance through the provision of affordable housing, public facilities, transport infrastructures, etc., the Postmodernist turn implied a return to the architectural fragment and the autonomy of the object. Postmodernism resituated the political sphere in the realm of representation –that is, in the idea that architecture expresses political positions or ideological stances and that, in turn, this expression politicizes space. Further, this re-conceptualization of the political was associated with a profound reorganization of the urban discipline which, essentially, implied a scalar retreat.[2]

Without neglecting the limits and disciplinary constraints of architecture and urbanism, revamping the claims for redistribution may be an adequate way of counteracting the retreat of urban planning into the realm of bureaucracy, and that of architecture into representation, which we have witnessed in the last few decades. An unattainable goal, unless the urban imagination is put back to work at a scale and ambition that supersedes the political and spatial downscale that came with the advent of Postmodernism. The fundamental challenges embodied in recent social and spatial transformations cannot be properly addressed through the conventional methodologies –or scales– of architecture and urban design. They require, instead, reframing the urban question as a territorial question. To that end, new forms of design practice capable of intervening at geographic/territorial scales must be developed: forms of practice that conceive the territory as the ground, support and tool for redistribution.

DENSITY AND CENTRALITY: OR HOW URBANITY IS DISTRIBUTED

Density and centrality have been primordial features of *urbanity* to the point of becoming key factors in defining normative models for the *good* city –or, for that matter, the sustainable, just, productive or efficient city, or any adjective one may add. Because of their extensive use, both terms tend to be used quite uncritically and have become major targets for mainstream urban planning. In the Sustainable Development Goals proposed by UN Habitat, for instance, the recommended density is over 150 inhabitants per hectare. This level of concentration has undoubted benefits, in particular for economic development or for transport infrastructures. Nevertheless, recent studies are revealing a more nuanced approach to density while acknowledging a number of drawbacks when it comes to well-being, psychological health, air quality, ecological balance or even social interaction.[3] In this regard, an understanding of density as a multivariable concept, one that pays attention to its configuration and to its redistributive potential, may lead to a more complex yet refined principle of organization.

Like any other form of agglomeration, high density be associated with highly uneven performances and does not necessarily imply a more efficient use of land. What high density does well is externalizing the consumption of land, although that does not necessarily mean the requirement for exploited land will be lower. The impacts and effects that high urban concentrations create in their external hinterlands has long been studied by ecological economists. As early as 1996, in their influential paper on 'Urban Ecological Footprints', William Rees and Mathis Wackernagel explained why cities cannot be sustainable habitats and why, because of that, they are a key to sustainability. As *dissipative structures*, modern cities "import available energy and material (essergy) from their host environments which they use to maintain their internal integrity. Such systems also export the resultant entropy (waste and disorder) into their hosts."[4] In this metabolic understanding of urban life, for all of its basic needs and cultural production, the city relies on "energy and material resources extracted from nature, and all this energy/matter is eventually returned in degraded form to the ecosphere as waste."[5] More recently, in the emerging field of Political Urban Economy, the notion of "metabolic urbanization" has been used to read the city as a material flux modulated by economic and political institutions. In this frame of analysis, the design and construction of any urban settlement is inextricably linked with ecological processes and capital flows.

Urban concentrations are not only embedded in a geographical space, but also have deep implications in the geological structure of the earth. The metaphor of the city as an "inverted mine" powerfully represents the dual process of *digging and dumping* that underpins urban density patterns, thus picturing the city skyline as the technological mirror of far distant sites of extraction.[6] The urban lifestyle is deeply entangled with other forms of life, regardless of their relative proximity to *city centers*. In this regard, to keep pursuing high-density agglomerations without, at the same time, scrutinizing their material and energy demands, seems fairly unreasonable.

Similarly, the reference to urban centrality has come to be understood quite simplistically in historical, geometric or economic terms. The central condition typically indicates a historical role in the development of the city, a high concentration and mix of activities, or a prominent economic role within a larger urban area. Its form and image can vary, although it is generally identified with a historical center, with a commercial street, or with a financial downtown. Nonetheless, as mentioned earlier, contemporary cities have expanded way beyond city cores and have clustered in large geographical areas where a dispersed urbanity is shaped and expressed in a variety of forms. The spread of urbanization and the rise of information and communication technologies have changed the patterns and experience of centrality, which now constitutes a hierarchy of centers in a sort of networked centrality that pervades urban systems.

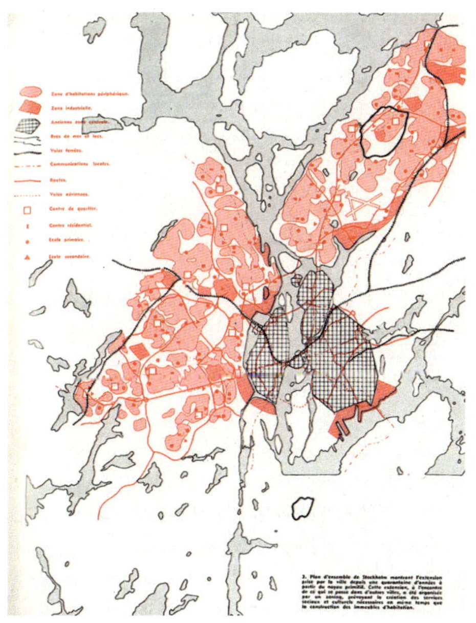

Figure 1: Stockholm's suburban development drawn as series of differentiated centers clustering along transportation lines. Source: *Architecture D'aujourd'Hui* 63, 1955.

Throughout the 20th century, a range of urban models addressing urban centrality were proposed by the disciplines of urban planning and urban geography. From Ebenezer Howard's Garden Cities to Fred Perry's Neighborhood Unit, from the discussion about the Heart of the City lead by Victor Gruen or Jane Jacobs in the United States to the Swedish ABC-towns proposed by Sven Markelius, most of these models were generally based on the replication of nodes of centrality, of urban nuclei periodically separated and linked by infrastructural transportation networks. In what could be called a model of *distributed centrality*, a dense and compact city core providing all of the main city functions was connected to a regional system of communication. One straight-forward example of a distributed centrality pattern is observable in the Stockholm metropolitan area. The urban *centrum*, a cluster of commercial, civic and cultural activities, was a major driver in the process of suburbanization promoted by Swedish functionalist planning. Despite the territorial scale of many of those projects, the urban unit remained largely the same. Moreover, the main focus of the distributed models tended to be the built fabric of the city, the *urban center*, rather than the spaces in between, external or peripheral to it.

Yet another approach to spatial distribution has been forming over the last decade. Providing an alternative to the *distributed centrality* models is the idea of a *distributive centrality*: a model of distribution that is not based on the repetition of a unit throughout a geographical space but emerges instead from an explosion of the *central* condition itself. Instead of identifying a clearly defined central nucleus comprising all the urban programs, a distributive centrality functions in a discontinuous and non-hierarchical manner. It distributes the "central" functions across a much broader territory. Furthermore, it can recognize a range of modes and conditions of what it means to be central, instead of designating a particular model of a normative centrality. Instead of a polycentric urban pattern, the central condition is thus assigned to a whole region or territory. It was Henri Lefebvre who, in his writings on space in the 1970s, opened up the possibility of thinking about centrality as a social logic that takes on a variety of forms: "To say 'urban space' is to say center and centrality, and it does not matter whether these are actual or merely possible, saturated, broken up or under fire, for we are speaking here of a dialectical centrality."[7] In this way, the central condition is defined as a fabric embedded in a flexible and adaptable pattern. Indeed, it emerges as an unstable centrality that is continuously reshaped.

Insist on a further concentration of highly densified urban centers could increase the existing polarization between center and periphery characteristic of metropolitan areas and would aggravate the strategy that has been pushing into the suburbs (or the region, or the county, or the territory… anywhere outside the "city") all those functions that generate tensions with urban life. This is, in fact, the principle that was commonly used in the industrial developments of the last century: productive and industrial activities, logistical spaces, energy infrastructures, waste management and recycling plants, inter-regional transport networks, large recreational hubs, commercial shopping centers, etc. were all periodically pushed further out, in order to preserve "good city life". Alternatively, an inclusive and distributive model for urban services and resources could offer a counter-proposal to the largely accepted models of *redensification* and *recentralization*, which tend to privilege exclusivity and limit the access to services. The work of Bernardo Secchi and Paola Viganò has been pioneering in an understanding of urbanity that operates horizontally and is inscribed in a metropolitan scale. By establishing new parameters and sets of relations that incorporate non-built spaces and infrastructural elements, this horizontal urbanity would supersede the culture of congestion exacerbated by industrial metropolises and their logic of accumulation. A distributive centrality would recognize central features in a discontinuous and scattered manner across a metropolitan area, thus defusing the traditional center/periphery dichotomy. Rather than replicating equivalent centers, this redistributive principle seeks out the intensity and simultaneity of interweaving uses and events, thus articulating the larger urban territory as a unified whole. Furthermore, a different way of measuring centrality could indeed incorporate non-human forms of life and pay attention to biotopes, water cycles, air quality, energy production or waste management as central urban elements.

BIOPOWER AND THE DISTRIBUTION OF LIFE

Proposing to conceive the space "external" to the city as fundamentally linked to urban life is hardly a novelty. The close bond between a city and its surrounding space has been conceived historically as one inseparable entity, something like two types of space forming a single whole. In ancient Greece, although this is often misunderstood, the space governed by the *polis* was actually not the city but the sum of the city and its countryside. The *polis* was formed by the unity of an urban territory and a rural territory -that is, the *asty* and the *khora*. This created an interdependent relationship between a dense and compact settlement and the cultivated lands around it. There is no need to travel that far, however, in search of examples of a symbiosis between ecological and urban systems. Despite the present urgency, concerns about the degradation of the environment and natural habitats and efforts to preserve various forms of life have a long history of precedents to draw on. In his study of the politics of space in Paris at the end of the *ancien régime*, Bruno Fortier developed the idea of the medicalization of the city with a concrete account of the policies and the shift in urban planning and design at the end of the 18th century. Characterized by a *substantialization of space*, where "water, air and, to some extent, light take on a new importance in the analysis of the urban reality",[8] the new city limits are essentially determined by their position in the flux of water and air. Anticipating Hausmann's systematic operations in the urban fabric, the planning of Paris at the end of the *ancien régime* was driven by principles of organization and distribution, not of relative location with regards to centrality or representation. Rather than a prominence of the symbolic presence in the city, questions of life, health and hygiene took a leading role, which required a comprehensive and systemic understanding of the city. Also in Paris, Sabine Barles has investigated how nitrogen became an asset in the first half of the 19th century when scientists and officials alike realized the need "to give back to the land what the city had taken".[9] Nitrogen from urban and industrial waste was converted into an agricultural fertilizer, which led not only to the improvement of hygienic and environmental conditions of the city, but to the reorganization of the entire region.

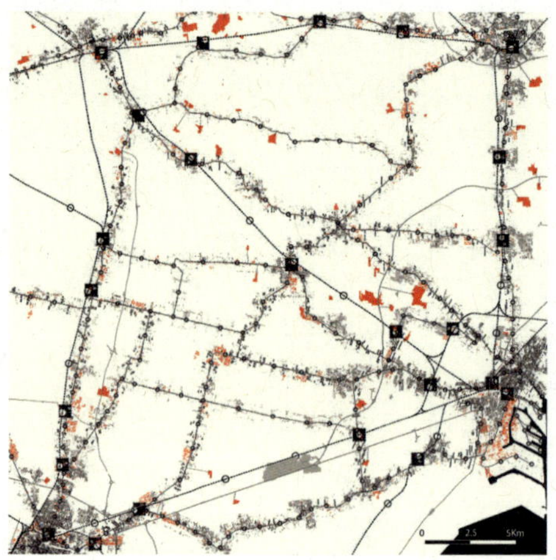

Figure 2: Paola Viganò has been studying territorial configurations beyond center-periphery dualisms. The diffuse urbanity described in her mappings resembles a case of a distributed centrality. Urban Switzerland in 2014: built (white). Source: Paola Viganò, *Horizontal Metropolis: A Radical Project*, Venice Architecture Biennale 2016, Atlases.

If we look at the case of Barcelona, we may find something of a distributive centrality at the core of Ildefons Cerdà's plan for the reform and expansion of the old city. In his own words, "[a city is] a great center of activities where the most positive realities of life can be found",[10] and the orthogonal grid proposed for the new *urbs* "is the only one able to uniformly distribute distances and capacities. This configuration is the clear and genuine expression... of mathematical equality, that is the equality of rights and interests, of justice itself".[11] So for Cerdà, as we claimed earlier, the proposal for a new type of space was developed within a framework of justice and the equal distribution of *urbanity* –in other words, the access to *centrality*. Following a meticulous and systematic method, Cerdà produced a vast set of charts and statistics to inform his design choices, including parameters of density and distribution of land uses. Metrics and statistics informed spatial arrangements, street widths and the occupation of urban blocks. In fact, Cerdà drew a direct correlation between density and mortality, from which arose his effort to *ruralize* the *urbs*, and the exact allocation of 40 sqm of city per inhabitant prescribed by his *Theory of the Construction of Cities* dating from 1859.

Figure 3: Urbanization of the Gran Via over the plain of Barcelona according to Cerdà's extension plan. Instead, ecological biopolitics could shift the logic of the colonization of nature toward a symbiotic relationship. Source: Barcelona Municipal Archive.

But the distribution of urban elements was not limited to demographics, land uses and physical elements. The street network was to provide "light to see, air to breathe, views to enjoy, and moreover all the necessary means to enable good communication and sociability", thus becoming an extension or an addendum to the house. But the street was also the space that made it possible "to import building materials, drinking water, and gas, to heat air or water, as well as to export rainwater and grey water, sewage and waste".[12] In this way, the urban structure could be viewed more like an irrigation system than a normative code regulating the built form. As Cerdà himself put it, "in addition to materiality, I needed to express the organism, the life, if I may call it such, which animates the material part."[13] In this logic, then, urban centrality is not contained in a central node, but in the urban fabric itself; it is embedded in its very layout and can integrate social, material and ecological elements.

One important clarification needs to be made, however. As Cerdà's foundational *General Theory of Urbanization* has gathered growing interest and international recognition in recent years, a misinterpretation of his vision is being increasingly disseminated. Besides being read as a biopolitical treatise intended to monitor and control the space of the population at large, his urban proposition is often described as endless and universal. Nevertheless, the reading of the city as an ever-expanding and all-encompassing square grid is a far cry from Cerdà's proposal. What he proposed was a territorial system of *ways* and *interways* that could extend across the planet, thus linking urban and rural spaces in the same process of urbanization. Furthermore, although he aimed to construct a science and a method that could be universally applicable, he never envisioned a single planetary city or a homogenization of global urbanity, but rather a planetary system of circulation connecting the multiple and individual urbs together. In his words:

> *Each urbs is a collective entity, with its own existence, independent and autonomous, only linked to the outside world by means of the main roads which take urban circulation to the universal road system, or bring into the urbs the circulation coming from other points of global social activity.*
>
> *Each individual urbs has the same elements as all others, yet not a single one among the many that make up the urban economy of the universe is like any other.*[14]

Cerdà clearly distinguishes between an *urbs* (which supersedes the limited term *city*) and rural land, although both types of space are integrated in a process of urbanization over the entire planet. It is precisely because of this important distinction that Cerdà's work is so premonitory and relevant today, when proponents of planetary urbanization like Neil Brenner claim that cities are entrenched in global circuits of extraction, distribution and consumption and must be understood in relation to their operational landscapes and global hinterlands. Parallel to Cerdà's effort to support *urban* life, expanding urban planning into territorial design may allow the inclusion of metabolic relations and larger circuits of life in a renewed ecological biopower.

The question of biopolitics requires a final note as well. At what point in history did *biopower* become the practice of monitoring and controlling the population, as opposed to serving as the space for litigation and reclamation, negotiation for a better life? This is obviously a rhetorical question, but it may help shift the angle of analysis in order to, again, bridge theory and practice, critique and proposition. Biopolitics and biopower are typically associated with a critique of the state and the administration. Yet, might we imagine a biopolitics that, beyond coercing and suppressing, also enables and promotes? As a political practice that pursues the possibility of a better life? From an ecological perspective, could the making and preservation of an environment –where life is not only possible but decent– be regarded as a counterforce against the excesses of capitalist production, extraction, pollution and the devastation of natural ecosystems?

It is important not to forget that power can be regarded as *oppressive* but also as *productive*. And that the great problems that contemporary societies are facing will not be solved by just leaving things as they are, but by mobilizing a different ethos and constructing a transformative political project. A project that, no doubt, must include all disciplines of design. As philosopher Reza Negarestani has bluntly put it, the responses to the anthropogenic environmental crisis, in order to succeed, must be equally anthropogenic. To do so, our inherited understandings of urban centrality may need to be rethought.

As it has been pointed out, urbanity is manifested in the dispersal of the city. Connecting back to Lefebvre, "as a form, the urban means simultaneity."[15] In turn, simultaneity implies assembly, encounter, which is what motivates the condition of urban centrality."In what does the dialectical movement of centrality consist? First of all, centrality, whether mental or social, is defined by the gathering-together and meeting of whatever coexists in a given space. What does coexist in this way? Everything that can be named and enumerated. Centrality is therefore a *form*, empty in itself but calling for contents –for, objects, natural or artificial beings, things, products and works, signs and symbols, people, acts, situations, practical relationships. This means that centrality closely resembles a *logical* form –and hence that there is a logic of centrality."[16]

Centrality, then, has a logic and contains both a formal and a social dimension. It is in this context that territory arises as a potential ground for a spatial practice engaging in processes of both redistribution and recognition of centralities. Here, territories must be conceived as unstable grounds defined by a mix of social, economic, environmental, technological, legal and administrative layers. As indeterminate spatial entities, territories are characterized by tensions and conflicts of interest that stretch across overlapping scales. Consequently, the production of architecture would consist in the very act of arranging and constructing its own sites of intervention, as opposed to the consolidation of an already defined place, program or scale. Territorial design necessitates a commitment to reality, both in its physical materiality and its administrative frameworks. Remarkably, this could open up new lines of intervention by developing forms of spatial practices that can operate at multiple scales and can inform new methods of mapping and design which integrate economic, social and environmental distributive analyses.[17]

At Aside, we believe that this approach to territorial design offers a window onto understanding how architecture contributes to processes of spatial and political coordination, thus revealing modes of organizing multiple agents around a particular concern. In this way, territorial design redefines architecture as a practice invested in the production of new scales of coexistence. In so doing, territorial design exceeds the administrative boundaries of urban design; it defines specific design interventions, rather than regional planning policies; it deals with ecological systems but surpasses landscape architecture by operating in the architectural, infrastructural, economic and ecological realms. In essence, it shifts the way in which architecture approaches urbanity and imagines the potential offered by processes of territorial restructuring and redistribution.

In this endeavor, an updated engagement with redistributive principles by spatial means may become a great support. Redistribution implies, by definition, a two-step action: first collect and later distribute. Whether the collected substance is people, money, data, matter, energy or any other quantifiable element does not change the nature of the concept, which indeed consists of assembling first, and then delivering back in a reshuffled form. Accordingly, the application of a redistributive logic to any form of spatial design should run parallel to the recognition of *territories*, *processes* and *agents*. These three terms are always relational and aim to expand the more traditional *site*, *program* and *user*, in order to contextualize them in a broader context and, thus, understand their entanglements and interrelations. *Territories* expand the physicality of the site; any intervention in the city is enmeshed in a spatial system that must be read through its material expression as much as through its normative frameworks and institutional structures. *Territories* are always constructed; they bring together the material and the legal spheres, the physicality of a given terrain with questions of power, sovereignty and jurisdiction. *Processes* expand the notion of program beyond functionality and use. The recognition of social processes aims to understand a program as it unfolds over time, what the prior necessities are as well as the subsequent effects. *Agents* can be very diverse; they expand the direct user to other forms of participation. They may include not only individuals and human activity, but also non-human actors enmeshed in a particular site: from material flows to biotopes, from administrative bodies to communities and social groups.

Interestingly enough, by bringing ecological systems alongside traditional "urban" elements, the practice of architecture and urbanism is expanded, not only in its multi-scalar dimension, but most importantly, in the inclusion of natural cycles, cultivated lands and functions typically associated with rurality, into a reshaped notion of urbanity. In a sort of thick fabric, the urban territory results from the synthesis of urban design, urban planning, rural planning, regional planning, landscape design and landscape ecology. Despite holding a design specificity, a distributive principle acknowledges the necessity to think and act *transversally*, *transdisciplinary* and *transcalarly*. Indeed, this opens up a path that can absorb contemporary critiques of modernity and the nature/culture divide into a more flexible but grounded spatial practice, and yet it avoids the naiveté of the pastoral narratives that claim a return to a pristine *nature* –one that is long gone.

NOTES

1 Fraser, Honneth 2003.
2 This thesis was developed in a conference paper presented at KTH School of Architecture in Stockholm: Carbonell, Adrià and Salgueiro, Roi (March 12, 2016). "The End of Planning and the Political Aporia of the Architectural City". *The Architecture of Deregulations: Politics and Postmodernism in Swedish Building 1975-1995*.
3 See for instance: Berghauser Pont, M Y et al, 2020.
4 Rees, Wackernagel 1996, 237.
5 *Ibid.* 225.
6 The idea of the 'inverted mine' was proposed by Gray Brechin in reference to the affluent skyline of San Francisco.
7 Lefebvre 1991, 101.
8 Fortier 1975, 40 (My translation).
9 Barles, Lestel 2007.
10 Cerdà 1863a, 58 (My translation).
11 Cerdà, 1864, 44 (My translation).
12 Cerdà, 1863b, 151 (My translation).
13 Cerdà 2018, 29.
14 *Ibid.* 631.
15 Lefebvre 1976, 68–69 (My translation).
16 Lefebvre, *The Production…*, *op. cit.*, 331-332.
17 We are currently developing this theme in a forthcoming publication: ASIDE (Salgueiro, Roi and Carbonell, Adrià), *Territorial Design* (Actar: Forthcoming).

The plug-ins that give this book its title operate in a different, complementary or even critical layer than the many other practices and fields of knowledge that have a bearing on the urban phenomenon (architecture, urban planning, economy, policy making, etc.). Design's interaction with these disciplines is not limited to a certain scale or a specific format (in terms of spatiality) or to a specific collective (in terms of the actors involved), and it does not come after other disciplinary agencies (in terms of temporality). Plug-ins perform a specific role with regard to design in the city, simultaneously assuming their autonomy and their constant interaction with many other fields, participating in a constant investigation of, reflection on, and practice of what a city is and how it operates.

THE MATERIALITY OF HYBRID SPACE

In the previous sections we have seen a series of plug-ins that are quite different in terms of purpose and dimensions, but they all share a consistent material component: they are systems whose ability to produce relationships is strongly conditioned by interactions that take place in the physical world, in proximity. For this reason, their material dimension, and the proximity interactions it generates, are a relevant aspect of their hybrid relational-material nature and, therefore, of the complex tangle of engendering process into which they are inserted.

In Chapter 2 we focused on an ecology of durations generated by the spatio-temporal interaction of bodies and things, unfolding both in concrete physical spaces and in the digital sphere, but always affecting the material makeup of the city. In Chapter 3, the city was posited as an intertwining web of relationships, and we saw that it is inseparable from the set of people, infrastructures, and relational objects that make it possible and sustain it over time. Finally, in Chapter 4, addressing the meanings the city conveys, we saw how they are connected to the materiality of the signifiers —that is, of the material entities that make it up. All this led us to discuss how and to what extent the materiality of bodies and things comes into play in the construction of the city.

These observations emerged with particular clarity in the design research that took place in Barcelona: a dense and dynamic city, where space, time, relationships and meanings are tangibly linked to the concrete reality of its citizens, its streets and squares. However, we believe that the lessons we have drawn have a general value. We also claim that this interaction between spaces, times, relationships and meanings is the link between the recognition of the complexity of the city and that of its materiality. Of course, this insistence on the material dimension of the city does not imply a return to the time when the city seemed to be made up only of buildings and streets. In short, to refer again to Richard Sennett's conceptualization,[105] it is not a question of returning to the *ville* and forgetting the *cité*. Instead, we need to recognize that the *cité*, the lived, relational city, cannot be separated from the *ville*, understood as the set of bodies, people and things, which intersect, collide, create frictions and generate relationships in a complex spatio-temporal arena.

Recognizing and accepting the irreducible complexity of the city means recognizing this coexistence of material and relational realities, acknowledging that the city is *also* an assembly of bodies and things —that is, of actors and actants— that interact in physical and digital space and produce what Donna Haraway[106] refers to as situated knowledge, based on the assumption that the perception of any situation always involves embodied, spatio-temporally located subjects.

With respect to this last point, we have also learned another important lesson. Reflecting on the growing role of digital space (a space in itself without distances and without matter), we have learned that it modifies the material dimension of the city, but does not eliminate it. The digitization of the city does not imply its dematerialization, but rather opens up novel ways of relating the material and relational aspects of cities, along with new ways of addressing civic agency.

Urban space today is already, and will increasingly be, a physical-digital hybrid space. But hybrid space has, and will likely always have, an irreducible material component. The question we need to address is what the quality of this hybrid space will be.

105 Sennett, *Building and...*, *op. cit.*
106 Haraway, *op. cit.*

We have seen that the times, spaces, relations and meanings of which the city is made would not exist if they were not incorporated into matter, if they were not materialized in bodies: the bodies of people, but also of things (in other words, houses, public spaces, products, services, or events). But we should add that the reverse proposition is also true: these bodies, of people and things, of actors and actants, exist and transact in specific space-times, creating landscapes with topologies that indicate different possibilities of life and, specifically, different types of cities.

In order to understand a city, and therefore its functioning and its meanings, we need to have a vision of how people and things are arranged in space and distributed in time, precisely because cities also have a material dimension. If this materiality were negligible, their location in physical space would be irrelevant because digital connectivity eliminates distances. As we have said, however, this is not the case, and therefore their distribution in space-time —that is, the topology of the landscape they generate— is important when it comes to defining how the short networks of proximity and the long networks of global connectivity are generated and, ultimately, how the city works and what meanings it produces.

In fact, people and things interact and build proximity systems: spatio-temporal systems of material entities which, given their proximity, can also interact physically. The proximity system thus introduces a topology of the material landscape that lets us to see and discuss, at the same time, people and things, and their relationships in the physical world. This makes it possible for us to qualify the urban systems we inhabit.[107] What we have seen is that the nature of these proximity systems is important in defining people's quality of life. Their density and variety determine what a person can or cannot find nearby, and what their chances are of meeting other people with whom to establish fruitful community relationships.

Moreover, proximity systems are also important in determining the environmental weight of the production activities taking place. This is

107 Manzini, *Livable...*, *op. cit.*

the case because their topology affects the intensity of transport, but also because the spatio-temporal characteristics can concretely limit or favor the practicability of a circular economy.

Ultimately, what we have learned in recent years is that it is precisely these proximity systems, the spatio-temporal topology of the material landscape, that decides whether and to what extent the city that is generated will be livable and sustainable.

TOWARDS A CITY OF CARE

Until recently, the belief that connectivity and digitization would lead to the dematerialization of the world dominated popular consciousness and led us into a sort of blindness. The inescapable reality of the ongoing social and environmental crises, however, currently exacerbated by the COVID-19 pandemic, have forced us to change our perception of the city. These crises have clearly shown that we have been blind to something that was actually quite evident: what might have seemed like an economy of services and deterritorialized and dematerialized experiences has actually required large amounts of energy, piled up mountains of waste, and led to the physical and social marginalization of an increasing number of people.

This inability to recognize the material dimension of bodies, things, cities and the world as a whole is also the cause and effect of the lack of care that sadly characterizes contemporary cities and society. The care we are talking about here must be understood in the broadest sense of relationships, attention, reciprocity between people, and between them and their surroundings, on all scales: from the hyper-local to the planetary. Understood in this way, care relates to everything we have talked about until now: the materiality of bodies and things and their situated existence in space-time.

As Maria Puig de la Bellacasa points out, there can be no care without physical contact and reciprocity[108] —that is, without proximity between bodies. This reciprocity and this necessary proximity are the direct expression of the interdependence that connects all the subjects who have a role in a care relationship. But they are also the key to under-

108 Puig de la Bellacasa, *op. cit.*

standing how and why conceiving the city as an abstract entity, as a dematerialized system, as a city of distances, translates into the practice of the city without care.

Working on these issues, and writing this book, we have learned not only that we cannot ignore the material dimension of the city, but that it needs to be our starting point: we need to recognize materiality as the substratum of every relationship, as a signifier of every meaning, as a necessary basis for establishing an ecological relationship with the world. Starting from there allows us to define the most appropriate plug-ins: the ones that, in various ways, make it possible for rich, dense and diversified proximity systems to emerge —plug-ins that are capable of stimulating and supporting care relationships between human beings and with the entire web of life to which they belong.

DESIGN AS PLUG-IN

Throughout this book, we have described *plug-ins* as part of a renewed approach to how design can be a key agent in city making. Plug-ins are situated design outcomes that aim to enrich the complex system of the city, accepting this complexity as positive and unravelling unexpected aspects as key agents for a desired city. By doing so, plug-ins extend the potentialities of the city, allowing individuals, collectives and built environments to reflect on their nature and perform in radical and active ways, pursuing their deserved position in the world.

As we laid out previously, based on the effects they produce in an urban system, the impact of plug-ins can be that of a *generator* (introducing new elements into a pre-existing context, transforming initial conditions and opening up new expectations and possibilities); a *mediator* (social condensers distilling existing practices into new landscapes and producing new relationships that activate the urban system); and an *identifier* (recognizing, visualizing and labelling spaces and practices, contributing to maintaining or enhancing a level of conscious awareness in the urban fabric). Plug-ins become a subset of agents to promote change in some deeply embedded inertias within the complex system of the city.

The texts and projects presented in this book assume that the key dimensions of these plug-ins are temporality, relationality and materiality.

Temporality is understood as the awareness of the diverse times that coexist in a city —from history to temporariness, from narrative to experience, from diachrony to synchrony, from memory to desire. By working on temporality, design plug-ins allow a multiplicity of individuals and collectives to find their own path and performance within the city. Furthermore, a critical, active use of temporality in design questions the abstract myth of innovation and the capitalist dependence on an ever-imminent promised future, while promoting a sense of co-responsibility for our urban environment through situated spatio-temporal practices. We claim that a focus on temporality results in a focus on civic life, situated experience and new forms of politics and of beauty.

Relationality establishes the social dimension of any design outcome, assuming the need to constantly question, reflect on and reframe the interactions between individuals and collectives. Attending to relational aspects, design plug-ins become key agents affecting the role human beings play in urban life —a role that is performed in both the physical and digital layers, and one that acknolwedges the potential of digital technologies and social media to develop infrastructures and services, at the same time that it is rooted in the caring dimension that underlies any human interaction.

Materiality, as the physical instance of this fundamental triad, recovers a deserved focus on human beings as embodied entities who interact critically with the built environment. Plug-ins address the concrete dimensions of the material interaction between bodies and their environment. This concretion not only questions and repositions any abstract policy or project implemented in the urban system, but also promotes an active re-semantization of the city led by individuals and collectives and a conscious care for the impact of any process related to matter and energy.

If they are to have an impact on the complex urban systems of contemporary society, design outcomes should be developed though these three key lenses, and, hopefully, the *design-as-plug-in* concept put forward by this book offers a clear yet open-ended way to do so, boldly positing design as a city making practice. ■

GREEN SPACES IN BARCELONA: FROM THE WALLED CITY TO THE SUPERBLOCK

Salvador Rueda

GREEN SPACES IN THE CERDÀ PLAN

Green spaces in the walled city were few and far between. When they did exist, they were owned either by the church or the wealthy classes. The dichotomy between compression and decompression was largely skewed toward the side of pressure.

Figure 1. Green spaces in Ciutat Vella in the mid-19th century. Source: Quarterons Garriga i Roca.

In the 19th century, it didn't make sense for the city to remain surrounded by a wall, even from the point of view of defense. The impact on health and the dysfunctions resulting from hyperdensification and very narrow streets (4.5 m) did not fit in with the needs of the new industrial age. Cities needed to tear down their walls and expand. After a process that we need not discuss here, the task of planning the new extension was assigned to Ildefons Cerdà.

The foundations of the Cerdà Plan were mainly rooted in theories on hygiene. In his quest to solve the serious public health problems of the time, he trusted in the scientific work of the hygienist movement, especially the ideas of the Frenchman Michel Levy.[1] His urban planning solution was based essentially on the parameters included in the following table:

	Proposal	References/author	Status Barcelona 1859
City surface area per inhabitant	40 m^2	Michel Levy	13.5 m^2
Street width	20 m^2	Michel Levy and Cerdà	4.19 m^2
Trees/open space	50% intervias	Cerdà	
Separation between trees	8 m	Cerdà	

Table 1. Hygienicist Parameters Used in the Cerdà Plan

Michel Levy proposed that there should be 40 m^2 of surface area in the city for every inhabitant. In Barcelona at that time, the average was only 13.5 m^2 per inhabitant. Another premise put forward by the hygenicist movement was that the width of the streets should be greater than the height of the buildings. Cerdà calculated that the average height of the buildings in Barcelona was a little over 19 m. The average width of the streets was 4.19 m. The proportions he chose for the Eixample were 20 m for the width of the streets and 16 m for the building heights.

Any morphological solution he chose would need to provide 40 m^2 of surface area per person and streets with a width of 20 m. To achieve this he devised various formal scenarios. The one he finally chose was in the form of a square made up of two buildings with chamfered corners (in red below) and a rectangle of open space in between, which creates the figure of an octagon, which he called an *intervia*. The dimensions of the square are justified by the following formula:

Open (with chamfers)

$$x = \frac{pv-2.db}{d} \pm \sqrt{\frac{pv(pvf-4.df-4b^2d)}{d2f}} = 113.3 \text{ m}$$

Where:

x = Length of the block

2b = Width of the street = 20 m

f = Depth of the plot for construction = 20 m

d = Façade of the plot for construction = 20 m

v = Number of inhabitants per unit = 4.3 and 43 per building

p = Amount of surface area corresponding to each individual = 40 m^2

The equation includes the surface area per individual and the width of the street, and it incorporates an assumption: it stipulates a plot of 20 × 20 m for 43 inhabitants. The total population per *intervia* is 444 (250 inhabitants/ha) in a built area of 4,131 m² with a surface area of 8,301 m² allocated for green space. The surface area of the *intervia* plus the surface area of the street is 17,763 m², which, when divided by 444 inhabitants, results in 40 m² per inhabitant. But there was a problem, the open spaces required by the *intervia* contain organic matter and moisture. At the time, it was believed that the effluvia that led to epidemics came from the combined action of the decomposition of organic matter and moisture. This belief —this misconception— is the foundation for much of Cerdà's proposal, which seeks out a way to neutralize the combination of organic matter and moisture (O/H) or, if that was impossible, to dissipate the effluvia it generated. The text from his *Teoría de la Construcción de las Ciudades* [Theory of the Construction of Cities] is very revealing in its justification of the planting of trees to combat the pernicious effects of organic matter and moisture from the soil:

> *Street trees. To a certain depth, the surface of the earth can be considered almost entirely composed of the remains of animals and plants that have inhabited it since time immemorial. To use Lord Byron's sublime expression, we could say that 'the dust we tread upon was once alive'.*
>
> *Those organic remains, some decomposed and others in the process of decomposition, combined with the moisture in the soil, are a continual and universal focus of decay and ill health, the effects of which must be neutralized —especially in large population centers where the residential areas are built atop land that was once agricultural. In those cases, planting trees is the most effective means of preventing the infection of the soil, sanitizing the ground and even purifying the air. Their roots, branching off endlessly, absorb the water —and the organic matter and the salts dissolved in it— from the earth with which they come into contact. And this absorption, upsetting the balance of moisture in the top layers of the soil, continuously pulls surface water deeper into the ground, which is extremely favorable for the purpose of maintaining healthy soil. At the same time, their leaves, when they are warmed by the sun, restore to the atmosphere part of the oxygen that is lost through respiration and combustion, thus contributing to the purification of the air. Thus, through what they take in, trees contribute to disinfecting the soil, and through what*

they release, they purify the city air. That is why it is not only advisable to plant street trees, but essential, in each city block, for trees to cover an area that is at least as large as the built area —especially in a country like ours with high levels of humidity. That said, the trees should be planted intelligently, taking care to choose the most suitable species for each orientation and ensuring their distribution is such that the roots will have the necessary space on the surface and underground to spread out without harming the foundations of the buildings or the sewage channels.

If the trees are very thick, they will keep the soil moist, but if they are spaced out so that the sun can filter down between them, some of the soil moisture will evaporate with the effects of the sun and the rest will be absorbed by the trees, which, as we have said, will act like sponges and absorb the harmful surface moisture.[2]

The proposal from 1859 ultimately allocated 8,301 m^2 of trees per intervia intended to neutralize the harmful effects of decomposing organic matter and moisture, while ensuring that the oxygen from the green areas and street trees (planted at intervals of 8 m) would 'purify' the air of the urban space. Additionally, the sun would handle any other remaining effluvia yet to be neutralized. In the same text, he writes: "On the other hand, by heating the earth's atmosphere, the action of the sun also brings about continuous movement of the air, which purifies it by carrying the harmful substances derived from animal respiration to the vegetation."[3]

The origin of the proposal for green space in the Cerdà Plan comes from providing the surface area needed to reach 40 m^2 per inhabitant and not so much from introducing urban green space as we would understand it today. It should also be noted that trees are cited as the only neutralizer of the organic matter/moisture combination. He never talks about other plant species. On the other hand, it is likely that the park Cerdà situated between the Besòs River and the new city was intended to neutralize the moisture from the river and the wetlands, while the northeast winds would provide oxygen-laden purifying air.[4]

The 113.3 m × 113.3 m *intervia* contains the parameters that formed the foundation of the urban model. To ensure that foundation would be maintained, Cerdà repeated the *intervia* endlessly, which is reflected in the plans from 1859 and 1863.

Cerdà considered it absolutely necessary to increase the amount of green space for hygienic reasons and to improve air quality, thus providing the ideal balance between relation and isolation, better known by his phrase "ruralizing the urban", which led him to recommend planting a tree every 8 m on streets while allocating half of the area of the *intervia* to green space.

The green area outlined in the 1863 proposal was 597 ha, reaching 1,311 ha if the calculations include the Parc del Besòs and Montjuïc. The presence of biodiversity in an urban space loses some of its meaning if it is not calculated in relation to other habitats. The system of green spaces should be organized based on street trees, the spaces of the *intervias*, green roofs, the greenery in parks, street-level greenery and/or agricultural vegetation, wetlands and riparian forests. With his proposal for green spaces, Cerdà managed to connect the river ecosystem of the Besòs and the agricultural area that surrounded it with the rich biodiversity of the mountain of Montjuïc and the agricultural delta of the Llobregat River, through the Parc del Besòs and the green network of the *intervias* and the street trees, resulting in a spectacular green continuum.

Cerdà took the *intervia* (space between roads) as the main mold for structuring the new city, replacing housing in that role. His octagonal city block allowed him to resolve of many of the conflicts he set out to address. The square shape of the blocks was derived from hygienic reasons, but it was also based on a legal, topological, architectural and transportation-related framework. Likewise, one of the biggest ideological motors were his egalitarian principles.

In his revised version of the plan from 1863, Cerdà proposed a parallel railway network every two streets. These alignments parallel to the sea crossing three-quarters of the Eixample pass through the center of a series of square superblocks made up of four L-shaped elements (he drew the first superblock in response to the need to incorporate the railway into the planning). These groupings continue alongside the train tracks in instances of large-scale Y-interchanges and run diagonally along the Avinguda Meridiana.[5]

The maritime-terrestrial articulation through the railway entailed a change of scale, interconnecting networks on a more global level. At the same time, the incorporation of the railway brought about a change in the relationship between transport and town planning, which was reflected in the phrase: *Each mode of locomotion generates a form of urbanization.*[6]

As we have said, Cerdà posited the city block as an elementary module for urban design, instead of the building, which became the elementary unit of architectural design. For the inventor of the concept of urbanism, the foundations for designing the city were the road network in its entirety, on the one hand, and city blocks on the other. The *intervias* provided an integrated response to the needs of habitability and transportation and served as the base module for the growth of the city.

THE GREEN SPACES IN LEON JAUSSELY'S PLAN AND IN THE PROPOSAL BY RUBIÓ I TUDURÍ

The incorporation of surrounding municipalities into Barcelona, including the large amounts of open land between them, made it necessary to study how the ensemble would be connected and linked together.

In 1903, the Barcelona City Council organized the International Competition for projects to connect Barcelona's Eixample with the annexed towns and with the rest of the municipal area of Sarrià and Horta (those two municipalities had not yet been annexed).

Of the five projects that were presented, Leon Jaussely's proposal "Romulus" was chosen at the end of 1907. It outlined the land-use planning (various residential areas, workers' housing, industry, facilities, parks, etc.) and the basic road network, organized around two ring roads and five radial axes. It also included a systematized proposal for connecting the different railway lines and burying the lines running through the interior of the city. The system of parks offered a distribution of green spaces similar to that of Paris or London, while offering the city a certain monumentality. In the preliminary design, the facilities were situated at focal points or central points in the road system.

The Jaussely Plan based its proposals on three criteria: the zoning of activities, the systematization of green spaces, and the design of streets and promenades —criteria that were applied to a territory that was poorly planned as a whole and, therefore, in need of a theoretical contribution that would make its urban continuity viable. On the other hand, the rejection of the Cerdà Plan was explicit, and Puig i Cadafalch kept insisting on that fact. The new plan manipulated Cerdà's orthogonal and isotropic layout and introduced oblique or diagonal elements.[7]

In Catalonia, the first "garden city" initiatives were developed between 1900 and 1920 under the influence of Cebrià de Montoliu and the magazine *Civitas*. Projects that date from this garden city period include Tibidabo and Park Güell, among others.

Montoliu —heavily influenced by Ebenezer Howard, Unwin and Parker— was the founder of the Sociedad Cívica, La ciudad jardín [Garden City Civic Society]. In 1912, he published the book *Modern Cities and Their Problems*, following on the reformist current of other countries. The book issued a criticism of the out-of-control industrial city and looked for formulas to support accord and decentralization to improve living conditions and environmental impact.

The systematization of green spaces would be accepted as necessary both to reduce conflicts in the city and for the sake of its beautification. The systematization would be pursued within a classical order, more neutral than the individuality suggested by modernism; it would incorporate characteristics specific to the Mediterranean condition, in which the Catalan current of *Noucentisme* was inscribed.

The connection plan had already defined the open spaces in Barcelona as a priority issue in the city —public places for activities such as walking, leisure and representation, but it was Rubió i Tudurí and the French landscape painter Forestier who systematically pursued the implementation of the Mediterranean garden.

The model seeped into the urban fabric of Barcelona in La Bonanova Ganduxer, Horta Campoamor, La Salut in Gràcia, El Putxet, Les Tres Torres, and Vallcarca.

GREEN AREAS IN THE CONTEXT OF FUNCTIONALISM: THE MACIÀ PLAN

After the Great War, zoning gave way to functionalism and, with it, the architects who belonged to rationalist schools began to intervene with force in the urban planning debate; the aim was to improve on the models of the functional city that had been defined by German urban planners. Le Corbusier said in 1930: *the garden city leads to an enslaved individualism* [...], *to a sterile isolation of the individual* [...].

The functional classification of the city into four basic functions —living, working, recreation and circulation— required a strict zoning of urban space. The Athens Charter generalized and rationalized principles and prescriptions derived from German town planning dating from 1870 to 1914.

The different elements of the urban system (open areas, road networks, housing) were hierarchized and distributed according to functionalist analysis and practices: the functions were separated, while the subsystems within each main system were analyzed (thus, daily, weekly and annual leisure activities were each associated with a different, appropriate space).

Functionalism entered Barcelona and its metropolitan area with the Macià Plan, also called the Plan for the New Barcelona, designed by Le Corbusier and the GATCPAC.

The Macià Plan respected the existing grid of the Cerdà Plan and reinterpreted it, pursuing a larger hierarchy in the road network —the three-street by three-street supergrid— which offered a more hygienic and less dense form of construction. Through the magazine *Arquitectura Contemporània*, which the group founded at the beginning of its existence, the GATCPAC criticized the abusive densification to which Cerdà's project had been subjected. The green space and recreational space inside the supergrid (superblock) accounted for 78% of the area.

Le Corbusier's proposal from 1932 embodied the function of circulation by proposing a grid of 400 m × 400 m for cars to circulate through.

Le Corbusier's efforts to urbanize the automobile were as revolutionary as Cerdà's plan to solve the urbanization of trains. This parallelism, while respecting the identity of the respective proposals, offers a very fertile point of view.[8]

The perimeter network of the *redents* makes it possible to connect one part of the city with another (the *function of circulation*) freeing up its interior for an urban planning proposal that, following the principles of the CIAM, seeks to develop the key functions: *living, working* and *recreation*.

GREEN SPACES IN TODAY'S BARCELONA

Outside the urban fabric, Barcelona has substantial natural heritage thanks to the size of the Collserola mountain range and, no doubt, its steep slopes. Collserola forms the border of the city (more than 8,000 ha in total), offering a mosaic of habitats that are home to a wealth of different species. The EU Habitats Directive from 1992 designates three of these habitats (holm oak groves, pine groves and dry meadows) as habitats for conservation. The rivers and the sea round out what might be called Barcelona's "natural environment", which is in truth very artificialized. In the city center, the public and private parks and gardens play a notable role (1,076 ha), forming the basis of the urban ecological infrastructure, with some particularly significant areas: Montjuïc (the cliff is listed on the Catalan government's Inventory of Geological Spaces), the Tres Turons, and the Parc de la Ciutadella (the largest flat park in the city, with just 15 ha for public use). There are some 153,000 street trees, including 150 different species and cultivars. Private green spaces represent 740 ha, but their contribution to the quality of life in the city is largely not stipulated. There are still 54 areas of natural interest within the city limits that have been inventoried but are not protected.

The analysis of green spaces since the beginning of the democratic period (urban green spaces between the end of the Spanish Civil War and the beginning of the democratic period do not warrant much comment) leads us to conclude that urban woodlands and green areas have grown in size and that farmland has come to have only a symbolic presence. During this period, the public sector intervened as a balancing agent, assessing the location of the interventions and addressing the added value generated by the new urban dynamics.

According to Busquets[9], the systematization of the urban planning process in Barcelona in the 1980s can be divided into three major categories according to the scale of the work. Here, we will deal only with the category of urban rehabilitation, which includes the actions carried out on green spaces and urban spaces, using public funds.

The green structure in question offers service to the entire urban fabric. The targeted areas include, on the one hand, interstitial spaces that are either empty, occupied with obsolete activities, or abandoned (industrial buildings in disuse, slaughterhouses, railroad dependencies, former barracks and military installations, etc.), across all districts of the city.

Of the available spaces, those that offer a greater centrality in each urban fabric are chosen following the criteria of opportunity and representation.

- *Squares and gardens*: more than 150 small-scale operations were carried out in the 1980s, which provided a strong start to the quality rehabilitation of Barcelona's urban space. As Busquets says, although their size may be small, their central position in each of the neighborhoods results in a very noticeable effect of urban diffusion.
  On the other hand, the inner courtyards of the Eixample blocks (nearly 500 of them) deserve their own chapter, not for the number of actions carried out, but for the number of potential gardens and their functions, taking advantage of the reconstruction or transformation of existing buildings. At the same time, residential uses in the district are encouraged as a component for rebalancing and neutralizing the pressures of functional specialization to which the centers of Western cities are subjected.
- *Gardens combined with facilities*: these are structures held over from the past, mostly in the upper part of the city, which are transformed into public spaces. The intervention involves adapting a private garden to the new functional and urban demands.
- *Urban axes*: certain linear axes with notable urban symbolism are given a new use; pedestrians are given a higher priority to the detriment of private vehicles. In these linear projects, the discussion is focused on the design of the transversal profile and on the implementation of different types of mobility and parking.
- *Urban parks*: covering anywhere from six to ten hectares, they arise as a consequence of generating benefit from old activities that have fallen into disuse.
- *Large-scale parks*: the larger size of the interventions allows for connecting part of the urban fabric with the surrounding physical or administrative boundaries.

The seafront, the western slope of Montjuïc mountain, the Parc del Diagonal, the Parc de la Vall d'Hebron, and the Parc del Besòs in Sant Adrià del Besòs run in a semicircle along the borders of the municipality. With the exception of the park in Sant Adrià del Besòs, the others were developed in the context of Olympic operations.

The mobilization of this large amount of land was made possible through direct purchase and also by virtue of the Special Plans for Internal Reform (PERI) that have operated through singular management, through the compensation of rights from prior planning, or through expropriation. The result of the initiatives listed above, combined with the pre-existing green spaces, gives rise to the current green spaces as seen in Figure 2.

Figure 2. Barcelona's Existing Network of Green Spaces.
Source: Barcelona City Council

The largest surfaces of greenery in Barcelona coincide with areas characterized by steep slopes. On the flatter surfaces, which is where people live, the figures decline significantly. The ratios do not meet the minimum.

The urban green space in the Cerdà Plan, which totaled 597 ha (reaching 1,311 ha if we include the green of Montjuïc and the Parc del Besòs), has been reduced 171.2 ha, with a ratio of 1.85 m^2/inhabitant in Cerdà's Eixample, increasing to 2.7 m^2/inhabitant if we add the area of Sant Martí included in the original plan.

The Cerdà Plan was subverted, eliminating the green spaces that had been planned; the Macià Plan was never carried out and cars invaded the city. In my opinion, the major mistake was the decision to use all the city's streets for mobility (85% of public road space today is occupied by vehicles for the purpose of mobility), especially after having occupied all the planned green spaces (in keeping with the regulations at the time), which resulted in generating an imbalance in the ratio of spaces for relation versus isolation. Today, the pressure on the central Eixample is intolerable. The error came from not having understood Cerdà's maxim: *Each mode of locomotion generates a form of urbanization.*[10] As a mode of locomotion, the car has very different characteristics from animal traction or the railway. When cars were introduced to Barcelona, the same layout was maintained for the Eixample that Cerdà had proposed in his plan from 1859, as though transportation were still powered by animals. The result is a city that is not prepared to tackle the great challenges of the 21st century: sustainability in the information age.

The rehabilitation strategy that began in the early democratic period was constrained, in my opinion, as soon as it failed to call into question the mobility model based on private vehicles, and 85% of the road was allocated to mobility —especially the mobility of motor vehicles. The *intervia* was maintained as a single city block and the urbanization was not adapted to cars and their characteristics. The dysfunctions of that decision are clearly visible today. It should be noted, however, that before the democratic period, renowned architects such as Antoni Bonet[11] and Oriol Bohigas, in preparation for the 100th anniversary of the Cerdà Plan in 1958, agreed that the logical evolution of the Plan was to implement 3 × 3 superblocks.[12] *The current problem involves finding a new scale. "Moving from the Cerdà block to a superblock nine times bigger... The module should be expanded so that it maintains the same relationship with respect to the new speeds as the Cerdá block provided for the speeds of his time. The grouping of 9 blocks (400 × 400 m) is entirely viable."*[13] The idea of implementing superblocks for the Eixample was in their minds. Unfortunately, the superblocks were not implemented, despite the technical and political responsibilities that Bohigas held in Barcelona City Council at the beginning of the democratic period.

GREEN SPACE IN THE SUPERBLOCK MODEL

Both the Cerdà Plan and the Macià Plan were designed as new developments. What we need today, in keeping with the steps begun by the post-Transition administrations, is not so much to produce a new city as to transform the existing one. As we have heard on more than one occasion, the battle for sustainability will be won or lost in the reorganization of existing cities. These days, the question is more about recycling and less about new developments.

We need a new ecosystemic model with its corresponding system of proportions that includes, at the same time, a reduction of contaminating emissions, noise, energy consumption, etc. and an increase in green spaces, leisure spaces, a diversity of legal entities, and entities with a high density of knowledge. An urban planning model that extends throughout the city and takes into account the current modes of locomotion.

Figure 3: Basic network of superblocks approved by the Barcelona City Council. Source: Barcelona City Council and BCNecology.

As in the case of the Cerdà Plan, the basic element of the city is not the dwelling, it is the *intervia*: the cell that serves as the basic piece in the mosaic of a road network, in which the continuity of movement makes it necessary to manage the road system in its entirety instead of on the basis of individual streets one by one. (The same goes for the structure of the network of green spaces.) This new cell defines a standard *intervia* of about 400 m × 400 m, which is meant as the basis for applying an urbanism centered on people, on living organisms and on the laws of nature,[14] while also developing the new model for mobility and public space.[15]

The dimensions of the new base module, naturally, are the same as the ones Le Corbusier proposed in the Macià Plan —the first plan to incorporate the urbanization of cars. The reason behind the dimensions of the 3 × 3 superblock has to do with the characteristics of car travel: at a speed of just over 20 km/h (the average speed of car travel in urban areas) the time it takes to travel around a superblock is equivalent to how long it takes a person walking at about 4 km/h (or in a vehicle pulled by an animal) to travel around one city block. With an arrangement based on main intersections every 400 m, the synchronization of traffic lights is much more efficient (with these distances, it is even possible to consider traffic light prioritization for public transport), and you avoid interrupting the main flow for turns (avoiding two out of every three turns), etc.

Connecting these cells gives rise to an orthogonal network of roads extending throughout the city; it is this network that defines the superblock model, not the blocks themselves. The perimeter of the superblocks includes the transportation networks: cars, public transport, foot traffic and the main bicycle network. The network for cars is defined by the perimeter of the superblocks. The rest of the city becomes a shared space with priority for pedestrians, for citizens' rights, and for the new network of green spaces.[16]

To maintain the same levels of traffic (at the same speed) with this network as with the current network, the number of cars would need to be reduced by between 13% and 15%. The Barcelona Urban Mobility Plan, based on superblocks and approved by the Barcelona City Council in March 2015, aims to reduce the number of cars by 21% in order to achieve air pollution levels at all measuring stations below the limits recommended by European legislation. This means that the speed of circulation on the roads around the superblocks would be faster than in the current situation. The amount of traffic would improve significantly, while improving air quality and noise levels, not only for those who live in the *intervia* but also those who live along the perimeter road. For those living on a perimeter road that defines a superblock, a 13% reduction in traffic would mean equaling the current environmental conditions. A 21% reduction would mean that environmental conditions would improve significantly compared to the current situation.

Perhaps one of the most important features of this new cell is its ability to integrate all the transport networks as well as the network of green spaces. By freeing up 70% of the space currently occupied by mobility, it is possible to design a network of green spaces that connects the different parts of the city, and the city with the surrounding metropolitan area.

A significant part of the almost 6.3 million square meters of space that is freed up can be used to renaturalize the city, creating a veritable connected green network. To exemplify this, and for the purpose of comparing between the different planning proposals that we have summarized thus far, we will focus the analysis of urban green spaces on the area of Cerdà's Eixample. To do this, the analysis focuses on the scale of the *intervia*.

If we compare the current surface area of green space and the area from the superblock model applied to the Eixample, we find that the surface area of green space increases significantly, arriving at 403.7 ha of potential green spaces, while maintaining the functionality of the city. Tabulating only the public space, it increases from the current 2.7 m^2/inhabitant (171.2 ha) to 6.3 m^2/inhabitant (403.7 ha) for the whole area of the Cerdà Plan. In areas of Sant Martí, the ratio rises to 7.6 m^2/ha.[17]

The square has been and continues to be the epitome of public space. It is the setting for the exercise of civil rights in general and/or some of them in particular. With the superblock project, broad extensions of surface area are freed up, and a large number of new squares appear at the intersections in the Eixample (see Figure 5). In a 3 × 3 superblock, there are four new squares, covering some 1,930 m² each.

Eixample 2017

Green space
169.4 ha (urban) 403.7 ha (urban)

Figure 4: Green space in the area of the Cerdà Plan in the current situation and with superblocks

The number of nodes that become squares in their entirety (1,930 m²) is 130, which is about 24.7 ha, and the number of new squares with an area of some two-thirds of the total area is 43, which adds 3 ha more. Potentially, then, there are 163 new squares that would cover an area of roughly 27.7 ha. Added to the 403 ha from Figure 4, that results in a ground level surface area of 431.4 ha.

Figure 5: Intersections that become new squares in the superblock model Source: BCNecology.

Public green spaces should be complemented by the green spaces in city block interiors and on green roofs. The environmental benefits increase with an augment in the surface area of urban green spaces both above ground and on ground level.

After combining public green space with green roofs (estimates for our purposes are based on an occupancy of 30%) and green spaces in city block interiors (counted as 1,500 m^2 per block), the surface area of green space per inhabitant increases to 9.6 m^2/inhabitant.

COMPARATIVE ANALYSIS OF THE SUPERBLOCK MODEL AND THE CITY COUNCIL'S PROPOSAL FOR GREEN AXES IN CERDÀ'S EIXAMPLE (2020)

In November 2020, the Barcelona City Council announced a "green axis" project for Barcelona's Eixample, which, generally speaking, is part of a project called Civic Axes that encompasses the entire city. The idea is simple: free up one of every three streets in the Eixample (that's the slogan; if you actually count the streets, the average is one in four). When the structure is forced on the other urban fabrics, it's a tighter fit. The internal logic is linear, still focused on mobility instead of a multiplicity of uses and citizens' rights. The fundamental right is still movement, even if it is on foot. With the proposed axes, the benefits of the superblock model are reduced by at least fourfold. The Green Axes project does not include, for example, key diagonals to structure a true network of green spaces: Avinguda de Roma (7.7 ha of potential linear park space, an area half the size of the Parc de la Ciutadella in an area with 1.85 m^2 of green space/inhabitant); Ronda de Sant Antoni is once again given over to vehicles, even though there has been no motorized traffic on two of its four sections for more than 10 years. The area around La Ronda has a population density of more than 800 inhabitants/ha. With a section similar to Avda. Mistral, La Ronda would be a key piece in building a green axis (30 m wide and almost 2 km long) that would stretch from Plaça Espanya to Avda Mistral, cross the superblock on carrer Tamarit, and run along La Ronda to Plaça Universitat; Pi i Margall, which could be a green corridor, will lose that status if buses are ultimately routed along it. This 30-meter-wide street is part of one of the main corridors approved by the City Council intended to connect the sea with Collserola.

To compare the Green Axes project in the Eixample with the superblock model, I will focus on the aspect of freeing up intersections to be converted into squares and freeing up surface area and intersections in the neighborhood of Sant Antoni. In the latter case, with the exception of one intersection, the intervention based on the Green Axes project is now practically finished.

The superblock model frees up 79 intersections that would become squares covering 1,934 m² each; the Green Axes project generates 21 squares of the same size. If we make the comparison extending the area to the include the entire fabric of the Eixample (including Poblenou, etc.), then the number of squares that are freed up in the superblock model is 163; for the Green Axes project, the number is 38. As we said earlier in this section, the benefits are reduced by a factor of four.

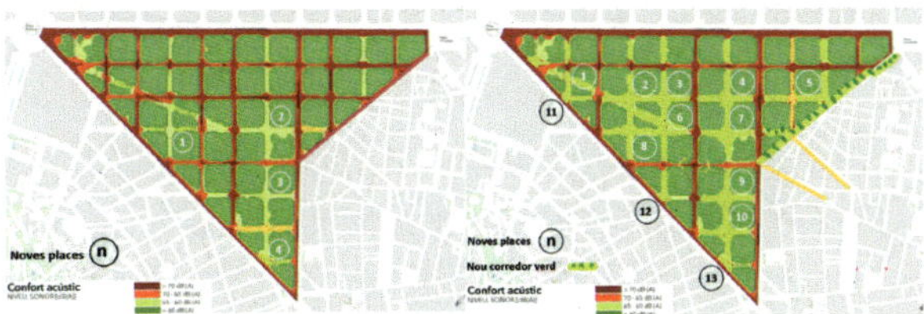

Figure 6. Noise levels and open space in the Green Axes project (map on the left) and the superblock model (right).

The comparison of the superblock model and the Green Axes in the area between Av. Paral·lel, Gran Via, Ronda de Sant Antoni and carrer Urgell (below) speaks for itself. The superblock model frees up 13 intersections and the Green Axes project, only 4.

	Civic axes	m²	Super-blocks	m²	Difference (m²)
Number of street sections freed up	23	52.118	40	90.640	38.522
Number of squares	4	7.602	13	23.644	16.042
Green corridor PÇA Espanya/ PÇA Universitat Nº of new sections	0		5	24.822	24.822
TOTAL		59.720		139.106	79.386 (8 ha)
Sections Avda Mistral	5	21.000	5	21.000	
Total surface area freed up		80.720		160.106 (16 ha)	

Table 2. Comparison of the Civic Axes project and the Superblock model: Characteristics and surface area of spaces freed up.

In the comparison, the total surface area that is freed up by the superblock model doubles. With the Axes project, 8 ha are freed up; with the superblock model it is 16 ha, an area larger than the Parc de la Ciutadella (15.5 ha, not counting the zoo). On the other hand, as explained earlier, the superblock model creates a 1.7-kilometer green corridor in this area that connects Plaça Espanya and Plaça Universitat through the Sant Antoni market superblock. The surface areas freed up for each type of space are detailed in Table 2.

If we extend the comparison to other aspects such as environmental variables with a high impact on health, it seems clearly unreasonable to abandon the superblock[18] model for a project that offers four times fewer benefits for the (elderly) population. Figure 14 describes the population density and the percentage of elderly residents by city block.

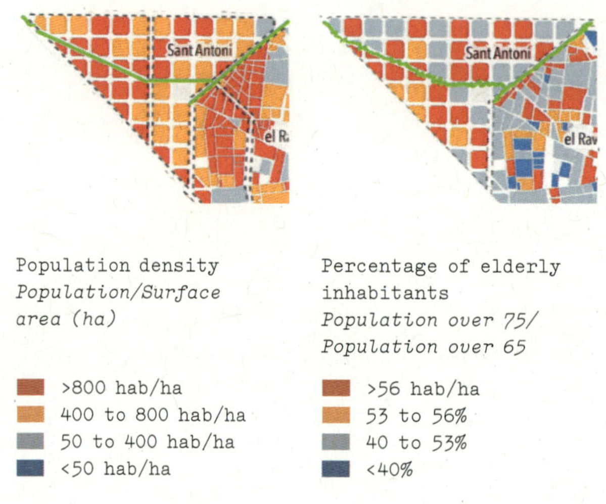

Population density
Population/Surface area (ha)

- >800 hab/ha
- 400 to 800 hab/ha
- 50 to 400 hab/ha
- <50 hab/ha

Percentage of elderly inhabitants
Population over 75/ Population over 65

- >56 hab/ha
- 53 to 56%
- 40 to 53%
- <40%

Figure 7. Population density by block and percentage of elderly inhabitants in Sant Antoni and part of the Raval.

If we compare these maps (Figure 7) with the ones in Figure 6, we can make an approximate calculation of the avoidable impact in relation to noise (permissible daytime values should be below 65 dB(A). The same can be said of the other variables included in the habitability index explained in the next section.

HABITABILITY IN PUBLIC SPACE: GREEN SPACE AND CONTROL OF ENVIRONMENTAL VARIABLES IN THE SUPERBLOCK MODEL

In their development (evolution), natural ecosystems tend to "control" the relationships among their members based on environmental variables –humidity, temperature, sun exposure/shade, paths crossing through, etc.– which are essential to increasing and/or maintaining their biodiversity.

In urban ecosystems, public space is the environment where the relationships between the components of the system occur: temperature, energy dissipation (noise, heat), air quality, attractiveness, safety, etc. are the environmental variables of the urban ecosystem.[19] As is obvious, in Barcelona these environment variables are not under control. Noise levels above 65 dB(A) are present in almost 50% of the city's public space; NO_2 concentrations above 40 micrograms/m3 affect 44% of Barcelona's citizens; on summer nights, temperatures can rise up to 8 ºC higher than in the periphery due to the heat island effect.[20] If we add to this effect the heatwaves that come with climate change, the conditions of habitability become dramatic, especially for the most vulnerable members of the population.[21]

With the introduction of the superblocks, the percentage of the population living in a place with acceptable air quality would reach 94%, and 73.5% of the population would live in a place with acceptable noise levels.

Urban green space slightly reduces air pollution and noise, but its role in regulating temperature and its positive effects on health are significant. The latent heat of the water in plants can help reduce the air temperature by between 4 and 5 ºC. Their role in regulating temperature is further increased with greater soil permeability.

The simulation of current surface temperatures and a superblock scenario shows a drop in temperatures due to the increase in urban green space on the street level and occupying one-third of the roofs[22].

THE GREEN AND BLUE NETWORKS IN THE SUPERBLOCK MODEL: THE MAIN GREEN CORRIDORS AND THEIR CONNECTION WITH COLLSEROLA

The naturalization of urban spaces involves infusing nature into the built environment by introducing greenery into the urban structure as much as possible. The continuity of urban green spaces replaces the grey, the asphalt and the cement, and provides a certain balance in the city's environmental and social demands.

Urban green corridors are strips where the presence of vegetation is dominant and the use is exclusive, or at least prioritary, for pedestrians and bicycles. They cross the urban fabric and guarantee connectivity and the connection between the different bits of green within the city. The series of corridors forms a functional green network connected to the surrounding natural spaces, a true ecological infrastructure within the city.

Likewise, urban green corridors are defined by the quality of the spaces they offer for walking or spending time, and by the presence of nature that is brought within the reach of city-dwellers. This makes the city more pleasant while also creating attractive habitats for fauna and incrementing the environmental and social benefits.

In order to define the main green corridors for Barcelona, the Barcelona Urban Ecology Agency developed a methodology that looked for the level of impedance (resistance) of each fabric with respect to the continuous passage of a green corridor.[23] The resulting maps identify the most critical areas with the greatest need for leisure spaces (in red).[24] For these areas, urban strategies are needed to alleviate the high rates of morphological and structural pressure to achieve, at the minimum, an equilibrium point in keeping with the city's average.Spaces on the margins are especially interesting from the standpoint of connectivity. These transition zones, called ecotones, are spaces where the environmental conditions allow for the coexistence of species that belong to different communities of organisms. Therefore, they need be addressed based on the principle of preserving the biological and environmental characteristics of those communities.

Requirements for leisure space m^2

- Less than -10,000 m^2
- from -10,000 to -5,000 m^2
- from -5,000 to -500 m^2
- from -500 m^2 to 500
- from 500 m^2 to 5000
- from 5,000 m^2 to 10,000 m^2
- more than 10,000 m^2

Figure 8. Calibrated Corrected Compactness: Requirements for leisure spaces, the foundation of the proposal for the network of main green corridors in Barcelona. Source: Barcelona Urban Ecology Agency.

Figure 7 shows the main green corridors and the connection of the green spaces through the "Gates to Collserola". Both green infrastructures would help connect with the natural park and link the green spaces of the municipality with the other large natural areas that frame the city: the coastline and the Besòs and Llobregat Rivers. On the other hand, a series of roads are highlighted, which, due to their character and section, form a network of secondary green axes in which nearly all the diagonals could be turned into green axes.

The number of green corridors in Figure 7, which have been included in Barcelona's Plan for Green Spaces and Biodiversity, could be incremented with the implementation of superblocks in the city (Figure 4 shows the potential corridors within the area of the Cerdà Plan). The navy blue color in the Calibrated Corrected Compactness in Figure 9 indicates a decrease in the impedance of urban fabrics as a result of freeing up 70% of public space currently used for motorized transport.[25]

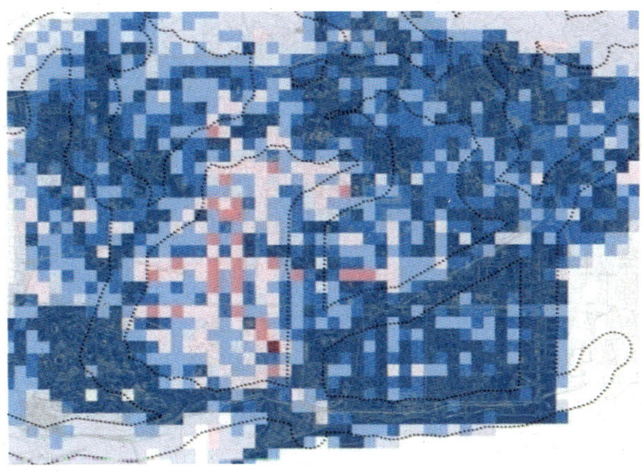

Requirements for leisure space m²

- Less than -10,000 m²
- from -10,000 to -5,000 m²
- from -5,000 to -500 m²
- from -500 m² to 500
- from 500 m² to 5000
- from 5,000 m² to 10,000 m²
- more than 10,000 m²

Figure 9. Calibrated Corrected Compactness: Requirements for leisure spaces in a superblock scenario for Barcelona. Source: BCNecology.

One of the green corridors that appears with the implementation of the superblocks stretches from the Besòs River to the Barceloneta beach, passing through five urban parks: the Parc del Besòs (Sant Adrià del Besòs), the Parc Central del Poblenou, the Parc del Nord, the Parc de la Ciutadella and the Parc de la Catalana. The axes that connect them are carrer Cristòbal de Moura, which has a width of 40 meters in some sections, carrer Pere IV and carrer Almogàvers until it reaches Passeig de Lluís Companys. A footbridge between the Ciutadella Park and the Barceloneta neighborhood would cross the Ronda Litoral.

On the other hand, in terms of the blue network, the natural poverty of the sandy and muddy sea bottoms along the Barcelona coastline (compared to the rocky sea bottoms) has been increasing as a result of the significant degradation to which they are –and have been, above all, in the past– subjected. Until recently, the Besòs river was an open-air sewer and, for decades, the mud from the Besòs sewage treatment plant intermingled there, mixed with quicklime, giving rise to an immense mountain of decaying organic matter, populated by the worm species *Capitella capitata*, *Spio sp* and *Mycronepthys sphaerocirrata*. The harsh environmental conditions, with an extraordinary contribution of organic matter which leads to anoxia in the sediment and the continuous precipitation of suspended solids, generate different typologies according to the organisms that live there, ranging from heavily polluted areas to degraded or altered areas, and transition areas. No sector of the benthic zone shows a correlation of organisms that corresponds to the desirable theoretical natural conditions of these sea bottoms.[26]

Figure 10: Proposal of superblocks for the urban cores of the municipalities in the Barcelona metropolitan area. Source: BCNecology.

Figure 7 shows the proposal for regenerating the seabed of Barcelona with the provision of a barrier of rough material forming a series of rocky reefs. The aim of incrementing the rough surfaces is to promote the regeneration of sea life. The rate of regeneration of an area as deteriorated as that of the seabed off the coast of Barcelona is significantly higher than it would be if no action were taken. The goal of regeneration is combined with another which justifies the proposal: transforming the area from the breakwater to the mouth of the Besòs River (10 km^2) into Barcelona's 12th district (the 11th is Sarajevo) –similar in size to the other districts in the city. This marine district would accommodate the uses and functions of recreation: fishing, diving, water sports, leisure, restaurants, etc. This would help regenerate and, where appropriate, enhance the activities on the seafront. No doubt, the implementation of the seafront district should be regulated through municipal ordinances in terms of both uses and services, such as waste collection. The proximity of a large recreational area is also intended to reduce the pressure from Barcelona residents fond of diving, fishing or water sports on vulnerable areas that are of high ecological value, such as the Medes Islands or other protected areas along the coast.

THE EXTENSION OF GREEN SPACES INTO THE URBAN CORES OF OTHER MUNICIPALITIES IN BARCELONA'S METROPOLITAN AREA WITH THE INTRODUCTION OF THE SUPERBLOCKS

The renaturalization of the urban areas in municipalities in the metropolitan area can be made a reality by introducing superblocks into each of them, in a similar way to the renaturalization of Barcelona based on superblocks. Figure 8 shows the proposed network of superblocks for municipalities in the metropolitan area of Barcelona.

By freeing up public space through the superblocks, it is not hard to imagine how greenery from the periphery could be brought into each of the municipalities creating a potential green network that can enter the urban fabric by replacing the uses currently reserved for mobility.

THE EXTENSION OF GREEN SPACES ACROSS THE METROPOLITAN REGION

In the Metropolitan Region of Barcelona, we have seen how the green matrix is being broken up across increasingly larger areas. At the same time the biodiversity is weakening, although we know that success in maintaining and, where appropriate, increasing the complexity of a space intended for preservation is largely dependent on the size of the area, the proximity of supply areas, and the real connection with other natural spaces that provide for the exchange of information between living organisms. The ecological stability of natural systems is supported by the non-isolation of these spaces and the promotion of a model for their distribution that tends toward forming a network of natural systems. When reserves are created or natural areas are isolated because of infrastructure or urban development, species are lost, and this loss is related to the size of the area and is the result of the differential rates of extinction and immigration. In consequence, such reserves should be as large as possible and barrier-free. Multiple small reserves will contain fewer species in equilibrium than a single reserve of the same total area; thus, they should be adjacent to one another in order for each to function as the origin point of species for the others. The effect is further enhanced if small reserves are connected by suitable habitat corridors.

On the other hand, the species most affected by fragmentation are the ones that tend to live in environments less affected by the presence of humans, such as in woodlands. Fragmentation results in a relative increase in edges or limit conditions and a reduction in the well-constituted interior areas of natural habitats. The consequence is the trivialization of flora and fauna: the species that can handle the change are more "anthropophilic", able to survive in environments that have been altered by a strong human presence and which are therefore common and easy to observe, while the numbers of species that are more associated with undisturbed environments, more skittish and difficult to see, sometimes more specialized and rare, can be reduced dramatically. Studies undertaken on the effects of fragmentation on American forests show that when residual forest patches in a landscape (whether rural or urban) are reduced to less than 50 ha, bird biodiversity falls by 50%. Marginal areas are suited to opportunistic species, which can find food in fields as well as in forests. This often includes birds and snakes that eat eggs, which helps us understand the decline in bird biodiversity.[27]

Additionally, there are other forms of fragmentation, from the inside or from the edges, resulting from human settlements or activities within or on the edges of natural areas, which generate disturbances that expand in growing halos, reducing the continuity of many species' habitats. Thus, it is easy to see how diffuse forms of urban growth have a greater impact on the biodiversity of a territory as a whole than more compact forms.[28] In order to maintain a certain biodiversity, there needs to be a clear dividing line between the countryside and the city. This entails breaking up the current mixture, which prevents us from knowing where the city ends and where the countryside begins. In that sense it seems reasonable, if the interest is conservation, to take the steps to develop a territorial model in which the countryside is wilder, and the city is more urban and less suburban.

To prevent the impoverishment and regression of biodiversity in the metropolitan area of Barcelona, existing green spaces should be extended and others, which are currently separated, should be merged by means of protected habitat corridors of different sizes and characteristics according to the spaces' natural interest. A minimum degree of protection (by way of regulation) would also be necessary for unprotected interstitial areas and habitats that are currently deteriorated or damaged: margins, hedges and green partitions. The structure of open spaces should guarantee the territorial balance between highly exploited, under-exploited and unused areas, in order to guarantee the desirable ecological diversity within our physical environment. This should also be taken into account when it comes to making decisions about land use planning and management.[29]

Expanding on the proposal by J.M. Carreras (1992), within the continuous structure of the network of green spaces in the Barcelona Metropolitan Area we could establish the following spatial typologies: 1) Large wooded areas in the Coastal and Pre-coastal mountain ranges. 2) Agricultural extensions such as in the Penedès region and, on another level but no less important, in the Llobregat delta. 3) Continuous corridors in the Llobregat and Besòs River valleys. 4) Maintenance of the strip of agriculture and woodlands in the north of the Vallès Oriental and Vallès Occidental and the stretches of agricultural lands and forest that are interspersed with the stretches of continuous city in the Vallès region. 5) Articulating threads, which may, in many cases, follow the secondary streams of the main hydrographic systems, the washes of the Maresme, etc., penetrating the built fabric and structuring possible urban park systems. In other cases, they may be paths or urban streets with the presence of greenery (gardens, trees). 6) Interstitial dividers that still make it possible to recognize the individuality of the different urban nuclei of the continuous city as a reference value in the territory. Among other things, this would include a role for the productive gardens of the Maresme. 7) A green structure connecting the different units of green in the compact city, with the creation of two layers, on street level and on roofs, forming a unit that is connected into the matrix of green.

The connections between the different typologies are threatened by the current urban expansion and have now become strategic spaces for the maintenance of the green matrix of the Barcelona Metropolitan Area. Safeguarding certain connectors and restoring others must be the priority conservation strategy, and some of the occupations that now compromise the articulation of the biodiversity network in the Metropolitan Area of Barcelona should be reviewed and reversed. Figure 8 shows the location and number of strategic connectors in the Metropolitan Region, i.e., those connectors that can maintain the interconnectivity between green spaces and the ones that are essential for maintaining biodiversity in the area. We should make it clear, however, that the articulation of a proposal like this one has no future unless steps are taken to develop a compact and complex settlement model that moves away from the current model of dispersal and the simplification of both biodiversity and organized urban structures.

NOTES

1 Today, we know that the proposed values do not hold up to scientific analysis. Science later refuted the assumptions on which they were based. We could say that the Cerdà Plan and the foundation for its system of proportions (which serves to justify the formal proposal) were derived from an error.
2 Cerdà, 1991.
3 *Ibid.*
4 Rueda, 2020.
5 Tarragó, Magrinyà, 1994.
6 Cerdà, 1968.
7 Busquets, 1994.
8 Tarragó, Magrinyà, *op. cit.*
9 Busquets, *op. cit.*
10 Cerdà, *Teoría general…, op. cit.*
11 Bonet, 1958.
12 Bohigas, 1958.
13 *Ibid.*
14 See the "Charter for designing new urban developments and regenerating existing ones" at charterbcnecologia.wordpress.com
15 Rueda, 2018.
16 Rueda, 2019.
17 Rueda, *Regenerando el Plan…, op. cit.*
18 The obstacles to the implementation of all the superblocks – whether in terms of traffic reduction (with less than a 15% reduction, the average speeds will be similar to the current scenario), or the investment required – can be overcome. The 500 superblocks can be implemented, using tactical solutions, at a cost of about €300 million over a period of four years. The City Council's budget for this four-year period is €5 billion (€3.3 billion per year).
19 Rueda, *Carta para…, op. cit.*
20 Martin Vide, 2015.
21 Mueller, Rueda, 2020.
22 Rueda, *Regenerando el Plan…, op. cit.*
23 Rueda, 2007, 14-49.
24 The color pink in the legend, for example, means that in order to arrive at an average surface area of mitigating spaces, it would be necessary to free up anywhere from 500 to 5,000 m² of space currently occupied by buildings.
25 Rueda, *El verd urbà…, op. cit.*
26 Rueda, 2004.
27 Terrades, Rueda, 2012.
28 *Ibid.*
29 Rueda, 2002.

ACHARNON FOR ARTS
SEE: *HABITAR EL VACÍO*

A LA PLAÇA
TEAM: Roger Paez, Toni Montes (faculty) + Shaun Barton, Lorenzo Damonte, Fiona Gather-Stammel, Marta Gutiérrez, Mira Kanj, Felix Köstinger-Lingitz, Ji-Qian Lai, Hung-Chi Li, Marcelo Reinoso, Laura Sánchez, Carlota Segú, Giulia Sportolari (students).
PROGRAM: Master in Ephemeral Architecture and Temporary Spaces, 2017-18.
STAKEHOLDERS: Civic-City, Théâtre Saint-Gervais (Genève), Centre Pompidou (Paris).

ALICE (LLUMBCN)
TEAM: Toni Montes, Roger Paez, Maria de la Cámara, Gabriel Paré (faculty) + Elise Chukri, Miquel Estany, Marta Esteban, Anna Gayete, Tatiana Glock, Laia Gonzalez, Laura Gusart, Mariana Magalhaes, Aida Pastor, Amalia Puga, Elisabeth Pujol, Albert Sanz, Valentí Soler, Marta Velasco (students).
PROGRAM: Master in Ephemeral Architecture and Temporary Spaces + Undergraduate Degree in Design/Undergraduate Degree in Industrial Design Engineering, 2018-19.
STAKEHOLDERS: LlumBCN 19
IN THIS BOOK: Plug-ins (D×CM in Barcelona), 214.

ALIMENTAR EL BARRI (A NEW CHANCE FOR THE RESIDENTS: THE NETWORK OF MERCATS DE PAGÈS)
TEAM: Giulia Damiani, Chiara Moretti (students) + Albert Fuster, Ezio Manzini, Roger Paez (faculty).
PROGRAM: Social Innovation Design Research Project.
STAKEHOLDERS: Slow Food Barcelona Vázquez Montalbán, Instituto italiano di cultura (Barcelona), Garcés-De Seta-Bonet arquitectes.
IN THIS BOOK: Plug-ins (D×CM in Barcelona), 114.

ANIMA (LLUMBCN)
TEAM: Roger Paez, Toni Montes, Maria de la Cámara, Gabriel Paré (faculty) + Berta Abad, Dalia Al-Akki, Jana Antoun, Juan Arizti, Marta Borreguero, Elena Caubet, Ines Fernandez, Rubén García, Tanvi Gupta, Stephanie Ibrahim, Tracy Jabbour, Yunling Jin, Jad Karam, Liam Kelly, Selen Kurt, Cristina Martí, Rubén Montero, Alexa Nader, Joelle Nader, Assil Naji, Mokshuda Narula, Miquel Pérez, Beth Pujol, Tiago Rosado, Eirini Sampani, Montserrat Sevilla, Judith Solé, Brentsen Solomon, Kuan Yi Wu (students).
PROGRAM: Master in Ephemeral Architecture and Temporary Spaces + Undergraduate Degree in Design, 2019-20.
STAKEHOLDERS: LlumBCN 20.
IN THIS BOOK: Plug-ins (D×CM in Barcelona), 214.

BIT-N-MUSIC
TEAM: Noelia Martín (student) + Ramon Faura, Mario Martínez (faculty).
Program: Final Degree Project in Design, 2020-21.

CAC
SEE: *HABITAR EL VACÍO*

CAN GUINEU
TEAM: Roger Paez, Jordi Queralt, Toni Montes (faculty) + Agustina Angelini, Momen Bakry, Dasstan Bissen, Malak Ghemraoui, John Gillen, Liana Kalaitzoglou, Gal·la Knoph, Julia Llorens, Elsa Romero, Chloé Rood, Giulia Tufariello, Irini Vazanellis, Aleksandra Zaitceva (students).
PROGRAM: Master in Ephemeral Architecture and Temporary Spaces, 2020-21.
STAKEHOLDERS: Aj. de Sant Sadurní d'Anoia.

CANVAS
SEE: *HABITAR EL VACÍO*

CARE SHARING
TEAM: Julia Benini, Ariel Guersenzvaig and Ezio Manzini (coord); Airi Dordas, Laszlo Herczeg, Lekshmy Parameswaran and Nuria Vilarasau (The Care Lab) + students.
PROGRAM: Master in Design and Communication (MUDIC), 2019-20.
STAKEHOLDERS: Aj. de Barcelona Area of Social Rights and The Care Lab.
IN THIS BOOK: Plug-ins (D×CM in Barcelona), 125, 130, 138, 139; Benini, 333.

CHASED
TEAM: Roger Paez, Jordi Cano, Marc Aliart, Eloi Maduell, Santi Vilanova (faculty) + Lorenzo Damonte, Marta Gutiérrez, Amira Ihab, Felix Köstinger, Cèlia Martínez, Esther Rodríguez, Kevin Rodríguez, Juan Alejandro Sánchez (students).
PROGRAM: Master in Ephemeral Architecture and Temporary Spaces + COM Elisava, 2017-18.
STAKEHOLDERS: Aj. de Girona, Vibra Festival.
IN THIS BOOK: Plug-ins (D×CM in Barcelona), 116.

CITY AND MAKER CULTURE
SEE: *PRODUCTIVE CITIZENS*

THE CITY OF INTERACTIONS. CONNECTING PEOPLE AND PLACES
An interactive community. Traditional residents as members of an interactive community. 30th April 2019. Pati Llimona. Roger Paez (coord)
Transient residents. Tourists as members of an interactive community. 6th June 2019. Les Golondrines. Ramon Faura (coord)
Recent residents. Migrants as members of an interactive community. 18th June 2019. Església de la Misericòrdia. Daria de Seta (coord)
Productive residents. Craftsmen as members of an interactive community. 18th June 2019. Nau Bostik. Oscar Tomico (coord)
[Final Event] Creative residents. Students as members of an interactive community. 23rd January 2020. Escola Elisava. Julia Claveria (coord), Albert Fuster
IN THIS BOOK: Plug-ins (D×CM in Barcelona), 139, 208.

COBOI SOCIAL INNOVATION LAB
TEAM: Danae Esparza, Sergi Frias (coord); Claudia Misteli (CoBoi)Program: Final Degree Project in Design, 2017-18, 2018-19.
STUDENT PROJECTS:
• *Formas de Compensanción.* Sara Porres (student) + Guillermo López (faculty), 2019.
• *Coboi 2.0 / centre d'innovació social.* Mireia Boix (student) + Guillermo López (faculty), 2019.
STAKEHOLDERS: Coboi, Municipality of Sant Boi de Llobregat.
IN THIS BOOK: Plug-ins (D×CM in Barcelona), 215.

COMMUNITY PLUG-INS
TEAM: Roger Paez, Bhavleen Kaur, Toni Montes, Atrey Chhaya (faculty) + Dalia Al-Akki, Jana Antoun, Juan Arizti, Marta Borreguero, Elena Caubet, Nishil Desai, Ines Fernandez, Tanvi Gupta, Stephanie Ibrahim, Tracy Jabbour, Yunling Jin, Jad Karam, Sajol Kinariwala, Louis Kurian, Selen Kurt, Alexa Nader, Joelle Nader, Assil Naji, Mokshuda Narula, Tiago Rosado, Eirini Sampani, Dhruv Seth, Rupal Shah, Montserrat Sevilla, Brentsen Solomon, Sajitha Varghese, Kuan Yi Wu (students).
PROGRAM: Master in Ephemeral Architecture and Temporary Spaces, 2019-20.
STAKEHOLDERS: Balwant Sheth School of Architecture (Mumbai).
IN THIS BOOK: Plug-ins (D×CM in Barcelona), 88, 116, 139.

CONVERSATIONS IN LES RAMBLES
TEAM: Danae Esparza, Silvia Escursell, Josep Novell, Noel Diaz, Raquel Llaberia, Pablo Figuera, Mariana Eidler (faculty) + Julia Bartrina, Helena Boet, Elsa Casanova, Jordi Farreras, Marco Gesualdo, Yara González, Jesús Jiménez, Nils Kamminga, Liam Kelly, Araceli Morand, Elisabeth Pujol, Albert Puertas, Ana Torrejon, Daniel Verano (students).
PROGRAM: Undergraduate Degree in Design, 1st year, 2017-18.
STAKEHOLDERS: Go Acció Cultural, KmZERO.
IN THIS BOOK: Plug-ins (D×CM in Barcelona), 52, 113; Faura, 101.

COOPER (RED DE COHESIÓN VECINAL)
SEE: *DIGITAL SERVICES FOR CITY MAKING*

COVID NICHES
TEAM: Roger Paez, Manuela Valtchanova, Toni Montes

(faculty) + Agustina Angelini, Alexandra Assinger, Momen Bakry, Mykola Balaban, Dastan Bissenov, Malak Ghemraoui, John Gillen, Lauren Harrington, Helena Jablonowska, Maciej Jasicki, Liana Kalaitzoglou, Gal·la Knoph, Karolina Kwiek, Júlia Llorens, Kinga Ostapkowicz, Natasza Pierzchala-Suska, Elsa Romero, Chloé Rood, Puja Sivamani, Giulia Tufariello, Irini Vazanellis, Aleksandra Zaitzeva, Mariia Zavertaliuk (students).
PROGRAM: Master in Ephemeral Architecture and Temporary Spaces + PJAIT, 2020-21.
STAKEHOLDERS: Polish-Japanese Academy of Information Technologies (Warsaw), EUNIC Warsaw.
IN THIS BOOK: Plug-ins (D×CM in Barcelona), 117.

CRISÀLIDES & GRESOLS: ELS BARS DE BARCELONA COM A TERRITORIS D'INSCRIPCIÓ CULTURAL
TEAM: Marc Aliart, Jordi Cano and Roger Paez (faculty) + Lucas Drobnitzky, Ximena Gamarra, Julian Laverde, Patricia Palacios, Raquel Pallejà, Francisco Palma, Luciana Pimentel, Adrián Pradon (alumni and students).
PROGRAM: Master in Design and Audiovisual Creativity; Master in Design and Art Direction and Master in Ephemeral Architecture and Temporary Spaces, 2019-20.
STAKEHOLDERS: Ministère de la Culture de la République Française, Musée de l'Histoire de l'Immigration, Montreuil.fr, Fondation Maison des Sciences de l'Homme (Collège d'Études Mondiales), Civic-City, dix-milliards-humains.

DEL FONAMENT A L'ESSENCIALITAT
SEE: *MARGES URBANS*

DIGITAL AND PHYSICAL PRODUCTIVE COMMUNITIES
SEE: *PRODUCTIVE CITIZENS*

DIGITAL SERVICES FOR CITY MAKING
TEAM: Rosa Llop, Ariel Guersenzvaig (coord) + Pablo Casals (faculty).
PROGRAM: Master in Design and Management of User Experience and Digital Services, 2018-19.
STUDENT PROJECTS:
• *Cooper (Red de cohesión vecinal)*. Alex Azagra, Raul Álvarez and César Castaño.
• *Fennec (Control del ruido doméstico)*. Mónica López, Gabriel Rivera, Gastón González and David Rojas.
• *Ona*. Cristina Iglesias, Helena Martínez and Giulia Surace.
• *Radars*. Lucía Ojeda, Julia Farkas, Laia Olivares and Sara Valdés.
STAKEHOLDERS: Radars, Fennec, Cooper.
IN THIS BOOK: Plug-ins (D×CM in Barcelona), 130, 138, 214.

DISSENYEM COMERÇ (SANTS-LES CORTS)
TEAM: Danae Esparza, Gastón Lisak (faculty) + María Eugenia Avilés, Maria Bladé, Helena Elizondo, Marta Esteban, Noelia Martin i Elisabet Sau (students).
PROGRAM: Undergraduate Degree in Design, 3rd and 4th year (workshop), 2019-20.
STAKEHOLDERS: Barcelona Activa, Disseny Hub Barcelona, Eix Comercial Sants-Les Corts (associació de comerciants).

DISSENYEM COMERÇ (LA SAGRERA)
TEAM: Danae Esparza i Ramon Faura (faculty) + Lia Alsina, Claudia Anguera, Irene Dominguez, Marcel Galtés, Gabriel Perez, Xavier Pons (students).
PROGRAM: Undergraduate Degree in Design and Simultaneous Studies Programme, 3rd and 4th year (workshop), 2020-21.
STAKEHOLDERS: Barcelona Activa, Disseny Hub Bcn, Sagrera Activa Associació de Comerciants.

EMERGING PLACES FROM NO-PLACES
SEE: *MARGES URBANS*

EMPOWERING LOCAL CRAFTS NETWORKS
SEE: *PRODUCTIVE CITIZENS*

EN MITJONS A LA PLAÇA (CIVIC PLACEMAKING 1)
TEAM: Roger Paez, Manuela Valtchanova, Toni Montes, Rodrigo Aguirre.
PROGRAM: Elisava Research, 2019,

STAKEHOLDERS: Aj. de Sant Boi, Fundació Marianao, Fundació La Caixa.
IN THIS BOOK: Plug-ins (D×CM in Barcelona), 98, 116.

FAR AWAY, SO CLOSE (CIVIC PLACEMAKING 2)
TEAM: Xevi Bayona, Toni Montes, Roger Paez (faculty) + Dalia Al-Akki, Jana Antoun, Juan Arizti, Marta Borreguero, Elena Caubet, Ines Fernandez, Tanvi Gupta, Stephanie Ibrahim, Tracy Jabbour, Yunling Jin, Jad Karam, Selen Kurt, Alexa Nader, Joelle Nader, Assil Naji, Mokshuda Narula, Tiago Rosado, Eirini Sampani, Montserrat Sevilla, Brentsen Solomon, Kuan Yi Wu (students).
PROGRAM: Master in Ephemeral Architecture and Temporary Spaces, 2019-2020.
STAKEHOLDERS: Aj. d'Olot.

FENNEC (CONTROL DEL RUIDO DOMÉSTICO)
SEE: *DIGITAL SERVICES FOR CITY MAKING*

FONERIA DE CANONS (2019)
TEAM: Ramon Faura, Ramon Garcia, Roger Paez (faculty) + Marc Casas & Myeng Lee (image), Rebeca Bonilla, Carlos Gerhard, Flavia Gütermann, Belén Jiménez, Arnau Merino, Javier Pradal, Ariadna Puig, Marina Subiràs, Jacqueline Vendrell (students).
PROGRAM: Undergraduate Degree in Design, 3rd year (Habitat), 2018-19.

FORMAS DE COMPENSACIÓN
SEE: *COBOI SOCIAL INNOVATION LAB*

GIRLS IN RAVAL
SEE: *RAVAL (IN)VISIBLE*

HABITAR EL VACÍO
TEAM: Daria de Seta (coord) with Anna Baldrich, Curro Claret, Luis Eslava, Anaïs Esmerado, Toni Llàcer, Pere Llorach, Francesc Pla, Robert Thompson (faculty); and the collaboration of Neus Arnal Dimas (Social Educator).
PROGRAM: Final Degree Project in Design, 2017-18, 2018-19.
STUDENT PROJECTS:
• *Acharnon for Arts*. Jacqueline Vendrell (2018)
• *CAC*. Daniel Benjamín (2018)
• *Canvas*. Eva Porcuna (2018)
• *The Human Flag*. Clara Vituri (2018)
• *Le damos la vuelta*. Marta Borreguero (2018)
• *Sava*. Silvia Sans (2018)
• *Projecte Diaspora*. Júlia Claveria (2019)
• *Topos*. Irati Azkue (2018)
STAKEHOLDERS: Aj. del Prat de Llobregat, Alencop, Asociación Amigos de Sárnago, CIDOB, Diandé Africa, Diomcoop, Provocant La Pau, Proactiva Open Arms, Comissió Catalana d'Ajuda al Refugiat, Sindicato Popular de Vendedores Ambulantes, Techo para Chile. The Human Flag de Clara Vituri.

INFRASTRUCTURES FOR PUBLIC SPACE INTERACTION (CIVIC PLACEMAKING 2)
TEAM: Curro Claret, Roger Paez, Manuela Valtchanova, Toni Montes (faculty) + Dalia Al-Akki, Jana Antoun, Juan Arizti, Marta Borreguero, Elena Caubet, Ines Fernandez, Tanvi Gupta, Stephanie Ibrahim, Tracy Jabbour, Yunling Jin, Jad Karam, Selen Kurt, Alexa Nader, Joelle Nader, Assil Naji, Mokshuda Narula, Tiago Rosado, Eirini Sampani, Montserrat Sevilla, Brentsen Solomon, Kuan Yi Wu (students).
PROGRAM: Master in Ephemeral Architecture and Temporary Spaces, 2019-20.
STAKEHOLDERS: Kn60Lab, Fund. Tot Raval, Fund. La Caixa.
IN THIS BOOK: Plug-ins (D×CM in Barcelona), 96.

INTERVENCIÓ O ACCIDENT: EXPLORACIÓ DE LÍMITS ESPACIALS
SEE: *TEIXITS DINÀMICS*

INVISIBLE MAKERS IN POBLENOU
TEAM: Danae Esparza, Toni Llàcer, Naomi Bueno de Mesquita, Marien Rios + students.
PROGRAM: Undergraduate Degree in Design, 3rd year (Producte, Context i Usuari), 2017-18.
STAKEHOLDERS: Ciutat Nova, Hangar, CR Polis, Direcció de Democràcia Activa i Descentralització, Ajuntament de Barcelona.
IN THIS BOOK: Plug-ins (D×CM in Barcelona), 213, 214.

INVISIBLE MAKERS IN CIUTAT VELLA
TEAM: Danae Esparza i Toni Llàcer, Julia Benini (coord) + students
PROGRAM: Undergraduate Degree in Design, 3rd year (Producte, Context i Usuari), 2018-19, 2019-20.
STAKEHOLDERS: Ciutat Nova, Taller de Yuu i Taller de Pinar Miró (ceràmica), Fundació Arrels, El Ciclo (Ramiro Sobral), Jorge Aragoné (Talles de Vitralls modernistes), Jaume Serra (Arlequí màscares), Joan Pozo (El ingenio), Grupo-Taller de Marionetas (Pepe Otal), Encuadernaciones Bermejo Dorados, Districte de Ciutat Vella.
IN THIS BOOK: Plug-ins (D×CM in Barcelona), 214.

LE DAMOS LA VUELTA
SEE: *HABITAR EL VACÍO*

LLACUNA (LLUMBCN)
TEAM: Roger Paez, Toni Montes, Maria de la Cámara, Gabriel Paré (faculty) + Esther Abad, Joana Bisbe, Clàudia Blanes, Carla Camín, Alberto Cantera, Joan Carreres, Maria Casadellà, Aina Engelhard, Aina Flores, Nils Kamminga, Sofía Martín, Cristina Peiris, Carme Roig, Ariadna Sala, Clara Viladecans (students).
PROGRAM: Master in Ephemeral Architecture and Temporary Spaces + Elisava Undergraduate Degree in Design / Undergraduate Degree in Industrial Design Engineering, 2017-18.
STAKEHOLDERS: LlumBCN 18
IN THIS BOOK: Plug-ins (D×CM in Barcelona), 214.

LA LUZ DE LAS INVISIBLES
TEAM: Antoni Ramal (student) + Daria de Seta (faculty).
PROGRAM: Final Degree Project in Design, 2020-21.

LUCES Y ACCIÓN
TEAM: Carla Masferrer (student) + Daria de Seta (faculty).
PROGRAM: Final Degree Project in Design, 2020-21

MANIFEST DE L'INVISIBLE
SEE: *TEIXITS DINÀMICS*

MARGES URBANS
TEAM: Daria de Seta (coord) + Ramón García, Francisco Manuel Muñoz and Manolo Laguillo (faculty).
PROGRAM: Undergraduate Degree in Design, 3rd year (Experimentació Espacial), 2019-20.
STUDENT PROJECTS:
• *Del fonament a l'essencialitat.* Lotte Gallardo, Belén Jiménez, Ariadna Puig.
• *El tiempo de espera en un momento stand by.* Paula Barragán, Ester Chen.
• *Emerging Places from No-places.* Mar Gené, Julia Llorens i Judit Tremosa.
• *Matèria fora de lloc.* Aida Pastor.
• *Recordar el pasado del Moll de Barcelona.* Clara Solà, Berta Soler i Marta Ventura.

MATÈRIA FORA DE LLOC
SEE: *MARGES URBANS*

SISTEMA RETICULAR PER A LA MATERIALITZACIÓ D'IDENTITATS MULTICULTURALS
TEAM: Hannah Adib (student); Danae Esparza (faculty)
PROGRAM: Final Degree Project in Design, 2020-21.
IN THIS BOOK: Plug-ins (D×CM in Barcelona), 209.

MI REALIDAD (VENDEDORES AMBULANTES EN BARCELONA)
SEE: *RAVAL (IN)VISIBLE*

[ ] (PAUSE SPACE, LA MONUMENTAL)
TEAM: Xevi Bayona, Toni Montes, Roger Paez (faculty) + Shaun Barton, Lorenzo Damonte, Fiona Gather-Stammel, Marta Gutiérrez, Mira Kanj, Felix Köstinger-Lingitz, Ji-Qian Lai, Hung-Chi Li, Marcelo Reinoso, Laura Sánchez, Carlota Segú, Giulia Sportolari (students).
PROGRAM: Master in Ephemeral Architecture and Temporary Spaces, 2017-18.
STAKEHOLDERS: Monumental Club.

MOVING PAPERS (SANTLLUC)
TEAM: Luz Broto, Roger Paez, Toni Montes (faculty) + Ihab Al Baraki, Sara Bhaty, Luis Cabrera, Elise Chukri, Estefanía Cortés, Paritosh

Hatolkar, Amira Ihab, Ridhima Malhotra, Camille Moins, Mariana Magalhães, Anna Piliugina, Èrica Soler, Priscyla Tallabas, Nieves Torbado, Lijing Wang (students).
PROGRAM: Master in Ephemeral Architecture and Temporary Spaces, 2018-19.
STAKEHOLDERS: Cercle Artístic Sant Lluc.

THE NEW URBAN VOCABULARY FOR THE SUPERILLA
TEAM: Roger Arquer, Jordi Canudas, Maria Charneco, Ivan Pomés, Reinhard Steger; Davide Fassi (faculty) + Anna Meroni (DESIS Lab) + students.
PROGRAM: Undergraduate Degree in Design, 3rd year (Projecte Global), 2019-2020.
STAKEHOLDERS: Aj. de Barcelona, DESIS Lab.
IN THIS BOOK: Benini, 333.

OFFSPACE (ARTS SANTA MÒNICA)
TEAM: Roger Paez, Toni Montes (faculty) + Hector Cosio, Natalie Franco, Virginia Gallo, Sara Guidi, Andrey Krel, Giulio Rampoldo, Sabrina Sturba, Ezequiel Torea, Manuela Valtchanova (students).
PROGRAM: Master in Ephemeral Architecture and Temporary Spaces, 2015-2016
STAKEHOLDERS: Arts Santa Mònica.

ONA
SEE: *DIGITAL SERVICES FOR CITY MAKING*

PAISAJES DE LA MEMORIA
SEE: *TEIXITS DINÀMICS*

PARTICIPATORY DEMOCRACY AND INTERACTION
TEAM: Tona Monjo (coord); Natàlia Herèdia i José Vittone (faculty) + Pau Adelantado, Carol Romero (Decidim) + students.
PROGRAM: Undergraduate Degree in Design, (Experiències Interactives), 2017-18, 2018-19, 2019-20.
STAKEHOLDERS: Ajuntament de Barcelona, Decidim.
IN THIS BOOK: Esparza, 308; Monjo, 322.

PARADISE NOW (TOWARDS A NEW WAY OF LIVING: SPECULATIVE DESIGN AND SOCIAL DREAMING)
TEAM: Claudia Blanes (student); Daria de Seta (faculty).
PROGRAM: Final Degree Project in Design, 2020-21.

PLAYABLE CIUTAT VELLA
TEAM: Toni Llàcer, Julia Benini, Naomi Bueno, Marien Rios, Blanca Callen, Carla Zollinger, Paolo Sustersic, Gaston Lisak, Tona Monjo, Juan J. Arrausi and Salva Fàbregas (faculty) + Students.
PROGRAM: Undergraduate Degree in Design, 3rd year (Producte, Context i Usuari), 2019-20.
IN THIS BOOK: Esparza, 308.

PRODUCTIVE CITIZENS
TEAM: Oscar Tomico (coord) + Valentí Acconcia, Adrià Arnaste, Javier Camino, Pere Llorach, Massimo Menichinelli, Ramon Sangüesa, Cristina Taverner, Miquel Tejero, Xavier Tutó, Sara de Ubieta (faculty) + Helena Calzado, Helena Estapé, Beatriz Guedán, Sergi Jansa, Laia Lloret, Aleix Martín, Ana Molés, Javier Jose Pajin, Júlia Puig, Carlota Puncernau (students).
PROGRAM: *City and Maker Culture:* Undergraduate Degree in Design; Undergraduate Degree in Industrial Design Engineering; and Simultaneous Studies Programme, 2017-18 *Empowering local crafts networks:* Undergraduate Degree in Design; Undergraduate Degree in Industrial Design Engineering; and Simultaneous Studies Programme, 2018-2019. *Digital and physical productive communities:* Undergraduate Degree in Design; Undergraduate Degree in Industrial Design Engineering; and Simultaneous Studies Programme, 2019-2020.
STAKEHOLDERS: Xarxa d'Ateneus de Fabricació, Ajuntament de Barcelona, FABLAB Barcelona, Adidas MakerLab.
IN THIS BOOK: Plug-ins (D×CM in Barcelona), 214; Tomico, 297.

PROJECTE DIASPORA – BARADA & CASILOOROO
SEE: *HABITAR EL VACÍO*

LA PROSTITUCIÓN EN EL RAVAL
SEE: *RAVAL (IN)VISIBLE*

RADARS
SEE: *DIGITAL SERVICES FOR CITY MAKING*

LA RAMBLA EVENT
TEAM: Maria Charneco, Laura Clèries, Joaquim Matutano (faculty) + students.
PROGRAM: Undergraduate Degree in Design, 3rd year (Narratives de l'espai), 2018-19.

RAVAL (IN)VISIBLE (EL LENGUAJE DE LA FOTONOVELA EN EL ESPACIO PÚBLICO)
TEAM: Mery Cuesta, José Luis Merino, Pedro Vicente, Joan Tomás (coords).
PROGRAM: Master in Illustration and Comics and Master of Arts in Photography and Design, 2019-20.
STUDENT PROJECTS:
• *Girls in raval.* Natalia Davtyan, Marta Gràcia, YaoRui Jiang, Charlotte Lambrecht and Annika Sapper (students).
• *Mi realidad (vendedores ambulantes en Barcelona).* Monica Karina Gomez, Alonso Chunga, Laura Mestre y Elsa Meza + Top Manta (Stakeholders).
• *La prostitución en el Raval.* Carissa Díaz, Alicia Fernández, Daniel Gómez, Paul Mjaes and Andrea Rosero.
• *La revelación de clara.* En Tránsito: Montse Abufarhue, Victoria Casalduc, Haidé Costa and Felipe Kehdi.
•*¿Salva vidas?* Adrià Baquer, Tessi Eng, Tomba Hoff and Vivian Lachner.

RECORDAR EL PASADO DEL MOLL DE BARCELONA
SEE: *MARGES URBANS*

REC POP-UP DAY
TEAM: Edouard Cabay, Toni Montes, Roger Paez (faculty) + Alba Julià, Daniela Meade, Andoni Zamora, Santiago Ríos, Claudia Ribot, Mariam Al Ali, Luciana Pimentel, Yuliana Leon, Pablo Viaplana (students).
PROGRAM: Master in Ephemeral Architecture and Temporary Spaces, 2016-17.
STAKEHOLDERS: REC.0 Experimental Stores
IN THIS BOOK: Plug-ins (D×CM in Barcelona), 116.

RED DE EMPODERAMIENTO DE MUJERES EXTRANJERAS
SEE: *DIGITAL SERVICES FOR CITY MAKING*

LA REVELACIÓN DE CLARA
SEE: *RAVAL (IN)VISIBLE*

REVIVIR, TEJIENDO TERRENO
SEE: *TEIXITS DINÀMICS*

¿SALVA VIDAS?
SEE: *RAVAL (IN)VISIBLE*

SAVA
SEE: *HABITAR EL VACÍO*

SLOW DOWN, STOP AND STAY
TEAM: Roger Paez, Jordi Queralt, Toni Montes (faculty) + Shaun Barton, Lorenzo Damonte, Fiona Gather-Stammel, Marta Gutiérrez, Mira Kanj, Felix Köstinger-Lingitz, Ji-Qian Lai, Hung-Chi Li, Marcelo Reinoso, Laura Sánchez, Carlota Segú, Giulia Sportolari (students).
PROGRAM: Master in Ephemeral Architecture and Temporary Spaces, 2017-18.
STAKEHOLDERS: MACBA.
IN THIS BOOK: Plug-ins (D×CM in Barcelona), 117, 139, 214.

SPECULATIONS ON A PANDEMIC
TEAM: Manuela Valtchanova, Roger Paez (faculty) + Dalia Al-Akki, Jana Antoun, Juan Arizti, Marta Borreguero, Elena Caubet, Ines Fernandez, Tanvi Gupta, Stephanie Ibrahim, Tracy Jabbour, Yunling Jin, Jad Karam, Selen Kurt, Alexa Nader, Joelle Nader, Assil Naji, Mokshuda Narula, Tiago Rosado, Eirini Sampani, Montserrat Sevilla, Brentsen Solomon, Kuan Yi Wu (students).
PROGRAM: Master in Ephemeral Architecture and Temporary Spaces, 2019-20.
IN THIS BOOK: Plug-ins (D×CM in Barcelona), 97.

SUBJECTIVE CARTOGRAPHIES (CIVIC PLACEMAKING 2)
TEAM: Roger Paez, Manuela Valtchanova.
PROGRAM: Elisava Research, 2020.

STAKEHOLDERS: Kn60Lab, Fund. Tot Raval, Fund. La Caixa.
IN THIS BOOK: Plug-ins (D×CM in Barcelona), 96.

TEIXITS DINÀMICS
TEAM: Daria de Seta (coord); Ramon Faura, Albert Fuster, Roger Paez (faculty).
PROGRAM: Final Degree Project in Design (Teixits Dinàmics), 2019-2020.
STUDENT PROJECTS:
• *Manifest de l'invisible.* Judit Tremosa (student) + Daria de Seta (faculty).
• *Intervenció o accident: exploració de límits espacials* Mar Gené (student); Albert Fuster (faculty).
• *Paisajes de la memoria.* Julia Llorens (student); Daria de Seta (faculty).
• *Revivir, Tejiendo terreno.* Laura Badia (student); Daria de Seta (faculty).
IN THIS BOOK: Plug-ins (D×CM in Barcelona), 113, 212; Faura, 101.

EL TIEMPO DE ESPERA EN UN MOMENTO STAND BY
SEE: *MARGES URBANS*

TOPOS
SEE: *HABITAR EL VACÍO*

TRANSFORMATION OF URBAN RUINS
TEAM: Francesc Pla, Ramon Faura, Ramón García (faculty). + students.
PROGRAM: Undergraduate Degree in Design, 2nd year, 2017-18.
STAKEHOLDERS: Nau Bostik, Welcome Refugees.

TURISME
TEAM: Tona Monjo (coord) + students.
PROGRAM: Undergraduate Degree in Design, 3rd and 4th year (Visual Narratives), 2019-20.

URBAN DOORS
TEAM: Marta Ventura (student) + Raúl Goñi, Maria Güell, Daria de Seta (faculty).
PROGRAM: Final Degree Project in Design, 2020-21.

VORA
TEAM: Roger Paez, Toni Montes, Noel Díaz.
PROGRAM: Elisava Research.
STAKEHOLDERS: EIT Urban Mobility, CARNET, Ajuntament de Barcelona, Escola Sagrada Família.
IN THIS BOOK: Plug-ins (D×CM in Barcelona), 96.

VULNERABILITY AND CONFINEMENT DURING THE PANDEMIC
TEAM: Danae Esparza, Toni Llàcer and Julia Benini (faculty) + Students.
PROGRAM: Undergraduate Degree in Design, 3rd year (Producte, Context i Usuari), 2020-21.
STAKEHOLDERS: Amics de les Rambles, Arts Santa Monica, Andreu Nin Library.
IN THIS BOOK: Esparza, 308; Benini, 333.

WHAT MONEY CANNOT BUY (LA PEDRERA)
TEAM: Roger Paez, Toni Montes, Maria de la Cámara, Gabriel Paré (faculty) + Ihab Al Baraki, Sara Bhaty, Luis Cabrera, Elise Chukri, Estefanía Cortés, Paritosh Hatolkar, Amira Ihab, Ridhima Malhotra, Camille Moins, Mariana Magalhães, Anna Piliugina, Èrica Soler, Priscyla Tallabas, Nieves Torbado, Lijing Wang (students).
PROGRAM: Master in Ephemeral Architecture and Temporary Spaces, 2018-19.
STAKEHOLDERS: Fundació Catalunya La Pedrera.

COMMUNITIES OF PRODUCTION: DESIGNING SOCIO-TECHNICAL SYSTEMS OF FABRICATION FROM A FIRST-PERSON PERSPECTIVE

Oscar Tomico and Danielle Wilde

Industrial and economic practices profoundly shape a city. In Barcelona, for example, craft and industrial practices impact personal behavior, infrastructure, and urban planning in profound ways. The everyday lives of the city's inhabitants are shaped by where and how they work; where people live in relation to where they work impacts how they live, travel, shop and enjoy leisure time. The city's infrastructure has been made for or by industrial production. Many iconic buildings have an industrial past; the materials used to construct the city's streets and public spaces and the decorations that give character to peoples' living spaces are largely industrially produced. At the level of urban planning, the names of neighborhoods and streets in Barcelona are based on guilds once located there, products sold or exchanged there, or industries that have their production plants there.

Technological development, social pressures and the ecological emergencies we face demand a re-evaluation of industrial and economic practices and their relation to cities. In recent decades, many have championed moving production out of the city.[1] In contrast, we advocate keeping industry in the city, reinventing industrial practices to contribute to economic, social and environmental sustainability and to play a much-needed regenerative role. For this to be possible, it requires a paradigm shift —a move from globalized and centralized mass-production practices to open, circular, local and distributed on-demand, even digital, manufacturing.[2] In this new paradigm, designing and making become key transformational agents, disrupting the life cycle of products and transform how we design, develop, produce, deploy, use and recycle them. Such disruptions transform so-called linear extractive processes into circular sustainable ones, create new pathways for reducing environmental impact, redistribute value among the community, and reinvigorate local craft and industrial practices to play a much-needed regenerative role.

To both realize and leverage such transformations requires considering production from a systemic perspective and approaching change from the bottom up. It isn't just the designed object that impacts society and the environment. How that object interacts with and creates the socio-technical systems of production necessary to its fabrication[3] must also be considered. We propose that being involved from a first-person perspective (1PP)[4] in the actions of *conceptualizing, developing, sourcing, producing, distributing, selling*, and *end-of-life* of a product service system (PSS)[5] can have a profound impact on a city. This impact depends on who collaborates in each step of the process: who finances it or provides digital infrastructure, where materials are sourced, where the product is produced, sold and used, and service touchpoints. As we will demonstrate, each of these actions can regenerate physical spaces, the economy, and the community in a neighborhood.[6] To exemplify our discussion, we focus on the project D×CM "Productive Citizens". This project included multiple design activities involving design engineering and design students at Elisava as part of final bachelor projects (City and Maker Culture, 2018), second-year bachelor courses (Empowering local crafts networks, 2019) and third-year bachelor courses (Digital and physical productive communities, 2020). Over three consecutive years, D×CM invited students to design, from a first-person perspective, regenerative socio-technical production systems for Barcelona.[7] D×CM begun from the bottom up and scales out rather than up. It did this by "being with" three foci (one per year), each building upon the knowledge generated the previous year(s). These foci: i) tapped into *material flows* of the city through material explorations; ii) focused on *community intra-relations*, leveraging them to support local crafts; and iii) critically engaged with *socio-technical systems of production*. We describe these foci and provide exemplary projects. The projects can be understood as alternative presents[8] —scenarios that can become a reality if adopted by local actors, including the municipality, other public institutions, the industrial sector, cultural associations, and grassroots movements. Before discussing our cases, we briefly characterize a 1PP approach to design.

When designing from a first-person perspective, the act of designing becomes personal.[9] It positions designers within communities. It situates and gives meaning to locally conducted research,[10] accounts for individual and communal situated experience, and empowers diverse, often marginalized actors in bottom-up transformation processes. The designers design for themselves, co-creating and sharing their outcomes; or they design for their community from within. These ways of designing require continually reassessing relationships that arise between people, places and purposes, in order to better understand and respond to the complex interplay of needs and values in situ.

BEING WITH THE MATERIAL FLOW

Being With the material flow means situating the design process in a local context and working with the available resources of a specific place. It requires shifting from "out-of-the-box thinking" to "inside-the-box thinking", transitioning from a perceived situation of overabundance to forced scarcity where resources are limited on purpose. With this stance, designing from a 1PP can assist a designer in working at a human scale and engaging with the ethics of how their professional practice can be more responsible.

Fig. 1. *The Extruder*. A project by S. Jansà, 2018.

In the first year, *City and Maker Culture* explored the possibilities of circularity in digital fabrication to make cities more economically, socially, and environmentally sustainable. This topic is broad. As a starting point, each designer was invited to begin from the skills, knowledge and attitudes that define their identity. Taking design explorations onto a personal level in this way —by designing for oneself with the materials at hand— allowed the final-year undergraduate students to frame their opportunities faster. Moreover, designing from and for where they live gave them the sense of reassurance needed for this open-ended exploratory project. The 1PP stance assisted the designers in focusing their explorations and achieving more robust outcomes. They experienced the implications of how people perceive the world and interact throughout the design process from a personal perspective.[11] The 1PP approach situated and gave meaning to the designers' activities. It gave a sense of direction, anchoring the designers when everything else was complex, undefined and unknown. The three projects that exemplify the work undertaken in the first year of D×CM are *The Extruder*, *This is not a temporary solution, this is Velt*, and *Inter-*. They combine material explorations and activities with reflections on personal interests, motivations, effort, place, ethical concerns and issues in the designers' everyday lives. The descriptions from the examples directly address the reader to make each designer's personal motivations and context easily accessible:

- *The Extruder* (Figure 1): If you like artists such as Erwan Bouroullec and Pierre Charpin, and your father knows about soldering, you might design something akin to "The Extruder". The Extruder transforms construction waste into sculptural public furniture pieces, to be shared and used in the area where you live, to create new meeting points for your community, in the streets and parks.
- *Velt*: If you are a graphic designer with an interest in experimenting with the materials you have at hand, a broken chair from your home can become the star of a communication campaign advocating for mending and repair. A modified "Velt" can become an easy-to-use repair kit advocating the act of repair as a permanent, rather than a temporary solution.
- *Inter-*: If your hobby is fashion design and you are passionate about textiles inspired by architectural structures, used bubble wrap can become a fancy tote bag. An "open source" bag, whose structural pieces can be produced in FabLabs and Maker Spaces at a minimum cost, breaks from the idea of exclusivity communicated by current fashion brands.

These examples demonstrate the added value of limiting material selection to the resources at hand and what the designer can work with accounting for their biographical legacy[12] and prior experience. The act of making is always personal. Involvement from a 1PP stance makes it possible for prototyping and material explorations to become a way to connect and integrate local crafts, resources, people, and infrastructures. The 1PP stance creates sustainable value flows to reinvigorate a city's local production, as exemplified in the example of *Inter-*'s material flow diagram (Figure 2).

BEING WITH COMMUNITY INTRA-RELATIONS

Taking the stance of being together with others in a neighborhood situates designers within the community as they work. A 1PP stance further positions them as community stakeholders. This stance, thus, adds the capacity to include and create bridges with others to the action of designing. Being in relation with the community doesn't just happen during the action of designing but throughout the day. It requires the designer to be vulnerable; to reframe the system from a relational attitude of care.[13] A 1PP stance supports this process. It demands the designer be responsible to personal, material, community and societal tensions and willing to teaching others to take a 1PP. Doing so strengthens design choices. It affords community-based ownership of the transformation process, including analysis and review of (interim and final) outcomes, giving rise to bottom-up transformation.

In Barcelona, local craftspeople rarely collaborate with artisans, designers, customers, public institutions, companies or other entities in the neighborhoods in which they work or live. This situation makes them vulnerable to changes in society and the economy. During the second year, *Empowering local crafts networks* examined the potential of digital communication and fabrication technologies to provide opportunities for establishing local connections for collaborations and services. Our interest encompassed the acts of designing, producing, buying, selling, promoting, distributing, teaching, sharing knowledge, utilizing a space, or any other activity undertaken in the neighborhood and in the act of designing.

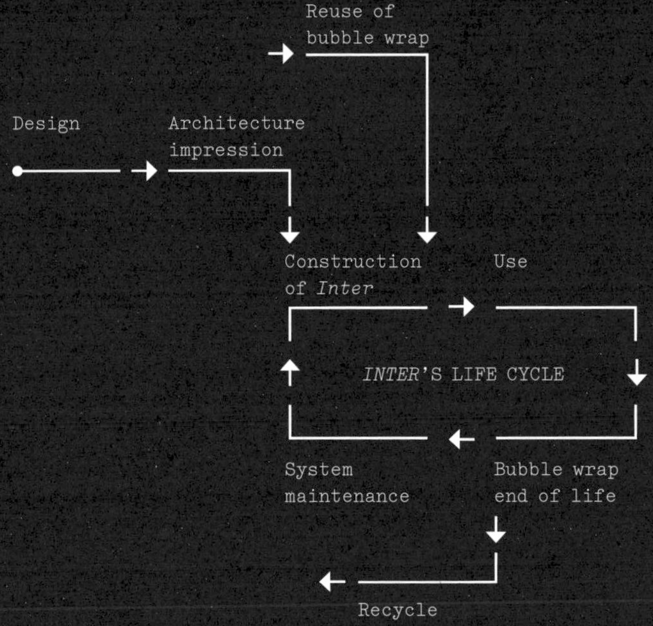

Fig. 2. *Inter*-'s material flow diagram

At first glance, taking a 1PP stance when collaborating with other designers and craftspeople might be considered strategic product design, service design or business innovation. Once multiple stakeholders are added to the equation, the "existential" need to know everything about the subject of study can push designers to take a top-down perspective. However, a bottom-up approach to mapping and articulating new "business" strategies can also be taken. 1PP in this context means becoming part of the community: being there, diving into the neighborhood, just being around. The designer as *local*, as *flâneur*, has the opportunity to become aware, to experience everyday personal relations and pre-existing collaborative activities. Having a coffee with the local clientele; allowing someone from the neighborhood to hang a poster on the studio door; explaining to customers what the craft is about; giving directions to a semi-hidden atelier that sells the same things; even taking care of lost tourists passing by. All of these activities can become design activities when the designer takes a 1PP stance

The three projects that exemplify the work undertaken in the second year of D×CM are *Hope*, *Instruma*, and *Atemporal*. All of them focus on empowering local craft networks by expanding the connections between different neighborhood actors.

- *Hope* (Figure 3): People at risk of social exclusion, such as homeless people that hang around near your design studio, can become part of your design process. In "Hope" the designer collaborates with vulnerable individuals in the production of jewelry, sold on the Ramblas in Barcelona. The collaboration provides a new source of income and dignity for the vulnerable individuals involved. This collaboration gives voice to a community. It makes visible an often-hidden characteristic of the neighborhood. It transfers craftsmanship skills, while offering possibilities for the craftspeople to work with NGOs and other public institutions. It thereby strengthens their identity and communication channels.
- *Instruma*: Knowledge sharing can help a luthier to develop new relationships with their neighborhood. They can keep local culture and traditions alive and vibrant, and educate the community, while promoting their business. In this example, inspiration was taken from the children you can see in the streets every day, walking around with their phones playing videogames. "Instruma" is a sensory video game tailored to school students and families, an interactive device that reveals the local production narrative of handcrafted instruments. The device enriches the experience of visitors to the local museum and others in the vicinity who can see this activity as a fun and active way of expanding their knowledge.
- *Atemporal*: Adding a new machine to the studio and collaborating with a junior designer-maker can support a radical change in how an established craftsperson sells and distributes locally made shoes. "Atemporal" combines established jute-sole making techniques with digital fabrication to raise interest in the community, strengthen product promotion, and support local transmission of

traditional craft techniques. Atemporal is a timeless product that fills a gap in the slow winter sales period. It meets locals' individual needs through personalization, achieved by implementing laser cutting techniques in design and production.

Fig. 3. *Instruma*. A project by C. Altube, A. Baéz and R. Prat. for a luthier in Barcelona, 2019.

Implicating themselves personally in the design process affords designers new relations at various levels —from the network, infrastructure and expertise that comes from their professional practice to the people, activities and things that fill the rest of their day. It is the combination of the individual and the place where the design action happens that acts as the connector, creating new relations in the neighborhood, both human and non-human. Figure 4 shows how augmenting existing practices and starting new ones from a bottom-up and emergent perspective can empower local networks.

BEING WITH SOCIO-TECHNICAL AND ENVIRONMENTAL INFRASTRUCTURES

If businesses are to be sustainable, they must shift from profit as the primary motivator to an interwoven, interdependent relationship between profit, people, place and purpose. Such a shift requires engaging with social structures, technical infrastructures, ecological systems, and cultural behaviors. In a profit-driven paradigm, few organizations can support designing from a 1PP stance.

However, in a people-, place-, purpose- and profit-driven paradigm, a 1PP stance ensures impact beyond the specific, situated, and temporally bound circumstances of the design process. This shift requires reevaluating vision and purpose as a space of opportunity and exploring new roles for iterations, multiplicity in action, and diversity in decision making.

During the third year, *the Digital and physical productive communities project* focused on regenerating Barcelona during COVID-19. Foreseeing the economic difficulties that industries faced due to the pandemic, the project explored how open, circular, local and distributed on-demand digital manufacturing could support the creation and distribution of value within local communities in the city. The goal was to bring a product service system (PSS) to market where the students live (Barcelona) and within their communities. The end-result was a Kickstarter campaign ready to be launched following a people-, place-, purpose- and profit-driven paradigm.

1PP design interventions at the level of the "socio-technical system of production" have the potential to reshape a city's infrastructure, identity and everyday life. They can support the transition from the current extractive economy to a more sustainable regenerative economy based on local, open, distributed and circular socio-technical production systems. The projects selected to exemplify this work are: *Entrega'm*, *Te invito a una copa*, and *Picante*. These projects all involve multiple local agents in Barcelona, including the municipality and other public institutions, the industrial sector, cultural associations and grassroots movements.

- *Entrega'm* (Figure 5): Designing a PSS around the symbolic act of giving away flowers and plants to show love, affection, kindness and well-being affords the opportunity to support habitat and biodiversity restoration where you live. Adding an online platform can help to create a lively community around the PSS for you and others to share articles and guides on plant care, recipes, and home harvesting. You might blog the stories of people who, like you, participate in the various activities offered or have a direct chat with botanical experts who can help you, and the others with you, to answer questions about your plants. "Entrega'm" achieves all of these things. It is a locally crafted seed bomb. Each purchase helps people to show gratitude to friends and family and supports small neighborhood businesses.
- *Te invito a una copa*: If you want to create a cocktail set (a trendy activity in Barcelona, during COVID-19 lockdowns), a PSS could help you find a market for your designs, while supporting local crafts, food and liquor production. "Te invito a una copa" creates a community around cocktail glasses designed by emerging local designers, recipes from local mixologists from local cocktail bars using local liquor brands, kilometer zero fruits and other ingredients.
- *Picante*: If you are interested in normalizing themes that

may cause shame to some, you might design “Picante, Picante, Picante”: a sex-themed board game that you can play with your friends. Apart from the standard game, you may like to create extra card collections produced by local organizations that deal with specific topics, such as feminism, LGBTQI+ or fetishism. You could collaborate with artists from those communities to create the cards and distribute them in various locations, from hospitals to sex shops. Taking this hyper-local approach can help communities and artists gain more visibility while supporting sexual health.

Fig. 5. *Te invito a una copa*. A project by B. Abad, M. España, L. Masdeu and G. Vilá, offers a unique experience with the best cocktails in town, 2020.

Mapping 1PP design interventions and scenario-building activities from a community of designers to their city (Figure 6) can assist us in reflecting on that city’s emerging and future production possibilities, taking into account materials, activities, actions, infrastructure, spaces, organizations, institutions, companies and other non-human agents. It shows the potential of scaling a 1PP to a series of collective actions. A 1PP stance on design does entail being individualistic or egocentric. On the contrary, it acknowledges the richness of differences among humans and non-humans, making the design process more inclusive. It means designing from within.

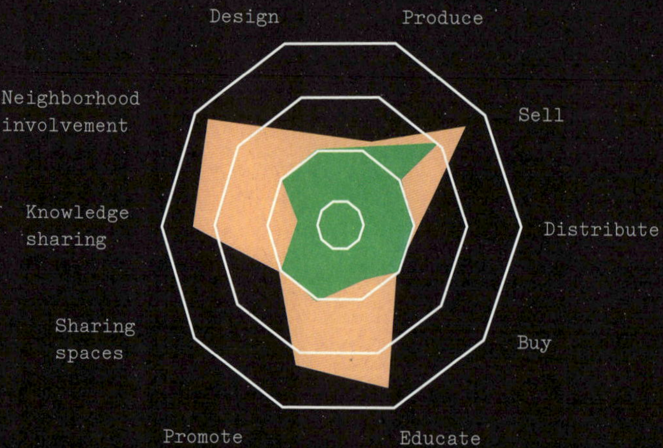

Fig. 4. New relations created in the local networks of a luthier in Barcelona by the design of *Instruma*, 2019. Green shows the web of relations before taking 1PP stance; peach shows an expansion of impact, with the addition of 1PP. This example clearly demonstrates how 1PP can transform a designers' relations with the community, to the benefit of all.

Fig. 6. Stakeholder mapping for *Picante, Picante, Picante* (blue), *Entrega'm* (purple) and *Te invito a una copa* (orange). Points on the maps represent schools, universities, maker spaces, craftspeople, local businesses, co-working spaces, designers, cultural centers and organizations, and public spaces.

TOWARDS A SOCIALLY, ENVIRONMENTALLY AND ECONOMICALLY REGENERATIVE PRODUCTION

Over three years, the D×CM Productive Citizens project opened design spaces for understanding the value of being with i) material flows, ii) community intra-actions, and iii) socio-technical and environmental infrastructures when producing designs in cities. The outcomes described here demonstrate how a 1PP stance can assist designers in actively reorienting production processes towards socially, environmentally, and economically regenerative communities of production. They work at the level of the individual, the community, and the city. They propose ways that we might live and design, moving forward, that are fair, just, and sustainable; that leverage technological advances; and that are people-, place-, purpose- and profit-driven. We see this work as a stepping stone towards a plurality of design propositions that can actively assist us in making this urgently needed paradigm shift.[14]

NOTES

1 Scott 1982, 111-141.
2 Nachtigall, Mironcika, Tomico, Feijs 2020, 274-292.
3 Sicklinger, Tomico, Pei, Buono 2021.
4 Tomico, Winthagen, van Heist 2012, 180-188.
5 Nachtigall, Mironcika, Tomico, Feijs, *op. cit.*
6 Wahl, Baxter 2008, 72-83.
7 Tukker 2004, 246-260.
8 Mackey, Wakkary, Wensveen, Hupfeld, Tomico 2020, 351-364.
9 Kirsh 2013, 1-30.
10 Lucero, Desjardins, Neustaedter, Höök, Hassenzahl, Cecchinato 2019, 385-388.
11 Desjardins, Ball 2018, 753-764.
12 Neustaedter, Sengers 2012, 28-33.
13 Puig de la Bellacasa 2017.
14 Acknowledgements: This project would not have been possible without the support of V. Acconcia, A. Arnaste, J. Camino, P. Llorach, M. Medichinelli, R. Sangüesa, C. Taverner, M. Tejero, and S. de Ubieta.

RESEARCH THROUGH DESIGN, DESIGN THROUGH RESEARCH (ACADEMIC EXPERIENCES WITH STUDENTS TO INTRODUCE RESEARCH INTO PROCESSES OF CO-DESIGN AND SOCIAL INNOVATION)

Danae Esparza

In recent years, design has positioned itself as a key element in taking on complex and global challenges that require working in transdisciplinary teams in areas as varied as transportation, community revitalization and resilience, energy systems, healthcare and policy design.[1]

These challenges have been called "wicked problems", a concept introduced by Rittel and Weber[2] to refer to *problems that are difficult to describe* and which, due to the complexity of the factors that make them up and the multitude of agents involved, *seem impossible to solve*. They are usually problems of a social, political or environmental nature such as inequality, poverty, sustainability, and education, among others. Therefore, there can be no definitive solution, and they can't be approached from within a single discipline.[3]

The change in scale of the projects in which designers have intervened in the last three decades shows "a move from the designing of things to interactions to systems, and from designing for people to designing with people and by people",[4] which is reflected in the emergence of new disciplines and working methodologies like interaction design, experience design, participatory design, co-design, service design and design for social innovation.

The public sector has also recognized the importance of incorporating design and its working methodologies in order to innovate in service design and policymaking. In that vein, the European Union highlights the work done by many of its members in spaces such as the Helsinki Design Lab, MindLab in Denmark, or the Cabinet Office Policy Lab in the UK, and points to the opportunity to lead this incorporation of design into the public realm.[5] The announcement by the President of the European Commission, Ursula von de Leyen, of the creation of the "New European Bauhaus" also draws on these experiences to propose the creation of a collaborative space for designers, artists, architects, engineers, scientists and students to work jointly on sustainability, accessibility and aesthetics: "It should experiment and provide practical answers to the social question of what modern life in harmony with nature can look like for Europeans. It will help to make our 21st century more beautiful and humane."[6]

In this context, several authors describe the new role that professional designers take on when leading multidisciplinary teams to address those issues. Manzini and Cipolla point out that "design experts may have a central role in bringing specific design competences to these larger co-design processes. That is to say, they may become *process drivers and facilitators* who use specific design skills to enhance the other actors' abilities to be good designers themselves."[7] Along the same lines, Sanders and Stappers look at the changes that have taken place in the business environment and point out the role that designers can play in facilitating creativity among other participants by inviting them to think creatively and critically about the future: "The people who are today's designers and design researchers are the facilitators and shapers of the collective dreams of the people in 2044."[8]

Faced with this evolution in the role of expert designers, at design schools it is worth asking ourselves: What skills will be necessary to address these new design challenges? How are schools preparing young designers to face new global challenges?

Design schools are the "places where the *next generation* of design experts are educated. This fundamental educational role can be considered as an *investment in the future*: if we want to build a better future, we have to ensure that its constructors are well prepared, thereby, in this case, producing suitably equipped designers."[9] However, Meyer and Norman point out that schools have not kept up to date with the new requirements of the 21st century and are not adequately preparing young designers with the necessary skills to deal with the increasing complexity and growing impact of global challenges.[10]

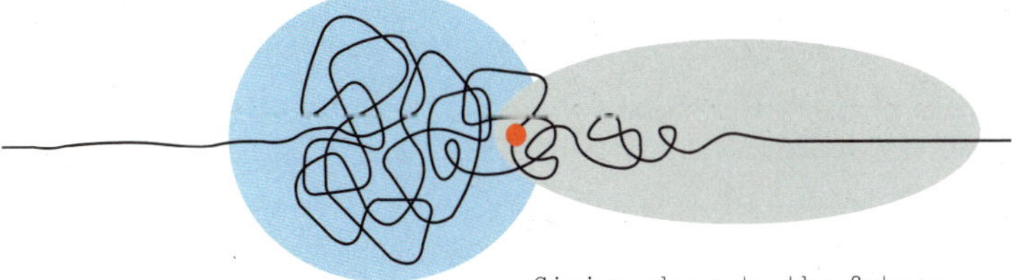

The design process today (Sanders 2017).

Elizabeth Sanders also highlights the existing difficulties, especially in the academic realm, of exploring the intersection between design education and practice. As a result, when designers graduate, they end up working in fields for which they have not been prepared: "The consequence of this lack of integration between education and practice in design is that designers and design researchers do not always have a seat at the table when the complex challenges that we face as a society are being discussed and explored."[11]

Sanders points out the need to prepare designers to be able to participate in (1) the initial part of the design process (in blue), also called "the fuzzy front end", in conjunction with stakeholders to explore the situation in a collaborative way and decide on what needs to be designed (red dot), while also (2) being able to "give shape to the future" (in grey) and involve others through to the end of the process. "But these changes mean that designers will need to learn to play new roles. They will need to learn how to facilitate the creativity of every stakeholder on their collaborative team. They will need to learn how to become process guides, provocateurs and activists who enable others to explore, express and test hypotheses about future ways of living in the world."[12]

In this context where everyone is learning to use design tools, Sanders warns us that it is also time to rethink the role of designers while, at the same time, encouraging teachers to be prepared to facilitate this change. She also adds that this initial phase of the design process is becoming increasingly important, due to the complexity of wicked design challenges, and that is why now is the time to explore the mutual benefits of the intersection between the academic and professional spheres: "I propose that we stop spending time and energy trying to straddle the line, or bridge the gaps, or fix the murky middle ground. Let's explore what it takes for a new space between education and practice to grow".[13]

One space where these explorations are taking place are the different Design Labs that are part of the International DESIS Network housed in design schools "*to behave as critical and creative actors in today's context*, i.e., to be agents of sustainable change in the ongoing social and environmental transition phase".[14] As Thorpe and Rhodes describe it, "the philosophy of the International DESIS Network, considers staff and students of design universities to be societal assets capable of bringing design skills and competencies to bear on societal challenges, and the community context to be an action-learning environment for all those involved. Participants share knowledge, skills, experience and expertise, working collaboratively to address local goals and challenges linked to the co-design and prototyping of public service and social innovations."[15]

Schools are understood as a space for experimentation that can contribute socially through a positive exchange in which, on the one hand, students have the opportunity to learn by participating in real challenges with collaboration from the community and, on the other hand, students share their working processes and skills: "In this scenario, the design school —a bastion of the diversity and redundancy of thinking and doing essential to experimentation, reflective learning and innovation— is a social resource with the capacity to bring redundancy in the form of a superabundance of creative resources to those to whom it is denied through austerity and efficiency."[16]

One of the leading schools that incorporates the approach to complex challenges into its curriculum is the School of Design at Carnegie Mellon University, promoted by Irwin through the "Transition Design" PhD program. As she describes it, "It is proposed as a new area for design research and practice as well as an area of higher education that aims to prepare a new generation of designers qualified to work in transdisciplinary teams on transition solutions." (…) It argues that design has a key role to play in these transitions and applies an understanding of the interconnectedness of social, economic, political and natural systems to address problems at all levels of spatio-temporal scale in ways that improve quality of life."[17]

Irwin highlights the role of design research —a field that has gradually been maturing— to complement research with other disciplines: "An important area for the expansion of design into 'transition' scale projects is the field of design research. Designers have evolved beyond their reputation as 'inspiration-based creatives' to work on higher order, increasingly 'wicked' problems that necessitate diverse, comprehensive and creative research methods."[18]

These new design practices require additional skills that are more focused on research. Therefore, *research* has become *a key skill* today for graduates in design: they must be able to demonstrate familiarity with research methods, have the ability to analyze and synthesize data, and communicate findings objectively and convincingly.[19]

Rodgers and Yee even observe a rise in the term "design researcher" in job offers both in multinationals and at technology companies: "Unsurprisingly, the job title of 'design researcher' has begun to emerge in the last few years in design consultancies, businesses, government agencies, research institutions and policy organisations. […] These jobs are the most direct representation and evidence of how academic research training can and is being used to inform professional practice in design."[20]

Design research is not based only on the quantitative and qualitative investigation typical of the social sciences but requires both "evidence and intuition". Designers need to be informed but they also need intuition to be able to imagine new possibilities: "Design research both inspires imagination and informs intuition through a variety of methods with related intents: to expose patterns underlying the rich reality of people's behaviours and experiences, to explore reactions to probes and prototypes, and to shed light on the unknown through iterative hypothesis and experiment."[21]

Writing about this double perspective that designers can bring to research, Yee reflects on how the skills developed from the point of view of research can benefit design practice and how design skills can benefit the practice of research, as seen in the following table:[22]

How a research lens can inform a design practice	How a design lens can inform a research practice
• *Articulating the why, how and what* • Developing critical thinking skills through writing • Understanding the importance of epistemology	• Being a creative researcher • Embracing uncertainty and ambiguity • Visualization as a research tool • Adopting a bricolage approach • Using empathic skills to uncover hidden insights

In design schools, it is worth reflecting on how those skills are put into practice in design studios. The following are three academic experiences from the 2019-2020 and 2020-2021 academic years, carried out for the BA in Design at Elisava. These two required courses, taken by students in the 2nd and 3rd year —Context and User I and II— introduce students to research in design. These courses form part of the Design for City Making program developed at Elisava's DESIS Lab with the aim of helping design and design schools become active agents in the process of designing cities.

INTRODUCTION TO DESIGN RESEARCH

Through the required course Context and User I, part of the 2nd year curriculum, students are introduced to design research. The objective of the course is twofold: on the one hand, for students to integrate social research into the design process as part of their search for opportunities and their decision-making; and, on the other, for them explore the contributions that design can make to research. We might say that the focus, in this case, is for them, as designers, to acquire the skills of a "design researcher" —meaning, to familiarize them with the researcher's point of view, to introduce the "research lens" posited by Yee,[23] through an analytical, rigorous, descriptive gaze intended to "inform a design practice". To that end, it is also necessary for the teaching staff to be multidisciplinary, so that each of the teachers can contribute their specific knowledge to a complex and non-linear process.[24]

The learning takes place through a research project undertaken in multidisciplinary groups based on a main research question, formulated at the beginning of the course, which each group uses to specify and formulate a secondary question. The course is taken simultaneously by 170 students, so the teaching team ensures that the research topics are not repeated so as to avoid overburdening a specific community with the students' questions.

During the course's lecture sessions, the research is directed, and the guidelines for social research are introduced to serve as the foundation for a quantitative investigation (consulting existing databases, developing surveys) and a qualitative investigation (observation and interviews). In addition to introducing these social science methods, we ask the students, as designers, to be able to represent the information graphically in a clear and understandable way, making use of photographs and infographics, and to synthesize their research through insights so that they will be able to lay out opportunities in sketch form.

Unlike other courses that students take throughout the degree, where learning focuses on a specific design typology and therefore the initial research focuses exclusively on similar results, in this case, the type of opportunities raised are open with the respect to the findings of the research. They may range from services to public facilities, strategies, mobile applications, communication campaigns, or what Sanders calls "the transition from a product perspective to the purpose perspective".[25]

The results of this work are shared in three different formats: (1) the entire research process is included in a research report. All the reports follow the same layout, to show that each project is part of the same overall research effort. The written information must be accompanied by images and graphics so that it can be shared clearly and understandably. (2) A collaborative digital map is created for all the teams to upload information about their work. This allows for collaboration and creating synergies between the different teams, and we also obtain a map of the whole investigation, like an in-depth analysis of the issue across the territory in question. (3) Finally, the results are shared publicly in an exhibition, to which the institutional collaborators or individuals who have participated in the research are invited.

The territory where the research was carried out in the examples described below is the district of Ciutat Vella, where the school is located. This choice was made taking into account that the school's network of contacts with the administration, institutions and neighborhood associations in the area are key actors and collaborators to aid in the research. Moreover, the proximity facilitates field work for students, who are expected to spend many hours in the field observing, photographing, interviewing, etc. The research process sparks interactions between students and different groups of people that would not have happened otherwise, resulting in mutual learning experiences. The students empathize with people whose realities are very different from their own and their families', and from the university environment.

The choice of this district is also a response to the fact that its characteristics make it a complex context. It is also the subject of many publications, not just studies, reports or books, but also features in the media, which gives students the possibility to use a variety of secondary sources. Ciutat Vella is the historic center of Barcelona, and in recent years it has suffered intense pressure from tourism. It is also the second-densest district in the city and has the highest concentration of foreign residents. That said, its population is currently falling significantly.

In the last two editions of the course, the research projects have shown two radically different situations in the district. In October 2019, a three-month investigation began that mapped recreational and sports activities to offer strategies to promote the use of public space as a space for social cohesion and the practice of sports. In October 2020, the context of the city had changed completely due to the impact of COVID-19, and we saw neighborhoods that were surprisingly devoid tourists, full of shuttered businesses, and the approach of the course focused on imagining strategies for its recovery.

Playable Ciutat Vella

The goal of the research carried out from October to December 2019 was to propose strategies to promote outdoor recreational activities in the public spaces of Ciutat Vella.

Barcelona is implementing a plan with an eye to 2030 that proposes a transition from a city equipped with play areas toward a "playable city", where the barriers to play are removed, and play becomes a priority in the urban planning for the entire city. A paradigm shift that aims to remedy some of the city's clear deficits, such as the lack of green spaces, high levels of air and noise pollution, and the lack of quality spaces for social coexistence: "In recent decades, the urban functions related to social gathering and leisure have shrunk noticeably or even disappeared from our streets, which were traditionally the quintessential place for children to play, for neighbors to meet, for people to stroll or take a break, for playing sports, or for economic exchanges."[26]

In order to reverse this trend and develop strategies so that play and sports can once again be present in the streets of the district, we suggested that students begin by detecting the recreational and sports activities that still take place in public spaces and analyzing them in depth. Due to the neighborhood's proximity to the sea and because it is home to the second-largest urban park in the city, a wide variety of activities were detected, ranging from water sports to swimming, beach volleyball, relaxation and fitness, as well activities that require specific equipment such as ping-pong, pétanque, cricket or children's games.

Some of the working teams pushed the limits of the brief, addressing controversial issues in the city such as public drinking or street art, which, despite being on the margins of the objectives set by the course, introduce activities that are both relevant and topical. We decided to accept all the issues that were brought up by the students, —young people who are often accused of causing conflict— who are capable of coming up with proposals that go beyond prohibition and reprimands.

Tertulia. A project by A. Reyes, C. Shin, S. Sustersic and S. Tarragona.

From this edition of the course, it is worth highlighting the autonomy shown by the students in identifying and contacting the relevant institutions or people in relation to their chosen activity, as well as their ability to fully immerse themselves in a complex issue such as public space. Through the research, students were able to understand the complexity of relationships that occur in public spaces, their value as a space for meeting and social interaction, and the role of physical and environmental qualities in supporting urban life.

The proposals put forward by the students were transversal in nature, often impossible to categorize within a single design specialty, including games, championships, celebrations, signage or communication strategies. Their proposals aimed to reactivate public space as a place for play and interaction, based on the investigation of recreational activities that already take place there, for the purpose of facilitating and promoting them.

The interest of the proposals lies precisely in their creative and transversal perspective, coming from young designers who are willing to move past the limits created by the municipal departments that intervene in public space.

Petanca. A project by M. Miquel, P. Perdiguero, J. Solé and C. Zabaco.

How Can We Recover Ciutat Vella?

In October 2020, the international health crisis was having a devastating effect on Ciutat Vella. The drastic drop in tourism resulting from mobility restrictions left behind a totally unprecedented image of the city, with empty streets, closed hotels and tourist apartments, and souvenir shops bereft of customers. In this edition, the research efforts were aimed at *detecting opportunities for the recovery of Ciutat Vella on the part of Barcelona residents* who, in recent years, have felt pushed out by the limited offer of products and services for local inhabitants.

The increase in tourism seen in recent years has been a source of tension, especially in Ciutat Vella, leading to complaints from residents and associations who highlight its negative impact (noise at all hours, illegal tourist apartments, monoculture in the retail landscape, increases in housing prices, pollution), which makes it impossible to lead a "normal" life in certain areas.

However, the pandemic presented opportunities for the streets of Ciutat Vella to once again be inhabited by locals and other residents of the city. Unexpectedly, the crisis became a vehicle for the reappropriation of the city by its inhabitants. This gave rise to the possibility of imagining the space, the activities and the forms of interaction from a new perspective, focused on the needs of the people of Barcelona, rather than the stereotypes of the tourism market.

The 45 teams of students participating in this research project each chose a community of people who usually live or work in the city center. Most of the groups analyzed the impact on commerce (souvenir shops, small neighborhood businesses, Pakistani-owned shops, municipal markets), bars and restaurants, the hotel sector, the cultural sector (museums, galleries). Only two groups focused their work on the residents who live in Ciutat Vella.

These projects showed an unprecedented image of the city center, unrecognizable after so many years of a tourism boom. Compared to the previous year, in 2020 there was a drop of 75% in passenger flights and an 81% drop in passengers arriving by sea, with the consequent reduction of 91% in the number of overnight stays in hotels in the city of Barcelona during the month of August 2020, compared to the same month the previous year.

Surprised by the data they were seeing, the students became invested in the course's objectives. They overcame their fear of contacting and talking with the people who were suffering the impacts of the changes to the neighborhood where they lived or worked. The students were surprised by the openness of the people they contacted and the positive reception of their research. They were able to empathize with the vendors, understand the work and effort that goes into many businesses, and in some cases they established enough trust to be able to do highly interesting in-depth interviews and accompany their subjects during a working day.

The research aimed to inspire and inform a series of ideas that might make it possible for citizens to help revitalize the offering in the city center. In that sense, the students themselves were the first possible users to recover those spaces in the city, presenting proposals aimed at a young audience that has always felt excluded from the city center because it has catered to tourism.

The final presentation of the research was held at the beginning of November 2020 in an exhibition of the posters that summarized the work done by each of the groups. The posters were hung on the façade of Arts Santa Mònica and the Andreu Nin library, two buildings located on Les Rambles near the school. This exhibition of posters marked the endpoint of the course, and, at the same time, shared the research and proposals with the public, despite the fact that due to sanitary restrictions, the communication of the event was restricted to avoid large gatherings.

This action was part of the program of activities called "Baixa a Les Rambles" [Come down to Les Rambles] organized by the Amics de les Rambles association and the Barcelona City Council during the same dates. The initiative coincided fully with the course objectives, scheduling a series of activities to invite citizens to reoccupy this emblematic space of the city. In that sense, it was an opportunity to collaborate with district agents to recover the city center.

After this first approach to design research, in which students introduce social science research tools into their design processes, in the following year, during the 3rd year of the BA in Design, students take another course dedicated to research. It is an opportunity to take it one step further and, in this case, recognize the “design lens” that can inform research practice, making use of experimental methods and introducing references and processes characteristic of co-design and participatory design.

The 2020-21 academic year was the first year that the Context and User II course was taught. The course is associated with a project that goes on at the same time, during the first quarter of the third year of the degree, which involves collaboration with social institutions and/or public administrations that participate in the process. Students can choose one project to participate in. In this edition they were able to choose between seven projects, which included: designing care services with the Barcelona City Council and The Care Lab; designing spaces for participation with Decidim Barcelona in the old Canòdrom [dog racing track]; transforming an industrial site into a shared dwelling with the Hospitalet City Council; working with the homeless in the Pere Tarrés shelter run by Fundació Arrels; carrying out an editorial project on aging with the Fundació Grífols; or, as we will see below, designing the signage for an industrial estate in collaboration with the Bon Pastor neighborhood association.

Approximately 25 students participated in each of these projects, with the possibility of interacting directly with the different agents. In most of the projects, unlike the previous course, a typology for the results was determined ahead of time by the teaching team and the participating institutions, in order to focus the process on what Sanders calls “giving shape to the future”, while involving the different agents as much as possible.[27]

Signage for an Industrial Estate

Among the different projects, this one focused on the creation of a signage system for the industrial estate in the Eix Besòs (Bon Pastor). Specifically, the Torrent de l’Estadella estate was selected as the project site. The briefing was defined in collaboration with the CR Polis research center and the Bon Pastor neighborhood association, in the context of the “urban cohesion” projects they carry out.[28] The gender perspective was also introduced because the Barcelona City Council is developing a Strategic Plan for Gender Justice for the estates in this area of the Besòs.

The Bon Pastor neighborhood is one of the few in Barcelona that maintains a productive industrial fabric. It is surrounded by a series of industrial estates built in the 1960s that remain active despite the deindustrialization processes that began in the 1980s. “As is common with industrial estates, their ‘urban quality’ is relatively poor, and they generate spaces of ‘disconnection’ or ‘barriers’ with the respect to the rest of the urban fabric. These phenomena are compounded by deficiencies in individual accessibility (due to layouts, poor condition of the urban design as a whole, inadequate signage) and a feeling of insecurity (insufficient lighting, lack of use)”.[29]

Aseñalus. A project by B. Baechler, J. de Mur, E. Avilés, J. Turú and M. Galtés.

The students in the course worked in teams of five. They all developed a research plan that, first off, was intended to survey the characteristics of the territory in addition to understanding the perception of safety on the part of the workers in the estate and the residents of the Bon Pastor neighborhood. The field work began right away, so that the students could get to know the territory first-hand. They walked through the industrial estate at different times of day and took photographs, maintained informal conversations and observed pedestrian routes.

To delve further into each of the projects, the different groups designed the necessary tools to incorporate the participation of different key agents from the territory. One of the groups took tours led by members of the Bon Pastor neighborhood association while they talked about the situation in the neighborhood and its relationship with the industrial estate. To learn about the different routes taken by the Bon Pastor residents, this same group made a collective map, asking people to draw their usual routes on a map of the area. Another group contacted one of the companies located in the estate and accompanied workers from home to work to find out how their perceptions of safety influenced the paths they took.

Most of the teams tested their signage proposals using 1:1 scale prototypes. The prototypes let them make decisions on the dimensioning and placement of the designed elements and, at the same time, observe people's reactions to the proposals. At the end of the project, the students had the opportunity to present their proposals at the industrial estate and receive feedback from companies, the Bon Pastor neighborhood association, and the CR Polis from the University of Barcelona, along with the team of teachers.

RESEARCH AND DESIGN AS INTERDEPENDENT PRACTICES AT THE SERVICE OF SOCIAL INNOVATION

These three academic experiences, carried out during the previous two academic years, involved projects that allowed students to reflect on their role as researchers in the design of the city, which requires a transversal approach in terms of the disciplinary areas they are accustomed to working in: i.e., the design of objects, space, communication, or interaction.

This takes place in two courses that are dedicated to giving them the skills they need to carry out research in complex, collaborative, and socially oriented projects. The first course introduces the point of view of research in design practice, making use of research methods, an analytical gaze and a critical spirit. The following course explores the perspective of a designer in the practice of research, harnessing creative abilities and visualization and prototyping techniques to create tools to share the design process with all the agents involved.

These projects are intended to contribute socially, either by sharing the tools of the design process with the community or by inspiring new opportunities through the proposals they develop. At the same time, these projects are meant to provide evidence —especially to local administrations and non-profit institutions— of design's potential not only as a discipline capable of developing products, services and their graphic communication, but also for its organizational capacity. While in the private sphere, companies recognize the contributions of design in terms of its strategic capacity, there is still a long way to go before this perception is also embraced by local administrations and social institutions.[30]

NOTES

1 Irwin, Tonkinwise, Kossoff, 2020, 31-65.
2 Rittel, Weber, 1973, 155-169.
3 Irwin, Tonkinwise, Kossoff, *op. cit.*
4 Sanders, Stappers, 2014, 24-33.
5 Design Council, London, 2013.
6 European Commission, 2020.
7 Manzini, Cipolla, 2019.
8 Sanders, Stappers, *op. cit.*
9 Manzini, Cipolla, *op cit.*
10 Meyer, Norman, 2020.
11 Sanders, 2017, 3-15.
12 Sanders, *op. cit.*
13 Sanders, *op. cit.*
14 Manzini, Cipolla, *op. cit.*
15 Thorpe, Rhodes, 2018.
16 Thorpe, Rhodes, *op. cit.*
17 Irwin, Tonkinwise, Kossoff, *op. cit.*
18 Irwin, Tonkinwise, Kossoff, *op. cit.*
19 Rodgers, Yee, 2016).
20 *Ibid.*
21 Fulton Suri, 2008, 53-57.
22 Research lens, based on: Yee, 2017.
23 *Ibid.*
24 In that sense, the course would not be possible without the contributions from a team of teachers, with different specialties and a variety of backgrounds. Thus, it is worth thanking the entire team of teachers and colleagues who have participated in the development of these subjects, contributing to the content and the definition of each of the briefings, as well as following up on the students' research: Toni Llàcer, Julia Benini, Naomi Bueno, Marien Rios, Blanca Callen, Carla Zollinger, Paolo Sustersic, Gaston Lisak, Tona Monjo, Juan J. Arrausi and Salva Fàbregas, along with all the students who participated in the course.
25 Sanders, Stappers, 2008, 5-18.
26 Barcelona City Council, Urban Ecology, Government Initiative, 2021.
27 Sanders, *op. cit.*
28 Remesar, Crespo, 2018), 3-51.
29 *Íbíd.*
30 Nusem, Wrigley, Matthews, 2017, 61-75.

DECIDIM × ELISAVA

Tona Monjo

In the 2017-18 academic year, Elisava and Decidim began a collaboration that continued for three years and, in a different form, is still ongoing.

This text describes the three occasions in which Elisava students and teachers were given the opportunity to reflect on the concept of participatory democracy and its implications for how we live in cities.

The 21st century began with a serious crisis in the concept of democracy. Citizens are identifying less and less with their representatives in political institutions. The 20th century seems to have carried away with it any remnant of faith in a system that was known to be perfectible but was generally understood as the best model from among the imaginable options.

In 2001, we were already seeing a growing disillusionment, on the part of citizens, with respect to their governments and public institutions. The growing, seemingly endless list of emerging corruption cases, the inability of the state to provide effective responses to citizens' needs, and the lack of a connection between representatives and the people they represent have been three major triggers for this situation.[1]

Social agents are beginning to recognize that citizens cannot simply wait for a government response. It is no longer a question of trusting the system to be able to act on its own. If there is going to be a change, it must come from a profound transformation on both sides, on the part of both institutions and civil society. There is a clear need for all agents to play an active role.

The economic crisis that began in 2008 supports this view. Millions of people around the world began mobilizing not only to demand answers from their governments, but also to take the initiative in building a real democracy. The 15-M movement (2011) was key in its attempt to reclaim public space as a site for politics to be carried out, and as a place to experiment with new democratic models. Information technologies, which fostered the globalization of a capitalist system in the late 20th century, are now becoming a popular tool for taking back politics.

DECIDIM

Decidim was founded in February 2016 under the auspices of the Barcelona City Council. It is defined as a "public-common's, free and open, digital infrastructure for participatory democracy", and its aim is to serve as a tool and a model for political transformation.

The digital platform, which is Decidim's main tool, is built with open source code. The platform can be consulted, commented on, improved and replicated from the public Github repository.[2] The first instance of its implementation, used for Barcelona,[3] was the starting point for its spread to other cities. As of July 2021, it is used by 40 municipalities and 44 organizations worldwide.

The motor behind Decidim is the Metadecidim community, which organizes participatory meetings and events, open to all citizens, to help define the platform's design and the evolution of the project. Metadecidim meets regularly through Metadecidim Operational Sessions and LAB Seminars centered on research. Since 2019, it has been organizing the Decidim Fest, a three-day global meeting to reflect on the relationship between technology and democracy in the network society.

THE PLATFORM

Through the Decidim platform, citizens can generate spaces for participation that can be configured based on various different components.

Spaces for Participation

Spaces for Participation are frameworks that define how a participation process will be carried out. They may be created by citizens or by members of an organization who are interested in compiling information on a particular issue. The different spaces for participation include:

- *Participatory processes*. Creating and configuring different types of participatory processes (e.g., electing board members, or publicly approving budgets).
- *Participatory bodies*. Constituting assemblies or decision-making groups that meet periodically in specific locations and manage the associated documentation.
- *Consultations*. Holding referendums and debates, using a secure electronic voting system that also allows for publishing the results.
- *Initiatives*. Creating initiatives using collaborative methods and defining specific objectives and phases. Setting up systems to communicate initiatives and gather support, in addition to convening open debates or in-person gatherings to collect signatures.

Components of the Participation Process

The components of the participation process are the mechanisms used in the interactions that take place within the platform's spaces for participation:

- *Proposals*. Generating proposals, comparing them with existing ones, publishing them on the platform and adding documentation.

- *Voting*. Activating and managing various systems for voting or expressing support for the different proposals.
- *Results*. Collecting the results of the proposals and confirming their acceptance or rejection.
- *Accountability*. Tools for communicating progress that has been made in implementing the results.
- *Meetings*. Calling meetings, keeping track of attendees, defining the structure of an in-person meeting and publishing the minutes and resulting proposals.
- *Participatory texts*. Combining different texts into a proposal or a unified set of proposals.

ELISAVA FOR DECIDIM

The experience during the first year of the platform's operation is positive: participation has gradually been increasing. However, there are aspects that need to be worked on more in depth: some support is needed help to increase participation and reach more users, and, on the other hand, some issues in the interaction design need to be fine-tuned.

With an eye to this situation, in July 2017, Decidim and Elisava begin a process of collaboration in the context of the Mention in Interactive Experiences as part of the BA in Design. This collaboration combines two main goals:

- Students will be able to work on all the stages of an interaction project applied to a real case, and
- In the process, they should generate proposals that will help improve Decidim's interaction and dissemination among residents of Barcelona.

The collaboration begins in the 2017-18 academic year and will continue for three years. In each case, the specific brief is different, but it is always related to improving the design of the digital platform.

Beginning in the 2020-21 academic year, a new phase begins in the relationship with Decidim, in which the scope of work is expanded, leaving behind the purely digital sphere to address the project's relationship with citizens in public space.

Methodology

Since its first iteration, the Decidim project has allowed students to work through all the different phases of an interaction design project based on a perspective of people-centered design (PCD). The project is carried out during a single academic quarter, over a 10-week period, with a frequency of three weekly sessions (3 hours per session).

Students are divided into groups of 3 or 4, with the aim of making it possible to address the multiple tasks that need to be undertaken during the project, but also to maintain a relatively small team size in order to make task sharing more manageable and to facilitate the internal debate that necessarily goes on during the design process.

The methodology using the PCD approach is divided in 4 overall stages: research, conceptualization, prototyping, and assessment. It should be noted that these stages are neither sequential nor independent, but rather interrelated: the tasks involved in one stage have an impact on the others and may even make it necessarily to rethink actions or decisions that were made previously.

Research

Based on the approach of a relatively open brief, the project begins with various research actions, which are intended to help students get to know the Decidim platform and the contexts for its use.

In this stage, the whole class group works in cooperation, such that both the design of the research actions and the results obtained are shared and developed conjointly. The aim is to work consistently with Decidim's open source ideology and to encourage information sharing and deliberation on the information that is obtained.

The methods and techniques applied during this phase vary according to the specific objectives defined for each academic year, but the common foundations include the following:

- *Desktop research*, based on an analysis of the Decidim platform and an understanding of its context and the community behind it. The starting point for this action, and in fact for the whole project, is a presentation given by members of Decidim, introducing students to the platform and to the issues that are the focus of action for the year in question. Students come into contact with the community behind the project from day one. This helps them to break the ice, get past the feeling of anonymity that might be associated with an analysis focused exclusively on digital aspects, and connect with the project. Knowing that there are people behind it, and being able to talk to them, knowing that they will be meeting again several times during the course of the project, helps students realize that their work will have an impact on a real project.
- *Benchmarking*, which involves an analysis of similar cases or platforms with functional or conceptual aspects that relate to the project. Students begin to understand the larger panorama beyond the specific case they are working on, and they can construct a critical perspective on their projects.
- *Interviews*. Students design and conduct interviews with individuals who match the user profile defined for their

academic year. The goal is for students to figure out what they need to know in order to carry out a project, and for them to learn how to collect and process qualitative information: not only the what, but also the why. The results of the interviews are shared in class, in order to discuss them, define common conclusions, and identify issues that have been left unresolved or that raise new avenues of inquiry.

- *Surveys*. After the interviews, students design and distribute surveys, which are intended to fill in the gaps left by the interviews, or to address new points of inquiry. The interviews are conducted using Google Forms and distributed via email. In general, a good number of answers are received, although it is important to keep in mind that the information gathered using this technique is quantitative: it focuses on how many people do what, and not so much on why.
- *Analysis of results*. Following the different research actions, two sessions are devoted to implementing various techniques for processing the results and identifying insights or discoveries (in other words, what they have learned from the research and which aspects are of central value). The aim is for students to formulate their working hypotheses —i.e., the actions that will orient their projects in line with the objectives they have set— and determine the following stages in conceptual terms.

Conceptualization

Following the research phase, students have a broad and in-depth view of the different aspects involved in the project. In the next stage, students articulate the knowledge they have obtained, in order to make it conceptually manageable and to help define the value proposition that will guide their project.

During this phase, students work in groups of 3 or 4 people, which will remain together through the end of the project. That being said, the follow-up for the different projects takes place in open debate in the classroom. The reasoning behind this is not only for the sake of knowledge exchange, but also so that the students can practice exercising a critical perspective, participating in the commentary on their peers' projects, while learning to assimilate the suggestions they receive and defend their decisions when necessary. The methods applied in this phase are divided into two main groups:

- *User modeling*. At the beginning of this stage, the students have a lot of information, which makes the task of managing it highly complex. What do we do with the information if we can't turn it into knowledge? In response, various user modeling techniques are implemented, with the aim of identifying the different user profiles for each project. A user group shares common needs and may experience similar difficulties or barriers to use.

User modeling leads to the generation of a fundamental working tool: the people, or archetypes that display all the characteristics of a group of users, are formalized into a character that is given a name, an appearance and a series of identifiable characteristics. Each of these people will "accompany" the students throughout the design process. This is complemented by other techniques, such as the description of use cases or the preparation of "happy path" user journeys —i.e., visual descriptions that define what an ideal interaction process should look like. This is already an initial design tool, in the sense that it defines the foundations for the design that will be developed later.

- *Definition of the value proposition*. Each team works with different tools that help them gradually arrive at the value proposition that will direct their design. There is an open relationship with Decidim in that regard, in the sense that there aren't any conditions that limit the possibilities: Decidim monitors the process by taking on an advisory role that enriches the results, but the students are free to define value propositions that bring their projects into an area that they are interested in exploring.

Prototyping

Once the teams have defined the conceptual foundations for their project, they move on to the prototyping phase, which helps the teams advance gradually in the definition of the design. Given that this is an interaction project, the phases they address are the following:

- *Information architecture*. Analysis of the different types of content that users can view on the platform and the actions they can take. Students can propose reorganizing the content to help users access it as easily as possible.
- *Sketching*. Although the project revolves around the design of a digital platform, students work off screens for at least two sessions. The goal is to use the simplest tools —pencil and paper— to generate ideas without committing to a particular solution simply because of the effort that has been put into it. It's a time for brainstorming, playing and working on a process of generating ideas that go in different directions without choosing any of them yet.
- *Wireframing*. After making a selection from the ideas that emerged during the sketching, the first fully digital prototype is completed. Wireframes let the students define the structure of the different pages or screens on the platform,

focusing fully on the interaction design before incorporating the graphic layer.

- *Mockups*. Once the wireframes have been developed and debugged over several iterations, work begins on the graphic layer, which defines the visual identity of the project.
- *Interaction design for other types of devices*. In order to push students to reflect on the ubiquity of interaction and move beyond the scope of traditional screens (computers, tablets and mobile phones), students are asked to work with in-context interaction channels, which make it possible to situate the point of contact with Decidim on the site of a participatory initiative or process.

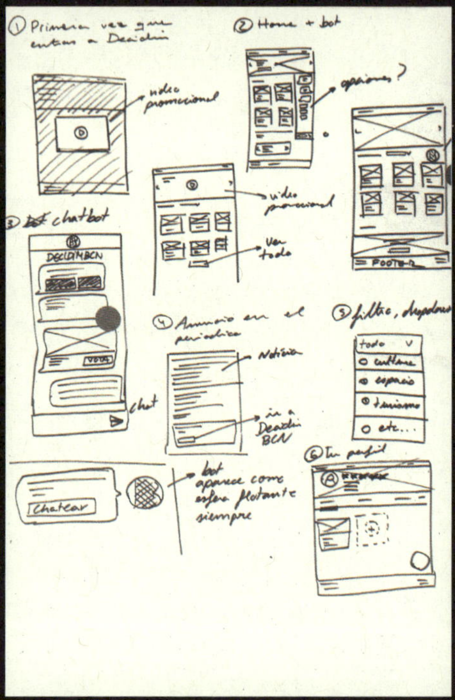

Sketches of the interaction for mobile phone. By E. del Moral, Ó. Morales and M. Moreso (2018-19 academic year).

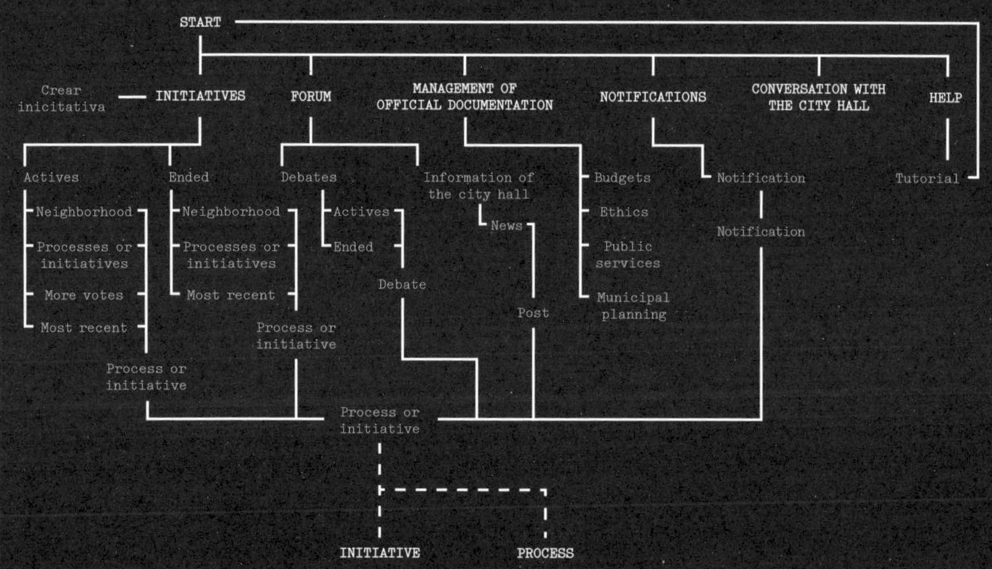

The content tree is a visual tool that represents the information architecture, i.e., the project's content structure. By A. Caruso, S. Giménez, J. Perez and M. Raurell (2019-20 academic year).

Design Assessment

Assessment isn't really conceived as a separate phase; rather, testing is carried out throughout the different stages of prototyping. Consistent with the people-centered design approach, a variety of dynamics are employed that let students put their proposals into the hands of users to see how they are actually used and to get feedback that will help them refine their designs.

Card sorting and tree testing techniques are employed to ensure that the information architecture is targeted toward the people who will be using it, which makes it possible to design the new structure together with the users.

To evaluate the interaction and visual design, tests with users are carried out, based on tasks that participants are asked to try to solve by using the wireframes or mockups (depending on the stage of the project). Successes, failures, or difficulties observed while carrying out this dynamic provide very useful information for students as they move forward with their projects.

Both Elisava teachers and Decidim tutors are involved in the entire process described above.

Elisava's teaching staff is made up of specialists in each of the areas involved in the project: research, interaction design and visual design.

As for Decidim, the tutors are involved at three key moments during the project:

- In the beginning, when they present the platform and Decidim's organizational model to the students.
- Checkpoint 1. Students present their research results and value propositions to Elisava and Decidim tutors. This checkpoint is critical in directing subsequent design actions.
- Checkpoint 2. Students present their proposals one week before the final submission. This presentation gives the working teams a final joint session, in which they receive feedback from the Decidim tutors in addition to the points of view of the Degree professors who have accompanied them throughout the semester.

Checkpoint 1 from the 2018-19 academic year held at Fabra i Coats (then headquarters of Decidim).

It is worth mentioning that each year, the results and students' final proposals are shared internally with the members of Decidim to provide them with ideas for improving the platform and how it engages with citizens.

As mentioned earlier, the collaboration between Elisava and Decidim began in 2017 and continued for three years. Although the guiding theme was always the dissemination of the Decidim platform and the improvement of the user experience, the specific focus for the work was reformulated in each edition.

2017–18 academic year

In the first edition, the main goal was to increase citizen engagement with the platform. This entailed two associated goals:

- Communicating the platform's existence to citizens who were unaware of it.
- Improving the user experience on the platform, to remove barriers to accessing the content and encourage participation.

While the demographic range of Barcelona's residents is very wide, in this first edition we focused on a specific group of users: young people aged 18 to 30, a group associated with a particularly low participation rate.

2018–19 academic year

The second edition focused on two main objectives:

- Encouraging in-context citizen participation, i.e., at the locations where an initiative was taking place. This involved not only designing interactions beyond the usual channels (desktop and mobile), but also working on issues related to the visibility of these devices and motivating citizens to participate.
- Promoting well-informed and thoughtful, quality participation. The aim is for students to work on the project from a critical perspective.

2019–20 academic year

The main goal this time was to encourage participation from senior users. Therefore, it addressed issues associated with inclusive design.

In addition to the advisors from Decidim and the Elisava teaching staff, this edition also incorporated participation from members of the project Vincles, an initiative promoted by the Barcelona City Council to strengthen social relations among the elderly, in order to improve their well-being through technology and social stimulation.

After the third edition and as a result of the launch of the new curriculum for the BA in Design, in the 2020-21 academic year the collaboration between Decidim and Elisava entered a new phase. It involved third-year students and expanded its scope, shifting the main focus of the project from interaction with the platform to an intervention on the part of Decidim in public space, in order to generate a direct relationship with citizens to support democratic participation.

As previously mentioned, during the three editions in which the project focused on digital interaction, a people-centered design methodology was adopted so that students could carry out a complete process of interaction design, putting into practice the main methods and techniques used in both professional and academic contexts.

However, the teaching goal was not only to provide students with working tools, but also to promote the construction of a critical perspective. Throughout the three editions, through reading and debate, the exercise promoted reflection on aspects of participatory democracy in relation to the students' projects. Questions like "Do we want more participation or higher quality participation?" or "What does quality participation mean?" open up spaces for reflection that push students to develop their own discourse, not only with regard to the specific topic of their own projects, but on the implications of the decisions they make as designers.

NOTES

1 Cornwall, Gaventa, 2001.
2 Access to the full documentation is open to everyone: www.decidim.org
3 www.decidim.barcelona

THE SILVER LINING OF A PANDEMIC: SOCIAL INNOVATION AWARENESS IN CITY MAKING FOR ELISAVA STUDENTS

Julia Benini and The Care Lab

In 2020, the Elisava community was set to explore how design could help co-create a vision for Barcelona's development of the superblock (*superilla*) beyond the issue of mobility. This systemic and eco-integrative approach presupposes that, in order to address the challenges generated by the growing urbanization of the planet, the ideal urban model is compact and diverse, has metabolic efficiency and social cohesion. Beyond the urban infrastructure, superblocks also aim to comprise independent but converging programs and services. The idea is that all basic services can be available to residents within the radius of a 10-minute walk.

One of the main interests of the City Council is to create services that support its most vulnerable residents, particularly caring services. This provides authorities the capacity to act in a more decentralized manner in order to reach citizens' specific care needs. It also allows citizens to access services independently of public transit or considerable movement between neighborhoods — decreasing carbon emissions and increasing neighborhood resiliency in the event of a social and health crisis, such as the one we are still experiencing due to the COVID-19 pandemic.

The beginning of the COVID-19 pandemic led to profound shifts in the way we taught at Elisava. Professors and students had to quickly adapt to the new normality of blended learning and the presence constraints in the school's workshops and prototyping facilities. But the drastic changes were not limited to these logistical issues. We had the social duty to adapt the syllabus to respond, as a design community, to the pressing needs of a health and social emergency. Within one year, the school has significantly expanded its teaching curriculum in the areas of service design and design research (i.e., exploratory and generative research) for social innovation.

For the duration of 2020, our students were busy thinking of new paradigms for caring services that can be delivered within the framework of superblocks. They explored how territoriality and digital technologies can be combined to create new community-based models of care that take into account the specific needs of a superblock's residents. Working closely with the Barcelona City Council, specifically the Area of Social Rights (Drets Socials, Justícia Global, Feminismes i LGTBI),[1] we were able to craft design briefs for our students to apply theoretical knowledge to the practice of addressing the pressing, complex problems that require multidisciplinary teams and close community collaboration to resolve.

Below, we describe the main initiatives that informed one another and helped the Elisava community respond, within the context of

Barcelona's new urban planning strategy, to the social and health crisis we experienced in 2020.

A NEW URBAN VOCABULARY FOR SUPERBLOCKS[2]

Elisava's third-year undergraduate design students were challenged to work in multidisciplinary teams to design a new urban vocabulary for the Germanetes Superilla, the newest superblock being implemented in the district of Esquerra de l'Eixample, in Barcelona's city center. This area is densely built and populated, with a particular deficit of greenery and neighborhood facilities.

The brief required students to think beyond the traditional elements that make up the urban vocabulary, such as urban furniture and signage, expanding their reach to a truly systemic outlook that included services and digital experiences to support the urban landscape changes yielded by the superblocks. As their work was developed at the height of the COVID-19 lockdown in Spain, the behavioral shifts we were all forced to incorporate into our relationship with public space were taken as both constraints and inspiration.

Collaborating with Professors Davide Fassi and Anna Meroni from the DESIS Lab at Politecnico di Milano, we exchanged the results generated by our students and their Master's students in Tactical Urbanism. The latter also explored experiments in the urban landscape, with a particular interest in the effects of the then new social distancing measures in the planning of public spaces. This exchange of experiences and fieldwork knowledge, along with their invaluable feedback for our students, inspired and improved our design work.

Engaging space, graphic, digital, and service design into their conceptual frameworks, they delivered their visions as well as complete design specifications for this new urban vocabulary. Below we present two highlights from the students' projects.

Students Blanca Ballesteros, Mariona Ros, Sara Unzueta, and Bernardo Vázquez developed a concept centered around mobility, community, activities and culture as the key pillars of their urban vocabulary. The project integrated the urban furniture and signage with services and digital touchpoints that explored interactions within the superblock's compact and diverse environment. The goal was to create a singular dwelling experience for citizens, nurturing community participation and citizen governance opportunities.

Miquel Comas, Roger Cos, Blanca Pérez, and Laia Moras highlighted sustainability, community building and wellness in their concept, bringing forth a vision where the urban landscape is conducive to incorporating services and digital touchpoints that offer citizens access to a healthier and more engaged neighborhood life.

THE EFFECTS OF THE PANDEMIC ON CARING BEHAVIORS[3]

While working on the new urban vocabulary for the Germanetes superblock, third-year design students were also being introduced to design research, i.e., the use of methods stemming from the social sciences to carry out exploratory research projects with the potential to inform design. We were in the thick of the COVID-19 pandemic. Students were experiencing first-hand the new constraints on personal freedom and the new social habits that limited the very sociable Spanish culture of getting together. They were experiencing fear for the lives of their loved ones and being faced with sudden shifts in behaviors to respond to the health and social emergency affecting the most vulnerable around them. We saw these shifts as an opportunity to build a capacity for critical reflection in those young designers, and we proposed they explore, in their first design research project, the shifts in attitudes and behavior related to care delivery during the pandemic in Catalonia, one of the hardest-hit areas during the pandemic.

Students were requested to analyze the consequences of the shelter-in-place orders in response to the COVID-19 pandemic on the care of the most vulnerable and susceptible to getting sick, such as the elderly, children, healthcare professionals, etc. The goal was to generate learning outcomes that could inform the development of the territorialization of care as proposed by the *social superilles*, a layer of social programming within the superblocks strategy. Our ultimate goal was to invite a reflection on how design could support better coordination and efficiency of care services (both formal and informal), while tapping into the rising relational care that has been generated among neighbors.

Some of the questions students were invited to answer were: What are the transformations that this situation has generated in the field of care? What role have digital social networks played? What shifted in people's attitudes and behaviors in relation to the care of the most vulnerable once the pandemic slowed down for the first time? How does the territorialization of care help increase superblocks' resiliency to health crises like the one we have just experienced?

Students delivered design research reports, presenting analyses of shifts in behavior and attitudes in relation to care among different groups that were particularly affected by the pandemic, opportunities generated by those shifts, as well as instances of design concepts that harnessed those opportunities.

Claudia Iglesis, Laia Homdedeu, Berta Soler, and Marta Ventura researched the impact of the pandemic on the homeless population of the city, shedding light on the emotional, physical, and especially gender-based, violence suffered by this population, and the overall lack of information about and care for their situation among communities in general. In their words: "The current situation of the homeless is a social injustice that has been subject to an enormous invisibilization, and a large number of solutions could be offered from the field of design."

Teresa Fainé, Tania Bonilla, Maricarmen Ramos, and Laia Carbonés researched the communication between families and seniors during the pandemic. They developed an understanding of and empathy for the problem at hand, despite the challenges of inaccessibility, even for family members, due to nursing homes being on lockdown. Then, they ran a design charrette, from which a few concepts emerged. One of them involved the use of augmented reality to bring seniors closer to families during the stricter moments of lockdown.

Laia González, Cristina Tous, Núria Estarlich, and Belén Moreno researched the immense burden that healthcare practitioners were enduring at the peak of the pandemic, withstanding a huge emotional impact. Having the lives and fates of so many people in their hands on a daily basis, struggling with the lack of resources and having to make life and death decisions due to the collapse of the Spanish healthcare system, students learned that this collective was not being cared for themselves.

DESIGNING CARING COMMUNITIES[4]

In this service design module taught for Elisava's Master's in Design and Communication (MUDIC), we partnered with The Care Lab and the Area of Social Rights at the Barcelona City Council to tackle the following challenge: How might we create a platform to engage youth and elderly citizens to team up to care for each other and their community?

Given the complex context of ageing and loneliness, the students used Service Design for Care as an approach to social innovation, to explore how to enable "caring communities" within the Barcelona Ageing Strategy supported by the Social Superillas project.

The superblocks pilot in Barcelona's Sant Antoni neighborhood was the selected site to explore opportunities around the care challenge proposed. As a one-day fieldwork research effort, the students identified existing care communities and potential care exchanges in the superblock through a neighborhood tour and observations. A co-creation session was organized with key stakeholders (youth and elderly citizens, and family and professional caregivers) as well as 1-on-1 interviews with each profile to uncover their care capabilities and care needs and identify opportunities for care exchanges.

In total, 12 opportunity areas were defined, and 3 different service concept scenarios were developed and validated with users.

Designing a first set of concept ideas and bringing them back into the community to validate them with potential users was a big realization for the students and a reality check for their concepts. They could better understand the enablers and barriers for both youth and elderly citizens, factors that might encourage them or prevent them from joining these initiatives, and this helped students to refine their final concepts. The learning outcomes included breaking the stigma and preconceptions that exist on both sides, empowering the elderly and preventing them from feeling vulnerable and weak, and engaging the youth by showing them the value of exchanging their time with the elderly, among others.

The MUDIC team in the field gathering insights with the community on the caring needs of elders in the Sant Antoni superblock.

Jhonson Quintero, Cinto Monsech and Gastón Lisak developed a service concept that connects youth with elderly people who need help with technology, social media and online bureaucracy. Using a common shared space in the neighborhood —cafes— and harnessing the youths' knowledge and interest in technology, the two generations are brought together into this caring encounter.

The second service concept, developed by Andrea Pazmiño, Alejandra Valle and Raúl Goñi, tackles the feeling of loneliness experienced by elderly people who cannot go out because of health problems, through a volunteering platform that brings part of the neighborhood events into their homes. This is achieved through the collaboration of neighborhood schools, who invite their students to participate in this initiative, and La Colla Cuidadora, a family and professional caregivers' organization that serves as the link between the volunteers and the elderly.

Laura Quesada, Allen Vallejo and Noel Díaz designed a third service concept that aims to create a tradition of care among young people, to develop caring capabilities and reduce the burden on family and professional caregivers. Through a series of workshops in the university curriculum, students have the opportunity to learn basic skills to support the elderly in the neighborhood, with the collaboration of the family and professional caregivers' association.

BARCELONA CUIDA: SERVICE DESIGN FOR SOCIAL WELLBEING IN THE SUPERBLOCKS[5]

The Fall 2020 class of third-year undergraduate design students was invited to participate in a service design bootcamp applied to social innovation. Students were challenged to explore how design could offer a vision for Barcelona's superblocks to extend their capacity to foster caring communities. Students built off the opportunity areas crafted by MUDIC Master's students and The Care Lab a few months earlier. The briefs were provided by the Barcelona City Council's Area of Social Rights, focusing on the key needs that emerged in the city's social services infrastructure during the COVID-19 pandemic.

Students worked on one of four design challenges, taking the Sant Antoni superblock as the setting for these potential services to unfold. The themes included: increasing the efficiency and the wellbeing of 1) professional and 2) family ("informal") caregivers, 3) new models of daycare for children aged 0-2 years old that can hold up to the uncertainties of new lockdowns, and 4) the flexible use of public spaces to support caring activities outdoors for different vulnerable populations. Dignification of care, gender equity within caregiving, and the leveraging of relational proximity between neighbors were some of the design principles that encompassed each brief.

During the prototyping phase, students collaborated with Master's students in Transdisciplinary Design at Parsons New School. Students of this New York-based program were then scattered all over the world due to the pandemic, so the collaboration was completely remote and spanned various time zones. Parsons students were paired up with Elisava groups and worked together on a two-week prototyping sprint. The very nature of service design, its prototyping strategies and tools, made this remote collaboration possible, and the design outcomes improved consistently throughout the collaboration.

Below we present a few highlights of students' work, some that embrace the systemic perspective that demonstrates the relevance of service design in social innovation.

Students Lia Alsina, Laura Català, Marta Moreno, and Manuela Quintero tackled the family ("informal") caregivers challenge. Working closely with community organizations of caregivers in the Sant Antoni superblock, they created a service ecosystem connected by an app and powered by and for the family caregivers in the superblock.

Through the app, family caregivers can connect in a network to coordinate help with caring tasks and to share emotional support.

Students Judith Vila, Nicole Bolón, Noé Eto, and Tomás Gonzalito tackled the challenge of improving the quality of work for professional caregivers in the municipal network. During the design research, they learned that a single person may have different caregivers —professionals and family members— and that there was an unmet need involving the proper hand-off of caring tasks from one caregiver to another. This lack of communication reduced efficiency and the quality of care provided. Their solution was a digital system that connects caregivers and centralizes the information on a person's caring needs.

Images of prototyping process by J. Vila, N. Bolón, N. Eto and T. Gonzalito.

At the end of the quarter, students Otto Bridgham, Gerard Garcia, and Nuria Granollers reflected on the process: "[Service design] was an experience that changed the way we are going to design from now on. Putting people at the center of our project helped us prototype around them; [they guided] us to where and what we had to design. This changed a lot of our previous ideas; it made us choose paths that we would never have chosen before. And this will always be with us while designing."

OPPORTUNITIES FOR A POST-PANDEMIC CITY

When the pandemic hit, we saw Barcelona, the bustling city, suddenly abandoned by 14 million tourists a year, leaving it calmer and poorer. In this sudden transition, we also glimpsed the seeds of new relational connections between neighbors generated by the pandemic. This has included more exchange with local commerce, vertical solidarity, use of social networks to provide care for those in need, more community awareness of the elderly and their needs, collective use of underutilized spaces (e.g., roofs and terraces), etc. Those were the silver linings of the health crisis, and they inspired our students to imagine a city that could emerge from the crisis more resilient, united, and compassionate.

As the city engaged in the urban planning transformation of superblocks in the midst of a pandemic, we were faced with the opportunity to deepen our students' critical thinking and ability to respond to social innovation challenges, particularly around care, inviting a reflection on design's potential for systemic impact. We built off the work already being carried out by the Barcelona municipality, involving young designers through conceptual design within their syllabus.[6] Their challenges focused on conceiving visions that can help consolidate this new model for the city, which promises increased sustainability and citizen participation.

The health emergency brought about by COVID-19 led to a socio-economic emergency whose impact we are still assessing. In the short term, the '10-minute city' approach of the *superilles* concept offers collaborative services and regenerative work opportunities to support each community's immediate social and economic needs. In the long run, it offers the prospect of vibrant and diverse neighborhoods that can become the building blocks of a more resilient society. Our role as faculty was to help our students create a vision for their roles as designers in creating a more just, caring, and resilient city for everyone.

NOTES

1 Àrea de Drets Socials, Justícia Global, Feminismes i LGTBI de l'Ajuntament de Barcelona: ajuntament.barcelona.cat.

2 Design course for third-year undergraduate students of the BA in Design carried out from January to March of 2020. The faculty included Jordi Canudas, Roger Arquer, Ivan Pomes, Maria Charneco and Rein Steger; the course was undertaken in collaboration with the Politecnico di Milano.

3 Design course in the Context area for third-year undergraduate students of the BA in Design carried out from January to March of 2020. The faculty included Danae Esparza, Toni Llàcer and Julia Benini.

4 Postgraduate course for the Master's in Design and Communication (MUDIC) carried out from January to March of 2020. The faculty included Ezio Manzini, Julia Benini and Ariel Guersenzvaig in collaboration with the team from the Care Lab (Lekshmy Parameswaran, Laszlo Herczeg, Nuria Vilarasau Creus, Airi Dordas Perpinya).

5 Design course for third-year undergraduate students of the BA in Design carried out from September to December of 2019 and January to March of 2020. The faculty included Julia Benini, Sofia Majan and Ariel Guersenzvaig in collaboration with The Care Lab, Parsons New School (Barbara Adams and Samuel Haddix), and the Barcelona City Council Area of Social Rights.

6 The bibliography includes some of the references we used in our work with the students.

SCALES OF DESIGN EXPANSION

Manuela Valtchanova

This research is based on the interest in understanding the phenomenology of the expansion of design approaches in contemporary city-making brought about by the critical imbrication between time, spatiality and intersubjectivity. To that end, the study builds a three-dimensional coordination system, in which each axis corresponds to one of the key concepts, and the system is then used to analyze a selection of design projects developed under the D×CM framework at Elisava.

- x-spatiality
  What is the format of the design action? There are six different formats distributed along the x-axis: knowledge, services, platforms, events, products and spaces.
- y-temporality
  What is the time duration of the action? The y-axis is organized by the following time intervals: 0 hours-24 hours-2 weeks-1 month-6 months-1 year-permanent-timeless.
- z-intersubjectivity
  What is the social and relational impact of the design action? How many people are affected and directly or indirectly involved in it? The z-axis is dimensioned by the following numbers of people: 0-100-500-1,000-5,000-10,000-25, 000-50,000.

The selection of design projects used for the study is divided according to the three categories of plug-ins outlined in the theoretical framework of this book: generators, mediators and identifiers. Each category is designated by a particular graphic code and nomenclature, such that all the projects under study are labelled with an identifying tag constituted by a letter (G-generators, M-mediators, I-identifiers) and a number.

Througha systematic research of all the projects, a group of key concepts considered crucial for the articulation of each design action are distilled. After that, the concepts are integrated into the three-dimensional study model by extrapolating them along the z-axis of each project. In this way, a visual landscape of words is constructed, in which multiple accidental superpositions create a strong visual haze. This haze evokes an attempt to trace intersubjectivity by enabling accidentality, relationality and disorder as operative graphic principles. Consequently, the result is a series of accidental cartographies of concepts, which, by way of their aesthetic impact, convey an idea of possible spaces for further expansion and experimentation based on potential cross-pollination between ideas.

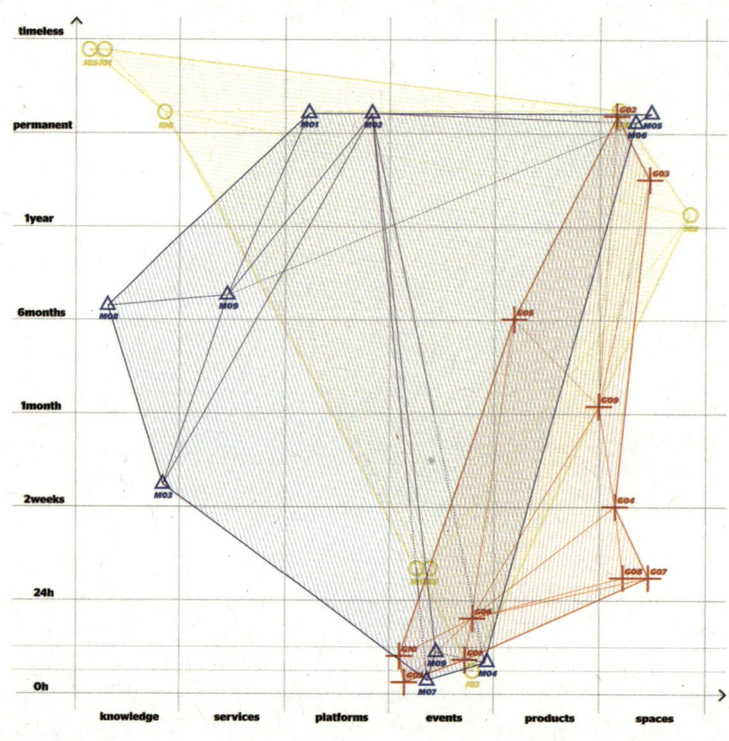

GENERATORS

G01 Slow Down, Stop, and Stay
G02 CoBoi Social Innovation Lab
G03 Community Plugin
G04 En mitjons a la plaça
G05 City and Maker Culture
G06 Tant lluny, tant a prop
G07 Chased
G08 LlumBCN
G09 Infrastructures for public space interactions (Civic Placemaking 2)
G10 COVID-19 Niches

MEDIATORS

M01 Participatory Democracy and Interaction / Decidim Barcelona
M02 Proyecto Radars / Control del ruido doméstico / Red de cohesión vecinal
M03 Tallers de cartografia subjectiva al Raval (Civic Placemaking 2)
M04 Cadires a la Rambla
M05 Transformation of Urban Ruins
M06 Foneria de Canons
M07 The city of Interactions: connecting people and places
M08 Raval (in)visible
M09 A new chance for the residents: The network of mercats de pagès

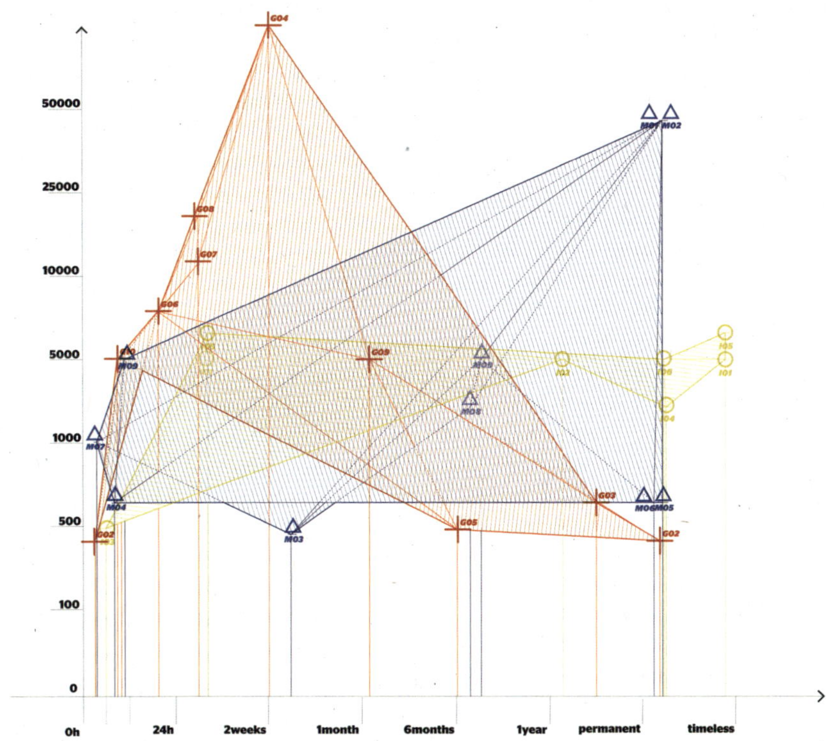

IDENTIFIERS

I01 A la Plaça: Modes of Public Space Appropriation
I02 Marges urbans / Lugares dialécticos
I03 Conversations in Les Rambles
I04 Habitar el Vacío
I05 Cocoons + Melting Pots: Barcelona bars as territories for cultural inscription
I06 Invisible Makers in Poblenou / Ciutat Vella
I08 Public space ludic activities

Interpretation of the results

The study selection is based on a heterogeneous collection of different projects, which shift and wash away the boundaries between formats, disciplines and methodologies. The results obtained after plotting all the projects onl the study axes (x-spatiality, y-time, z-intersubjectivity) show certain interdependences between the conceptual objectives of the design action and the position on the three-dimensional research grid. We propose to call these interdependences scales of design expansion. Some general tendencies can be observed:

- *Ephemeralization*: A tendency toward radical temporality in the material formats of the design interventions, with a more persistent social imbrication.
- *Dematerialization*: The longer the duration of the design action, the more immaterial the format becomes and the higher the social impact.
- *De-aestheticization*: A tendency toward the development of strategies and infrastructures for socio-spatial interaction in which the aesthetic dimension of the action is secondary to its socio-cultural performance.
- *Transversality*: A tendency toward the transversal cross-pollination of concepts among the multiple spatiotemporal formats of the design actions.

Scale – Accidental interactions:
Radically ephemeral and collaborative

The design actions on this scale operate within the dynamics of immediacy and direct interruption in the socio-spatial context, recalling formats like events, happenings and spontaneous interactive environments. They create accidental contexts of interaction, which are radically temporary (from 2 to 24 hours) and generate spontaneous collaborations. Negotiating mainly with the politics of the everyday and reinventing the relationships between the individual and the urban habitat, these projects can be considered to comprise direct transactions with human agency. The active civic body is intended to be emancipated by experiences, which enable mechanisms of direct action and the subjective transformation of memory and the dynamics of a place. In this sense, different design strategies (G01, G06, G04, G07, G08) on this scale develop game-based protocols or relational infrastructures, which build new collectivities and instill collaborative urban behaviors through a spontaneous playful experience. Another transversal issue that triggers accidental transactive environments is dissent or dialogical interaction, in response to which the dynamic exchange of subjective narratives, urban illusions and personal memories charges the urban habitat with plurality and intersubjectivity (M04,

M07, M09, I03). Accidental interactions trigger civic imagination by inspiring alternative visions of the place, where new possible realities can be rehearsed. In these accidentally available spaces of opportunity, the preestablished socio-spatial politics are temporarily disrupted in order to offer new terrains for interaction, in which emancipated human agency is enabled to subvert and reinvent the logics of the place.

Scale – Temporary Collectivities:
Temporary relational platforms

The design practices developed on the scale Temporary Collectivities happen in a range of extended temporality, e.g., 2 weeks–6 months, and create systemic experiences based on a periodic citizen involvement. These temporary relational platforms operate as disruptive venues, where new communities of action are built in order to consolidate counter-collectivities, and otherness and radical plurality are enabled to emerge. In this regard, diversity and relational antagonism are crucial to the articulation of these design strategies, which prompt plural situated narratives, both personal and collective (M03, M08). Another design strategy from this scale of expansion is the activation of mechanisms and infrastructures for public space interaction, which have the capacity to operate reiteratively, consolidating models of self-initiated and self-managed interventions (G09) and processes of cultural inscription and civic interconnectedness (G05,I05). A common feature of this type of design actions is the consolidation of shared rituals, repetitive formats of social interaction, or new forms of collective civic behavior. The temporary relational platforms harness plurality and heterogeneity in accumulative processes of imbrication between space, politics and affect, which take place as time-limited experiences but trigger long-lasting effects of social inclusion and a diversification of the urban sphere.

Scale – Timeless Networks:
Permanent spaces of knowledge and democratization

On the scale of Timeless Networks, the design practices operate within the so-called politics of capacities, where the creation of knowledge or conditioning of new spaces of opportunity builds new collective capacities for emancipation and democratization. Social justice is a common axis of articulation for design behaviors, which tend to create de-aestheticized spaces, where the intervention is either totally dematerialized (I05, I01, I06), in order to build networks of cultural vindication, or materially consolidated as spaces that act as permanent articulators of socio-spatial open-endedness (G02, G03, M06, M05). Although this scale encompasses both radically immaterial interventions and solid

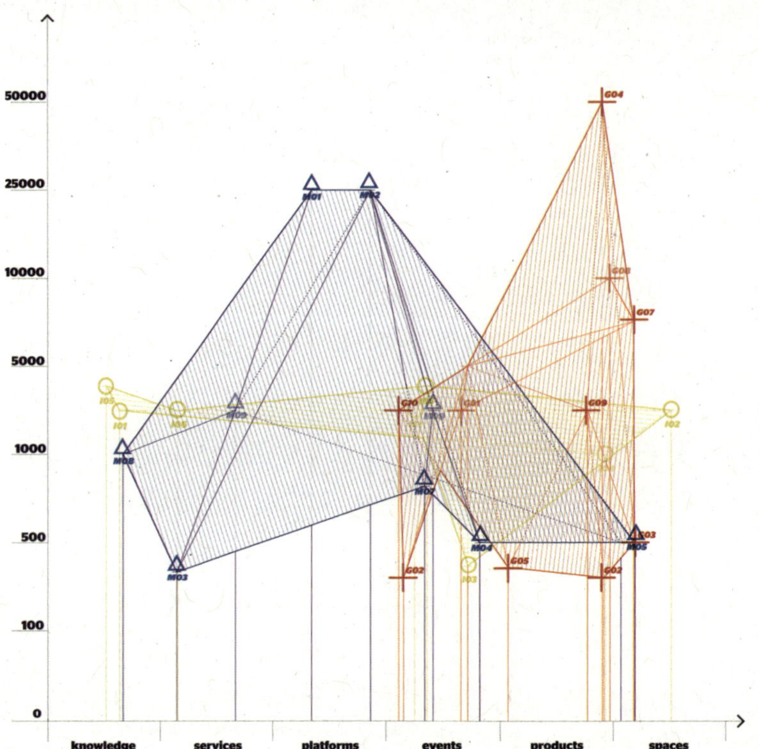
50000
25000
10000
5000
1000
500
100
0
knowledge
services
platforms
events
products
spaces

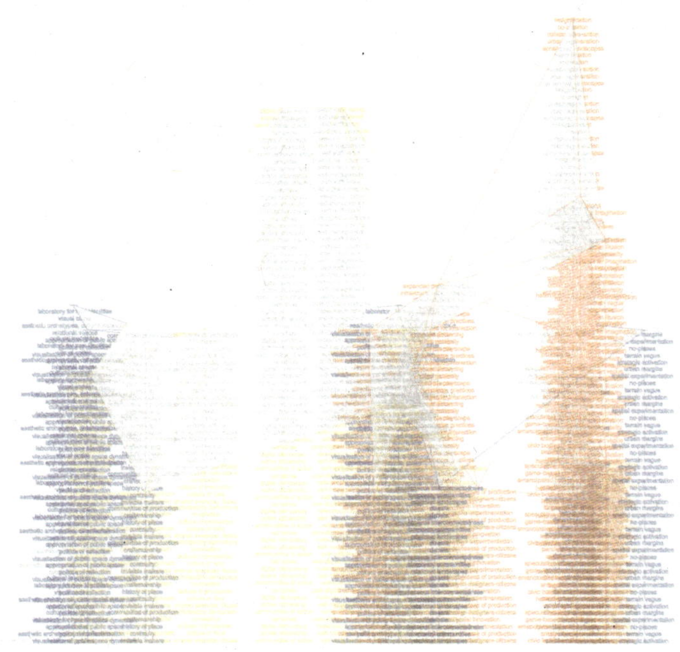

spatial experimentation
no-places
terrain vague
strategic activation
urban margins
spatial experimentation
no-places
terrain vague
strategic activation
urban margins
spatial experimentation
no-places
terrain vague
strategic activation
urban margins
spatial experimentation
no-places
terrain vague
strategic activation
urban margins
spatial experimentation
no-places

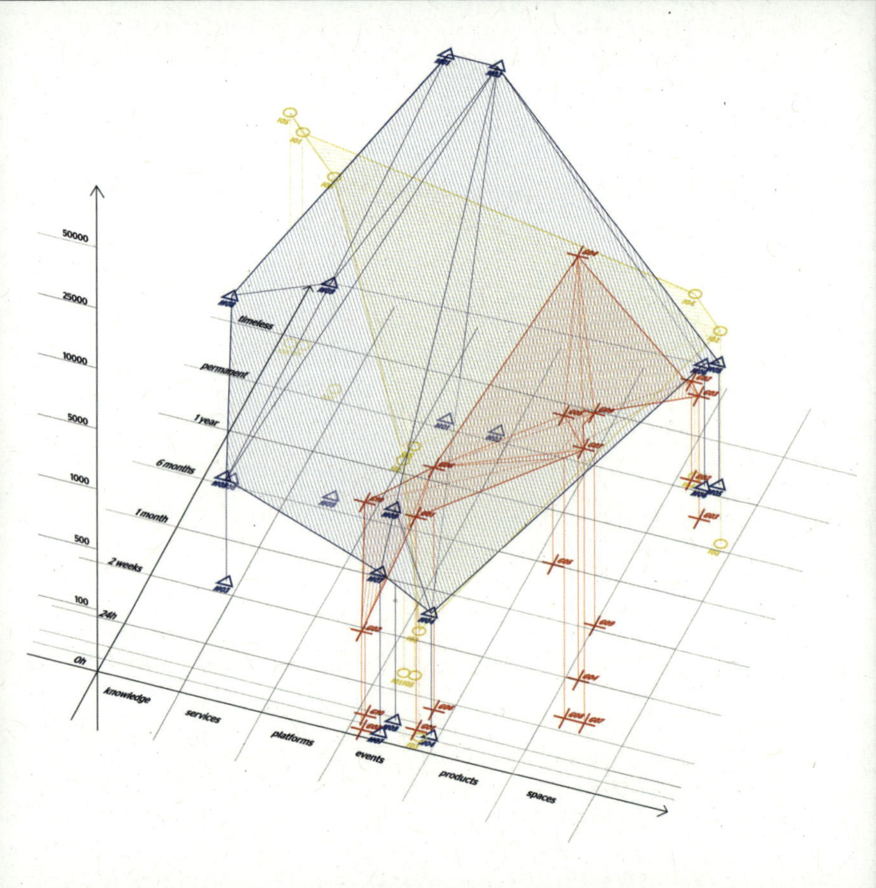

50000
25000
10000
5000
1000
500
100
0h
24h
2 weeks
1 month
6 months
1 year
permanent
timeless
knowledge
services
platforms
events
products
spaces

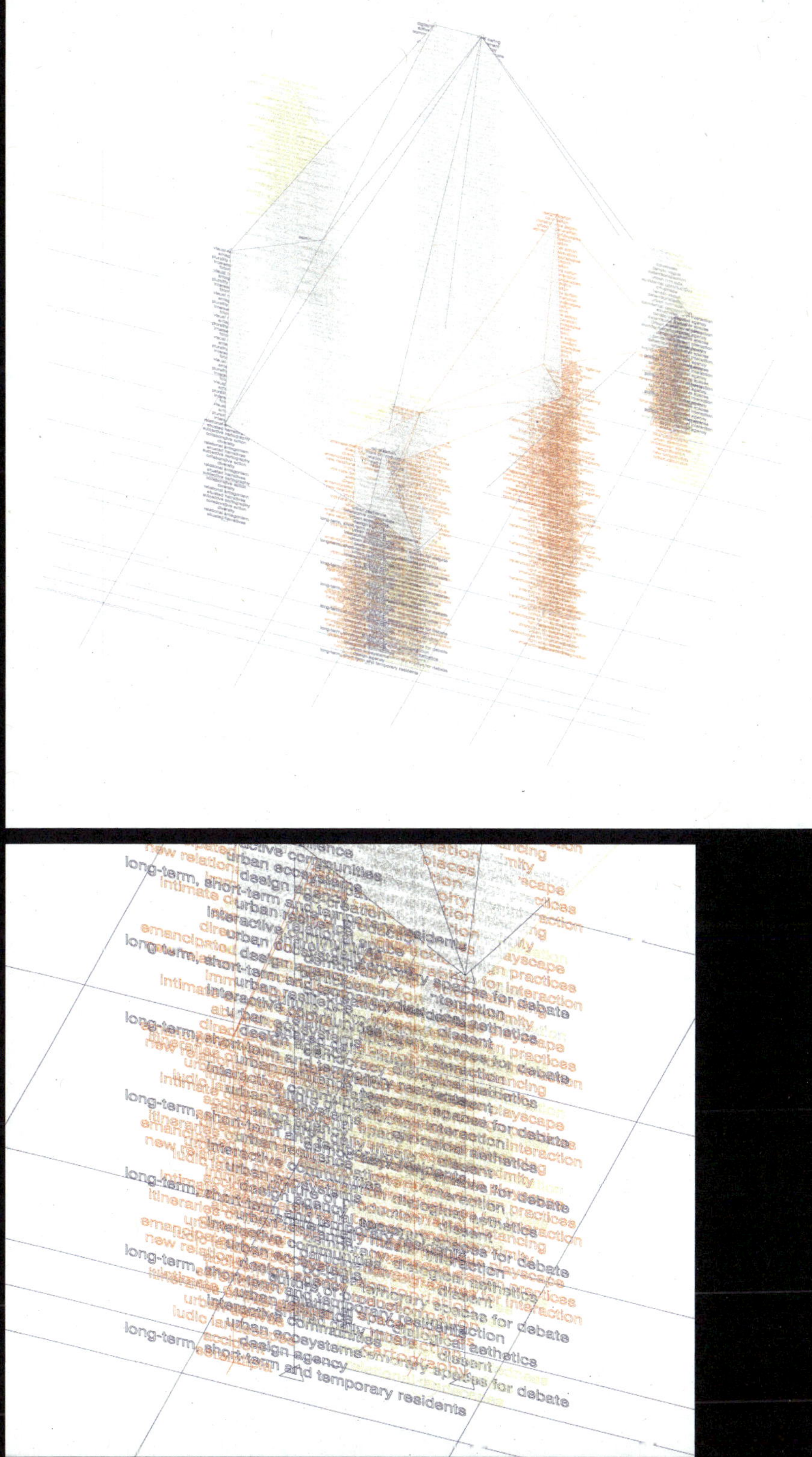

urban ecosystems
design agency
long-term, short-term and temporary residents
interactive communities
dialogical aesthetics
dissent
spaces for debate
playscape
practices
interaction

spatial rearrangements, both of them establish permanent, or rather timeless, spaces of networking, where democratization is enabled as both a social and a spatial process of negotiating the coexistence between humans and non-humans. This type of design actions proposes different strategies for addressing deterritorialization, which refers to the decodification of space brought about by the suspension of the stable patterns of inhabitation and the generation of dynamic temporary codes and meanings. In this sense, some of the strategies take part in consolidating the cultural identity of places in danger of cultural extinction through critical mapping or cataloguing (I01, I05) and others develop new modes of inhabiting the non-places or urban terrain vagues through infrastructures for plural appropriation (M06, M05). All of them, however, offer a response to the instable identity of the place. Overall, timeless networks of democratization are networks of spaces of opportunity, both material and immaterial, real and virtual, ephemeral and permanent, which trigger a continuous open process of transaction between social justice, cultural identity and civic empowerment.

Accidents: tracing intersubjectivity

Following a rigorous protocol, all the projects are positioned in the three-dimensional grid of study. Once the key concepts are extrapolated to the z-axis for each of them, the result becomes a complex visual haze of words, which suspends any analytical logic of interpretation and enacts mechanisms of accidentality, plurality and visual disorder. In this accidental cartography of concepts, intersubjectivity is traced in the unintentional interconnections between ideas and conceptual issues. In this way, harnessing randomness and multiplicity as graphic principles of representation, the research explores accident as an opportunity. Chance-based graphic relationships open up a new field of critical interpretation, which examineso new spaces for conceptual expansion that emerge from accidentality.

Allen, S. *Points + Lines: Diagrams and Projects for the City*. New York: Princeton Architectural Press, 1999.

Amin, A. and Thrift, N. *Seeing Like a City*. Cambridge UK: Polity Press, 2017.

Appadurai, A. *The Social Life of Things*. Cambridge: Cambridge University Press, 1986.

Aragon, L. *Le paysan de Paris*. Paris: Gallimard, 1926.

Baran, P. *On Distributed Communications*. Santa Monica, CA: The RAND Corporation, 1964. Memorandum RM-3420-PR (August, 1964).

Barthes, R. *Mythologies*. Paris: Éditions du Seuil, 1957.

Baudrillard, J. *Le système des objets*. Paris: Gallimard, 1968.

BCNecologia. *Charter for the Ecosystemic Planning of Cities and Metropolises*. Vilassar: Icaria editorial, 2019.

Benevolo, L. *Corso di Disegnoper i licei scientifici (1. La Descrizione dell'ambiente. 2. L'arte e la città antica. 3. L'arte e la città medioevale. 4. L'arte e la città moderna dal XV al XVII secolo)*. Roma; Bari: Laterza, 1975-76.

Benjamin, A. *Working with Walter Benjamin: Recovering a Political Philosophy*. Edinburgh: Edinburgh University Press, 2013.

Benjamin, W. "Theses on the Philosophy of History". *Illuminations*. New York: Houghton Mifflin Harcourt, 2019.

Best Cities. "Rankings". n.d. Accessed March 2, 2022.

Bhabha, H. 2004. *The Location of Culture*. Oxford: Routledge.

Björgvinsson, E., Ehn, P. and Hillgren, P.-A."Participatory Design and 'Democratizing Innovation". *Proceedings of the Participatory Design Conference, 29 November-3 December 2010, Sydney*.

Bonneau, M. and Jégou, F. *Social Innovation in Cities*. Brussels: Urbact, 2015.

Bravo, D., Schrader, C. and Yera, L. "Debate interdisciplinar: La ciudad como lugar de representación." *URBS: Revista de Estudios Urbanos y Ciencias Sociales* 2, 1 (2012): 119-136.

Buber M. *I and Thou*. New York: Simon and Schuster, 1996.

Cacciari, M. *Adolf Loos e il suo angelo*. Milano: Electa, 1981.

Calvino, Italo. *Invisible Cities*. New York: Vintage Classics, 2019. [1972]

Capel, H. "Los Problemas de las Ciudades: Urbs, Civitas y Polis". *Ciudades, Arquitectura y Espacio Urbano*, 9-22. Almería: Caja Rural Intermediterránea, Cajamar, 2003.

Chakrabarti, V. *A Country of Cities: A Manifesto for an Urban America*. New York: Metropolis Books, 2013.

CIAM (Congress Internationaux d'Architecture moderno), *La Charte d'Athenes* or *The Athens Charter, 1933*. Paris, France: The Library of the Graduate School of Design, Harvard University, 1946.

Cipolla C. "Relational Services and Conviviality". *Designing Services with Innovative Methods*. Satu Miettinen (ed).Helsinki: TAIK Publications/University of Art and Design Helsinki, 2009.

De Certeau, M. *L'invention du quotidien*. Paris: Gallimard, 1990.

De Landa, M. *A New Philosophy of Society*. London: Continuum, 2006.

De Landa, M. *A Thousand Years of Nonlinear History*. New York: Zone Books, 1997.

Deleuze, G. and Guattari, F. *A Thousand Plateaus: Capitalism and Schizophrenia*. Minneapolis: University of Minnesota Press, 1987.

Dell, C. *The Improvisation of Space*. Berlin: Jovis, 2019.

Dobson, A. (ed). *Fairness and Futurity: Essays on Environmental Sustainability and Social Justice*. Oxford: Oxford University Press,1999.

Dollphijn, R. and Van der Tuin, I. *New materialism: interviews & cartographies*. Ann Arbor: Open humanities press, 2012.

Douglas, M. and Isherwood, B. *The World of Goods*. London: Allen Lane, 1979.

Dunne, A. and Raby, F. *Speculative Everything: Design, Fiction, and Social Dreaming*. Cambridge, MA: The MIT Press, 2013.

Dupuy, G. *Urban Networks – Network Urbanism*. Delft: Techne Press, 2008.

Eames, C. "What is Design?". *Eames Design. The work of the office of Charles and Ray Eames*. Neuhart, J., Neuhart, M. and Eames, R (eds). 14-15. New York: Harry N. Abrams, 1989. [1972]

Ehn, P. "Participation in Design Things". *Participatory Design Conference Proceedings* (September 30-October 4, 2008, Bloomington, Indiana).

Eisenman, P. *Diagram Diaries*. New York: Universe Publishing, 1999.

Eriksen, T. H. *Overheating: An Anthropology of Accelerated Change*. London: Pluto Press, 2016.

Floch, J.M. *Sémiotique, marketing et communication: sous les signes, les stratégies*. Paris: PUF, 1990.

Franck, K.A. and Quentin S. *Loose Space: Possibility and Diversity in Urban Life*. London: Routledge, 2007.

Gehl, J. *Cities for People*. Washington-Covelo-London: Island Press, 2010.

Gehl, J. *Life Between Buildings*. Washington: Island Press, 2011.

Glasersfeld, E. von. "An Introduction to Radical Constructivism". *The invented reality*. Paul Watzlawick (ed), 17-40. New York: Norton, 1984.

Haraway, D. "Situated Knowledges: The Science Question in Feminism and the Privilege of Partial Perspective". *Feminist Studies* 14, 3 (Autumn, 1988): 575-599.

Harman, G. *Towards Speculative Realism: Essays and Lectures*. John Hunt Publishing: 2010.

Harvey, D. Rebel Cities: From the Right to the City to the Urban Revolution. London, Verso Books, 2012.

Harvey, D. "The Right to the City". *New Left Review* 53 (2008): 23-40.

Haydn, F. and Temel, R. *Temporary Urban Spaces: Concepts for the Use of City Spaces*. Basel: Birkhäuser, 2006.

Heidegger, M. "The Question Concerning Technology". *Basic Writings*. David Farrell Krell (ed), 308-341.London: Routledge, 1994. [1953]

Jacobs, J. *The Death and Life of the Great American City*. New York: Vintage, 1992. [1961]

Jousse, M. *L'anthropologie du geste*. Paris: Gallimard, 1974.

Koolhaas, R. *Delirious New York. A Retroactive Manifesto for Manhattan*. New York: Oxford University, 1978.

Koolhaas, R., and Mau, B. *Small, Medium, Large, Extra-Large*. Rotterdam: 010 Publishers, 1995.

Kostoff, S. *The City Shaped*. London: Thames & Hudson: London, 1991.

Landry, C. *The Art of City Making*. London: Earthscan, 2006.

Latour, B. "Bruno Latour Tracks Down Gaia". *Los Angeles Review Books* (july 3, 2018a)

Latour, B. *Down to Earth. Politics in the New Climate Regime*. Cambridge: Polity Press, 2018b.

Latour, B. *We Have Never Been Modern*. Cambridge: Harvard University Press, 1993.

Le Corbusier. "Excellence". *Ronchamp, Oeuvre de Notre-Dame du Haut*. Stuttgart: Verlag Gerd Hatje, 1957.

Lefebvre, H. *The Production of Space*. Oxford: Blackwell Publishers, 1991. [1974]

Lefebvre, Henri. "The Right to the City". *Writings on Cities*. Kofman, E. and Lebas, E. (eds.). Cambridge, MA: Wiley-Blackwell, 1996. [1968]

Leroi-Gourhan, A. *Gesture and Speech*. Cambridge, Massachusetts & London: MIT Press, 1993.

Manzini, E. *Design When Everybody Designs*. Cambridge MA: The MIT Press, 2015

Manzini E. *Livable Proximity*. Milano: Egea, 2022.

Manzini, E. *Politics of the Everyday*, London: Bloomsbury, 2019.

Manzini, E. and Thorpe, A. "Weaving People and Places: Art and Design for Resilient Communities". *She Ji: The Journal of Design, Economics, and Innovation* 4, 1 (Spring 2018).

Mauss, M. "*Les techniques du corps*". Journal de Psychologie, XXXII, 3-4 (15 mars - 15 avril 1936). Communication présentée à la Société de Psychologie le 17 mai 1934.

McNeill, D. "McGuggenisation? National Identity and Globalisation in the Basque Country". *Political Geography* (May 2000): 473-494.

Mercer."2019 City ranking". n.d. Accessed March 2, 2022.

Muñoz Carabias, F. "Límites precisos difusos. Arquitecturas paradójicas en la era postCOVID". *RITA Revista Indexada de Textos Académicos* 14 (2020): 110-115.

Numen/For Use. "Stepping Out of One's Field". *Oris* 101 (2016): 126-146.

O'Sullivan, F. "Paris Mayor: It's Time for a '15-Minute City'". *City Lab*.

Paez, R. "Design as Playground: Exploring Design Through Game-based Formats", *Space and Culture*, special issue: Cities as Playgrounds / Playgrounds as Cities: Rethinking Urban Play, Civic Engagement and Socio-Spatiality (in press).

Paez, R. *Operative Mapping: Maps as Design Tools*. New York: Actar, 2019.

Paez, R. and Valtchanova, M. *Civic Placemaking 2: Disseny, Espai Públic i Cohesió Social. Raval, Barcelona*. Barcelona: Elisava, 2021a.

Paez, R. and Valtchanova, M. "Harnessing Conflict: Antagonism and Spatiotemporal Design Practices". *Temes de Disseny 37: Invisible Conflicts: The New Terrain of Bodies, Infrastructures and Communication* (2021b): 182-213.

Pelletier, N. "Environmental sustainability as the first principle of distributive justice: Towards an ecological communitarian normative foundation for ecological economics". *Ecological Economics* 69, 10 (August 2010): 1887-1894.

Perez Galí, A. *Sweating the Discourse*. Geneva: Motto Books, 2015.

Plaza, B. (2000) "Evaluating the influence of a large cultural artifact in the attraction of tourism: the Guggenheim Museum Bilbao case". *Urban Affairs Review* 36 (2000): 264-274.

Price, C. *The Square Book*. Chichester: Wiley, 2003.

Puig de la Bellacasa, M. *Matters of care: Speculative ethics in more than human worlds*. Minneapolis, London: University of Minnesota Press, 2017.

Rilke, R.M. *Die Aufzeichnungen des Malte Laurids Brigge*. Leipzig: Insel Verlag, 1910.

Rogers, R. *Cities for a Small Planet*. New York: Basic Books, 1998.

Rose, J.P. *The Well-Tempered City: What Modern Science, Ancient Civilizations, and Human Nature Teach Us About the Future of Urban Life*. New York: Harper Wave, 2016.

Rossi, A. *L'architettura della città, di Aldo Rossi*. Padova: Marsilio, 1966.

Rueda, S. "La ciudad compacta y diversa frente a la conurbación difusa". (june 1997). See: *Ciudades para un Futuro más Sostenible*.

Saraceno, T. "Where is Everybody?". *Domus* 962 (October 2012)

Sennett, R. *Building and Dwelling: Ethics for the City*. New York: Farrar Strauss & Giroux, 2018.

Sennett, R. *Flesh and Stone. The body and the city in western civilization*. New York, London: W. W. Norton, 1994.

Sheets-Johnston, M. *The Primacy of Movement*. Amsterdam: John Benjamins, 1999.

Smithson, A. (ed). *The Emergence of Team 10 out of C.I.A.M.*. London: Architectural Association, 1982.

Smithson, A. and P. *Charged Void: Architecture*. New York: The Monacelli Press, 2001.

Soja, Edward W. *Thirdspace : Journeys to Los Angeles and other real-and-imagined places*. Cambridge, MA.: Blackwell, 1996.

Solà-Morales, M. de. *A Matter of Things*. Rotterdam: Nai Publishers, 2008.
Solà-Morales, Ignasi de. "Terrain Vague". *Anyplace*. Cambridge, MA: The MIT Press, 1995.

Star S.L and Bowker, G.C. "How to Infrastructure". *The Handbook of New Media*. Lievrouw, L. A. and Livingstone, S.L. (eds), 151–162. London: Sage, 2006.

Star, S.L. and Griesemer, J.R. "Institutional Ecology, 'Translations' and Boundary Objects: Amateurs and Professionals in Berkeley's Museum of Vertebrate Zoology, 1907–39," *Social Studies of Science* 19, 3 (1989): 387–420.

Star, S. L. and Ruhleder, K. "Steps toward an Ecology of Infrastructure: Design and Access for Large Information Spaces". *Information System Research* 7 (1996): 111–134.

Stockholm Resilience Centre.

Strebel, I., Bovet, A. and Sormani, P. (eds.). *Repair Work Ethnographies: Revisiting Breakdown, Relocating Materiality*. Singapore: Palgrave Macmillan, 2019.

Streek, J. "Gesturecraft. The Manu-facture of Meaning". *Gesture Studies* 2. Amsterdam: John Benjamins, 2009.

Tafuri, M. and Dal Co, F. *Architettura Contemporanea*. Milano: Electa, 1976.

Torrens, L. *Ageing and Improving Public Management. The Case of Barcelona and the Social Superblocks*. Barcelona: Institut de recerca TransJus (Universitat de Barcelona), 2018.

Torrens, L., Retort, S., Juan, M. "Towards a new social model of the city: Barcelona's integral superblocks". *Future Urban Habitation*. Oliver Heckmann (ed). Chichester: Wiley, 2020.

TRANSIT. "Doing Things Differently".*Transit Brief #1* (2017).

Tschumi, B. *Architecture and Disjunction*. Cambridge, MA: The MIT Press, 1996.

United Nations. *Sustainable Development*. Department of Economic and Social Affairs of the United Nations (2015).

United Nations. *UN World Urbanization Prospects 2018*. Department of Economic and Social Affairs of the United Nations (16 May 2018).

United Nations. *UN World Urbanization Prospects 2019*. Department of Economic and Social Affairs of the United Nations (17 June 2019).

Verbeek, P.-P. *What Things Do. Philosophical Reflections on Technology, Agency, and Design*. University Park USA: Penn State University Press, 2005.

Wakkary, R. "Things We Could Design in More-than-Human-Centred Worlds." *Summary retrieved from Elisava Tech Day 20: Biotech & Future Sustainable Societies*. (2020).

Weber, M. *The City*. Glencoe (IL): Free Press, 1986.

Winograd T. "A Language/ Action Perspective on Design for Cooperative Work." *Human Computer Interaction* 3, 1 (1987–1988): n.p.

Wright, F.L. "The Destruction of the Box". *Writings and Buildings*, 284-289. New York: Meridian Books, 1960.

RAMON FAURA COLL

Anders, G. *Más allá de los límites de la conciencia. Correspondencia entre el piloto de Hiroshima Claude Eatherly y Günter Anders*. Barcelona: Ediciones Paidós Ibérica, 2003. [1961]

Barthes, R. *Essais critiques*. Paris: Éditions du Seuil, 1964.

Berman, M. *All that is Solid Melts Into Air: The Experience of Modernity*. New York: Simon and Schuster, 1982.

Han, B.C. *Ausencia, acerca de la cultura y la filosofía del Lejano Oriente*. Buenos Aires: Caja negra editora, 2019.

Han, B.C. *La desaparición de los rituales, una topología del presente*. Barcelona: Herder, 2020.

Isozaki, A. *Japan-ness in Architecture*. Cambridge: The MIT Press, 2006.

McLuhan, *The Global Village: Transformations in World Life and Media in the 21st Century with Bruce R. Powers*. Oxford: Oxford University Press, 1989.

McLuhan, M. *El medio es el masaje*. Buenos Aires: La marca editora, 2015. [1967]. Žižek, S. *Acontecimiento*. Madrid. Editorial Sexto piso, 2014.

LLUÍS TORRENS

Baumol, W.J., et al. *The Cost Disease: Why Computers Get Cheaper and Health Care Doesn't*. New Haven: Yale University Press, 2012.

Jacobs, Jane. *The Death and Life of Great American Cities*. New York: Random House, 1993. [1961]

Torrens, L. *Ageing and Improving Public Management. The Case of Barcelona and the Social Superblocks*. Barcelona: Institut de recerca TransJus (Universitat de Barcelona, 2018).

Torrens, L. "Barcelona for older people. The social superblocks". *Barcelona Societat (Journal on social Knowledge and analysis)* 25 (March 2020).

TOMÁS DÍEZ

Brewer, J. "Culture Design Labs—Evolving the Future." *Age of Awareness* (July 2016).

Díez, T. "Personal Fabrication: Fab Labs as Platforms for Citizen-Based Innovation, from Microcontrollers to Cities". *Nexus Network Journal* 14 (2012): 457-468.

Díez, T. and Tomico, O. (2020). "Master in Design for Emergent Futures". *Fab Lab Barcelona at IAAC Education Programs* (2020)

Gershenfeld, N., Gershenfeld, A. and Cutcher-Gershenfeld, J. *Designing Reality, How to Survive and Thrive in the Third Digital Revolution*. New York: Basic Books, 2017.

Papanek, V. *Design for the Real World: Human Ecology and Social Change*. New York, Pantheon Books, 1971.

Patel, R. and Moore, J.W. *A History of the World in Seven Cheap Things: A Guide to Capitalism, Nature, and the Future of the Planet*. Berkeley: University of California Press, 2017.

Phillips, J. (1997). "Humans as Geologic Agents and the Question of Scale." *American Journal of Science* 297, 1 (1997): 98-115.

Van Newkirk, A. (1975). "Bioregions: Towards Bioregional Strategy for Human Cultures." *Environmental Conservation* 2, 2 (August, 2009). [1975]

Wahl, D.C. "Cosmopolitan Bioregionalism." *Age of Awareness* (April 2017).

ADRIÀ CARBONELL

Barles, S. and Lestel, L. "The Nitrogen Question: Urbanization, Industrialization, and River Quality in Paris, 1830-1939", *Journal of Urban History* 33, 5 (2007).

Berghauser Pont, M.Y. et al. "A Systematic Review of the Scientifically Demonstrated Effects of Densification", *IOP Conference Series: Earth and Environmental Science* 588, 052031 (2020).

Carbonell, A. and Salgueiro, R. "The End of Planning and the Political Aporia of the Architectural City". *The Architecture of Deregulations: Politics and Postmodernism in Swedish Building 1975-1995* (March 12, 2016).

Cerdà, I. "Edificación", *Revista de Obras Públicas* 12, 4 (1864).

Cerdà, I. *General Theory of Urbanization 1867*. Barcelona: Actar Publishers, 2018.
Cerdà, I. "La calle", *Revista de Obras Públicas* 11, 5 (1863a).

Cerdà, I. "*Necesidades de la circulación y de los vecinos de las calles con respecto a la vía pública urbana, y manera de satisfacerlas*", *Revista de Obras Públicas* 11, 13 (1863b)

Fortier, B. "La politique de l'espace parisien à la fin de l'ancien régime", *Journal of Architectural Research* 4, 1 (1975).

Fraser, N. and Honneth, A. *Redistribution or Recognition? A Political-Philosophical Exchange*. London: Verso, 2003.

Lefebvre, H. *The Production of Space*. Oxford: Blackwell, 1991.

Lefebvre, H. *Espacio y política: el derecho a la ciudad , II*. Barcelona: Ediciones península, 1976.

Rees, W. and Wackernagel, M. "Urban Ecological Footprints: Why Cities Cannot Be Sustainable and Why They Are a Key to Sustainability", *Environmental Impact Assessment Review* (1996).

SALVADOR RUEDA

Bohigas, O. "En el centenario del Plan Cerdà". *Cuadernos de Arquitectura* 34 (1958).

BCNecologia. *"A Charter for designing new urban developments and regenerating existing ones" . n.d. Accessed March 2, 2022.*

Bonet, A. "Carta Abierta al Director". *Viviendas Unifamiliares. Cuadernos de Arquitectura* 33 (1958).

Busquets, J. (1994). *Barcelona. Evolución urbanística de una ciudad compacta*. Barcelona: Ed. Mapfre, 1994.

Cerdà, I. *Teoría General de la Urbanización. Reforma y ensanche de Barcelona*. Madrid: Instituto de Estudios Fiscales, 1968. [1867]

Cerdà, I. *Teoría de la Construcción de las Ciudades aplicada al proyecto de Reforma y Ensanche de Barcelona*. Madrid: Ed. Ministerio para las Administraciones Públicas, 1991. [1859]

Martin Vide, J. 2015. *Causas y factores que influyen en la isla de calor, áreas críticas del territorio metropolitano y propuestas urbanísticas para su mitigación*. Presentation at the Taula de Metabolisme de l'AMB, 2015,

Mueller, N., Rueda, S. et al. "Changing the Urban Design of Cities for Health: The Superblock Model." *Environmental International* 134 (January 2020).

Rueda, S. *Barcelona, ciutat mediterrània, compacta i complexa. Una visió de futur més sostenible. Barcelona:* Ed. Ajuntament de Barcelona, 2002.

Rueda, S. "Carta para la planificación ecosistémica de ciudades y metrópolis." ETSAV, 2018.

Rueda, S. et al. *Projecte Biotop*. Barcelona: Ed. BCNecologia, 2004.

Rueda, S. *Regenerando el Plan Cerdà. De la intervía de Cerdà a las supermanzanas*. Barcelona: Ed. AGBAR, 2020.

Rueda, S. "Les Superilles per al disseny de Noves Ciutats i la Renovació de les Existents: el cas de Barcelona." Papers 59. *Nous Reptes en la Mobilitat Quotidiana* (2019).

Rueda, S. et al. *El Verd urbà: com i per què? Un manual de Ciutat Verda*. (col·lecció "Gestionar per conservar"). Barcelona: Ed. Fundació Territori i Paisatge de l'Obra Social de Caixa Catalunya, 2007.

Sotoca, A. and Carracedo, O. *Naturbà. Barcelona-Collserola, Una relació retrobada*. Barcelona: Ed. Col.legi d'Arquitectes de Catalunya, 2013.

Terrades, J. and Rueda, S. *Libro Verde de sostenibilidad urbana y local en la era de la información*. Madrid: Ed. Ministerio de Agricultura, Alimentación y Medio Ambiente, 2012.

Tarragó, S. and Magrinyà, F. *Catàleg de l'exposició: Cerdà, Urbs i Territori. Una visió de futur*. Barcelona: Ed. Departament de Política Territorial. Generalitat de Catalunya, 1994.

TOMICO - WILDE

Desjardins, A. and Ball, A. "Revealing Tensions in Autobiographical Design in HCI". *Proceedings of the 2018 Designing Interactive Systems Conference (DIS '18)*. Association for Computing Machinery, New York, 2018.

Kirsh, D. "Embodied cognition and the magical future of interaction design". *ACM Transaction on Computer Human Interaction* 20, 1 (March, 2013).

Lucero, A., Desjardins, A., Neustaedter, C., Höök, K., Hassenzahl, M. and Cecchinato, M. E. "A Sample of One: First-Person Research Methods". *HCI. In Companion Publication of the 2019 on Designing Interactive Systems Conference 2019 Companion (DIS '19 Companion)*. Association for Computing Machinery, New York, 2019.

Mackey, A., Wakkary, R., Wensveen, S., Hupfeld, A. and Tomico, O. "Alternative Presents for Dynamic Fabric". *Proceedings of the 2020 ACM Designing Interactive Systems Conference*. Association for Computing Machinery, New York, 2020.

Nachtigall, T., Mironcika, S., Tomico, O. and Feijs, L. "Designing ultra-personalized product service systems". *CoDesign* 16, 4 (2020).

Neustaedter, C. and Sengers, P. "Autobiographical design: what you can learn from designing for yourself". *Interactions* 19, 6 (November + December 2012).

Puig de la Bellacasa, M. *Matters of Care: Speculative Ethics in More than Human Worlds*. Minneapolis: Univ Of Minnesota Press, 2017.

Scott, A. J. "Locational patterns and dynamics of industrial activity in the modern metropolis". *Urban Studies* 19, 2 (may, 1982).

Sicklinger, A., Tomico, O., Pei, E. and Buono, M. "Designerly ways of making". *Proceedings of the Cumulus conference 2021*, 2 (July, 2021).

Tomicom O., Winthagen, V. and van Heist, M. "Designing for, with or within: 1st, 2nd and 3rd person points of view on designing for systems". *Proceedings of the 7th Nordic Conference on Human-Computer Interaction: Making Sense Through Design (NordiCHI '12)*. Association for Computing Machinery, New York, 2012.

Tukker, A. "Eight Types of Product-service System: Eight Ways to Sustainability? Experiences from SusProNet." *Business Strategy and the Environment*, 13, 4 (July, August, 2004).

Wahl, D.C. and Baxter, S. "The Designer's Role in Facilitating Sustainable Solutions". *Design Issues*, 24, 2 (Spring, 2008).

DANAE ESPARZA

Barcelona City Council, Urban Ecology, Government Initiative. *Estratègia Cap a una política de joc a l'espai públic* (2021).

Design Council, London. *Design for Public Good.* (2013).

European Commission. *A New European Bauhaus: op-ed article by Ursula von der Leyen, President of the European Commission* (2020).

Fulton Suri, J. "Informing our intuition. Design research for radical innovation". *Rotman Magazine* (Winter, 2008).

Irwin T, Tonkinwise C, Kossoff G. "Transition Design: An Educational Framework for Advancing the Study and Design of Sustainable Transitions". *Cuadernos del Centro de Estudios en Diseño y Comunicación* 15 (2020).

Manzini, E. "Making Things Happen: Social Innovation and Design". *Design Issues* 30, 1 (2014): 57-66.

Manzini, E., Cipolla, C. "Design for Social Innovation and Cities". *DESIS NETWORK - Design for Social Innovation and Sustainability* (2019).

Meyer, M.W., Norman, D. "Changing design education for the 21st century". *She ji: The Journal of Design, Economics, and Innovation* 6, 1 (Spring, 2020).

Nusem, E., Wrigley, C., Matthews, J. (2017). "Developing design capability in nonprofit organizations." *Design Issues* 33, 1 (Winter, 2017): 61-75.

Remesar, A., Crespo, B. (2018). "El sistema espacial de memoria cívica del barrio de Bon Pastor (Barcelona). Estudio del Centro Blanco". *On the w@terfront* 60, 4: 3-51.

Rittel, H; Weber, M. "Dilemmas in a general theory of planning". *Policy Sciences* 4, 2 (1973).

Rodgers, P., Yee, J. "Design Research is Alive and Kicking". *Design Research Society* 7 (2016).

Sanders, L., Stappers, P.A. "Co-creation and the new landscapes of design" *CoDesign: International Journal of CoCreation in Design and the Arts* 4, 1 (2008).

Sanders, E. "Design Research at the crossroads of education and practice" *She ji: The Journal of Design, Economics, and Innovation* 3, 1 (Spring 2017).

Sanders, L., Stappers, P.A. "From Designing to Co-designing to collective dreaming. Three slices in time". *Interactions* (Nov-Dec, 2014): 24-33.

Thorpe, A., Rhodes, S. "The Public Collaboration Lab - Infrastructuring Redundancy with Communities-in-Place". *She ji: The Journal of Design, Economics, and Innovation* 4, 1 (Spring 2018)

Yee, J. "The Researcherly designer/the designerly researcher". *Practice based design research*. Vaughan, L. (ed), 155-164. London: Bloomsbury Academic, 2017.

TONA MONJO

Barandiaran, X., Calleja, A., Monterde, A., Aragón, P., Linares-Lanzman, J., Romero, C., and Pereira, A. "Decidim: redes políticas y tecnopolíticas para la democracia en red." *RECERCA. Revista de Pensament i Anàlisi* (2017).

Cornwall, A., and Gaventa, J. "Bridging the Gap: Citizenship, Participation and Accountability". PLA Notes, 40 (February 2001): 32-35.

Mosque, N.B.D., Cila, N., Groen, M. and Meys, W. "Socio-technical Systems for Citizen Empowerment: How to Mediate between Different Expectations and Levels of Participation in the Design of Civic Apps." *International Journal of Electronic Governance*, 10, 2 (August 2018): 172-195.

Pateman, C. "Participatory Democracy Revisited". *Perspectives on politics* 10, 1 (March 2012): 7-19.

BENINI - THE CARE LAB

BCNecologia. *Charter for the Ecosystemic Planning of Cities and Metropolises*. Vilassar: Icaria editorial, 2019.

Manzini, E. *Design When Everybody Designs*. Cambridge MA: The MIT Press, 2015
Mueller et al. "Changing the urban design of cities for health: The superblock model". *Environment International*. (January 2020).

Puig de la Bellacasa, M. *Matters of care: Speculative ethics in more than human worlds*. Minneapolis, London: University of Minnesota Press, 2017.

Sennett, R.; Sendra, P. *Designing Disorder: Experiments and Disruptions in the City*. London: Verso.

10
Sagales
35
36
37

NO
SUPERILLA

TRAM

RUSO

P
P

STOP